THE COMPLETE IDIOT'S GUIDE® TO

Socially Responsible Investing

by Ken Little

ALPHA

A member of Penguin Group (USA) Inc.

This book is dedicated to my wife Cyndy who continues to inspire me with her confidence.

ALPHA BOOKS

Published by the Penguin Group

Penguin Group (USA) Inc., 375 Hudson Street, New York, New York 10014, USA

Penguin Group (Canada), 90 Eglinton Avenue East, Suite 700, Toronto, Ontario M4P 2Y3, Canada (a division of Pearson Penguin Canada Inc.)

Penguin Books Ltd., 80 Strand, London WC2R 0RL, England

Penguin Ireland, 25 St. Stephen's Green, Dublin 2, Ireland (a division of Penguin Books Ltd.)

Penguin Group (Australia), 250 Camberwell Road, Camberwell, Victoria 3124, Australia (a division of Pearson Australia Group Pty. Ltd.)

Penguin Books India Pvt. Ltd., 11 Community Centre, Panchsheel Park, New Delhi—110 017, India

Penguin Group (NZ), 67 Apollo Drive, Rosedale, North Shore, Auckland 1311, New Zealand (a division of Pearson New Zealand Ltd.)

Penguin Books (South Africa) (Pty.) Ltd., 24 Sturdee Avenue, Rosebank, Johannesburg 2196, South Africa

Penguin Books Ltd., Registered Offices: 80 Strand, London WC2R 0RL, England

International Standard Book Number: 978-1-59257-729-3
Library of Congress Catalog Card Number: 2007906892

10 09 08   8 7 6 5 4 3 2 1

Interpretation of the printing code: The rightmost number of the first series of numbers is the year of the book's printing; the rightmost number of the second series of numbers is the number of the book's printing. For example, a printing code of 08-1 shows that the first printing occurred in 2008.

Printed in the United States of America

Note: This publication contains the opinions and ideas of its author. It is intended to provide helpful and informative material on the subject matter covered. It is sold with the understanding that the author and publisher are not engaged in rendering professional services in the book. If the reader requires personal assistance or advice, a competent professional should be consulted.

The author and publisher specifically disclaim any responsibility for any liability, loss, or risk, personal or otherwise, which is incurred as a consequence, directly or indirectly, of the use and application of any of the contents of this book.

Most Alpha books are available at special quantity discounts for bulk purchases for sales promotions, premiums, fund-raising, or educational use. Special books, or book excerpts, can also be created to fit specific needs.

For details, write: Special Markets, Alpha Books, 375 Hudson Street, New York, NY 10014.

Publisher: *Marie Butler-Knight*
Editorial Director: *Mike Sanders*
Managing Editor: *Billy Fields*
Senior Acquisitions Editor: *Paul Dinas*
Development Editor: *Julie Bess*
Senior Production Editor: *Janette Lynn*

Copy Editor: *Jeff Rose*
Cover Designer: *Becky Harmon*
Book Designer: *Trina Wurst*
Indexer: *Brad Herriman*
Layout: *Brian Massey*
Proofreader: *Mary Hunt*

Contents at a Glance

Contents

Introduction

"Un-American."

That's how socially responsible investing was summarized by a well-known stock market icon a number of year ago. The idea that a company had any responsibility other than to make as much profit for its owners as possible was totally alien to this Wall Street tycoon. His sentiments were not alone. But another group of people—investors—didn't feel that way. They had strong personal feelings about certain issues and wished for a way to express those feeling through their investments. The Quakers had found a way during the 1800s to oppose slavery by not doing business with companies that profited from slave labor. Modern (Twentieth Century) investors carried that torch forward. Their opposition gelled around two major issues: Apartheid in South Africa and the war in Vietnam. Their vocal opposition to companies doing business in South Africa helped end that repressive government. Their efforts of pulling investments from defense contractors drew attention to the movement and raised it to a legitimate investment form.

Socially responsible investing today is still on a small segment of the total investment pie, yet the dollars involved are over $1.5 trillion invested. Most of the money, as in the traditional investment market, comes from institutional investors such as charitable organizations, religious groups, pension funds, insurance companies, and so on. These investment heavy weights have billions of dollars to invest.

The issue that has dogged socially responsible investing (SRI) for years is the idea that you will sacrifice performance if you choose this form of investing. The truth is that SRI mutual funds have their hot and cold streaks just the same as traditional mutual funds. Under some market conditions, the large cap growth SRI funds will flourish, while in different scenarios they may not. More SRI funds were added each year and with the new funds come new options and opportunities. One negative has been the fewer choices of SRI funds compared to traditional funds, but that's changing.

A key issue for SRI investors is the environment. With global warming and greenhouse gasses a major issue, it would seem the investing community has discovered SRI. Investors, both individual and institutional, are recognizing that companies without an environmental plan have an unaccounted for liability on their books. When the market begins discounting stocks for this and other flaws that socially responsible investors follow, the movement will gain even more popularity.

When something gains a lot of media attention, you can count on people trying to take advantage of the situation. One issue SRI investors encounter is companies who make a token effort at changing their environmental policy and then spend more money on a media blitz to tell the world what a good steward of the earth it is. This is known as "green washing" and you will see more of it as unscrupulous companies try to gain points without actually doing anything.

What to Expect

This book is an introduction to socially responsible investing. It covers the movement and its history, where it is now and where it is going. The basic parts of socially responsible investing (screened investing, shareholder advocacy, community development) are covered. Mutual funds are the backbone of investing options for SRI investors and we explore those in-depth. We look at major issues addressed by SRI and why they are important. We also tell you how to get started in socially responsible investing.

What this book does not do is sell you on the idea of socially responsible investing. We try to present a basic idea of what SRI is all about, how it works, what to expect, and what some of the critics say. Whether you choose to pursue SRI is up to you. That is a very personal decision that only you can make. If, after reading this book, it feels right to you, then you'll have a good start on the process and some resources to continue your education. If you read the book and SRI doesn't work for you, at least you have made an informed decision based on facts and you are ready to move on to some other strategy.

How to Use this Book

This book is divided into five parts.

Part 1, "What Is Socially Responsible Investing?" defines SRI and talks about its history and the myths surrounding performance. It also includes a discussion of the role of corporations and those who are affected by its actions.

Part 2, "Important Issues to SRI Investors" discusses the five broad issues that are important to the SRI movement.

Part 3, "SRI Strategies" discusses two important strategies: stock screening and shareholder advocacy.

Part 4, "SRI Investment Opportunities" looks at the main investment options of mutual funds, stocks, and bonds.

Part 5, "How to Do SRI" helps you prepare to make the decision about SRI investing, including working with a financial professional and the personal and financial commitment.

Extras

Scattered throughout the chapters are the following sidebars, which will add to your knowledge of SRI and help you with terms that might not be familiar. Watch for these:

Success Stories
Presents interesting facts and insights about the SRI industry.

def•i•ni•tion

These are definitions of industry terms

Red Flag

Beware of false information about SRI or warnings about potential traps.

Responsible Tip

Gives advice on how to get the most out of your SRI investment.

Acknowledgments

Thanks to Paul Dinas, Senior Acquisitions Editor of Alpha Books, for another opportunity to contribute to *The Complete Idiot's Guide* series. I am especially grateful for this opportunity because I believe in the topic. Thanks also to Julie Bess for her hard work as development editor on this project.

Trademarks

All terms mentioned in this book that are known to be or are suspected of being trademarks or service marks have been appropriately capitalized. Alpha Books and Penguin Group (USA) Inc. cannot attest to the accuracy of this information. Use of a term in this book should not be regarded as affecting the validity of any trademark or service mark.

Part 1

What Is Socially Responsible Investing?

Socially responsible investing puts your money where your heart is. It avoids profiting from activities that are contrary to your personal values. It has a long and active history marked by avoidance of investments in certain industries and activism against social injustice But must you sacrifice investment performance to honor your values? The answer follows.

Chapter 1

Socially Responsible Investing Defined

In This Chapter

◆ Weight of social values and traditional investment options

◆ Traditional and nontraditional opportunities for investments

◆ Investment options

◆ Differences among the social objectives of SRI practitioners

Socially responsible investing (SRI) makes either perfect sense or no sense at all, depending on whom you ask. A traditional approach to investing leaves no room for considering any factors other than those you can quantify: earnings, revenue, expenses, market share, and so on. These numbers can be proved, tested, and projected into the future to validate a stock's current price and predict where the price might go. Socially responsible investors consider these factors, too, but they are also concerned with other matters—most easily quantifiable, others less so. SRI looks at a set of issues (which vary from one group of investors to the next) that are as important as earnings per share. SRI investors generally seek to invest in enterprises that contribute to a clean, healthy environment, treat people fairly, embrace equal opportunity, produce safe and useful products, and support efforts to promote world peace. They will generally avoid alcohol and tobacco, and have limited exposure to gambling, nuclear power, weapons systems procurements, and companies known to have major environmental, social, and governance (ESG) concerns.

Socially Responsible Investing Defined

Socially responsible investing is a broad term that describes an approach to investing as opposed to any specific strategy. The simplest and most accurate definition of SRI is an approach to investing where an investor includes personal, religious, moral, or ethical values in investment decisions.

Responsible Tip

Socially responsible investing is about reflecting values that are personally meaningful to the investor and applying these values into investment decisions.

A socially responsible investor gives equal weight to these values when considering an investment, often excluding (or including) possible candidates strictly on how well they reflect their personal values or how well they measure up to benchmarks of corporate responsibility. This investment approach foregoes investing in any industry sector if the business or business practices of companies in that industry are in conflict with the investor's values. Socially responsible investing says that if a set of values is important to you, those values should also guide how you invest your money. For example, it makes no sense to be morally opposed to the consumption of alcohol, yet profit from investments in companies that make and sell alcoholic beverages. If you dutifully recycle, drive a high gas mileage car and work hard to do no harm to the environment, profiting from investments in companies that have criminal histories of polluting is incongruous. Socially responsible investing can be more than just avoiding investments that conflict with your values. Some practitioners take a proactive stance with their SRI and work to change companies that have poor records in those values important to the investors. Owning stock in a company gives investors certain rights and access that nonstockholders don't enjoy. Proactive socially responsible investors use this access to work for change within the corporation. The other example of proactive SRI is community investing, which seeks to direct investments to low-income communities traditionally overlooked by mainstream financial institutions.

How Is SRI Different

Socially responsible investing means many things to many people, however, its basic difference from traditional investing is in the approach to selecting (or rejecting) potential investment candidates. The traditional investment approach may select an investment candidate based on a set of criteria: industry, size, growth projections, earnings estimates and much more. An investor can do most of the analysis without ever knowing the name of the company. While the quality of management is given some weight in the decision, ultimately the numbers are more important to most analysts.

Responsible Tip

Socially responsible investors may avoid certain companies because of the products or services they make or sell. Once companies make the SRI cut, they are subjected to the same analysis used by traditional investors.

Socially responsible investors pay attention to the numbers, and they also give weight to those areas that are important to their values. For example, some socially responsible investors look for companies with good records of environmental impact, while others will not invest in any company that makes or sells alcohol or tobacco products. This extra layer of scrutiny means that if two companies look about the same by the numbers, but one fails the socially responsible test, the investor will choose the other for investment. Some socially responsible investors will make a conscious decision to accept a lower return rather than invest in a company that violates their personal values. While this happens, it is not a given that SRI is always a second-best return on investment and there is something of a myth about this in the investment community. We'll look at that more in Chapter 3.

Value and Values

Investing in a company is a process of deciding if the stock market has correctly valued its stock. In other words, if the stock market says a company's stock is worth $30 per share, is this an accurate and fair representation of the company's value today, and is purchasing the stock at that price a good investment base on future growth potential?

Investors are most interested in a company's growth potential, because this is where they will make their profit. As the company grows, its stock should increase in value. If investors pay too much for that potential growth in the form of a premium over the company's actual current value, it may be years before they realize the growth in share value they expected. Investors who find a stock with good growth potential that is not over-priced may reap significant rewards as the company grows in future years.

Investors use many different calculations based on company financial statements to help them determine the company's current value. This information is combined with industry and economic information to give investors an idea of the company's growth potential. When put together an investor has a target of how much to pay for the stock to give him a good chance at earning a profit in the future as the company grows and the share price increases.

The socially responsible investor adds another step to this process, sometimes at the beginning of the investigation. This step checks the company to see if it fits the investor's socially responsible criteria. As we'll see in more detail later, socially responsible investors come with a wide variety of issues that drive their investing decisions. For example, one investor may exclude all companies that manufacture, sell,

Red Flag

Just because a company does well on your tests for socially responsible investing does not necessarily make it a good investment candidate. You must consider whether the company is viable, has growth potential and all the other characteristics of a good investment beyond the SRI features.

Success Stories

Socially responsible investing is robust, but diverse. Investors should be certain they understand all the features of an SRI investment (mutual fund, for example) before sending money, since values and interpretation of values can vary greatly.

or earn revenue from alcohol and/or tobacco products. Another investor may be more concerned about a company's environmental policies.

In either case, companies that failed the investor's socially responsible test would be excluded from consideration, in most cases. This statement is qualified because there is a branch of SRI that is pro-active. Advocates of this form of SRI invest in companies that fail socially responsible tests to work for change from within as an owner of the company.

SRI Investment Options

Socially responsible investors have most of the same investment options available to them that traditional investors enjoy, plus some that are unique to SRI.

◆ Individual stocks

◆ Mutual funds

◆ Bonds

◆ Community investments

◆ Hybrid investments

The previous section briefly outlined how a socially responsible investor might approach an individual stock investment. Some investors prefer owning individual stocks to *mutual funds* because the potential for gain can be higher, with a corresponding increase in risk. For socially responsible investors, finding individual stocks that meet your value criteria may not be as hard as you imagine. There are abundant resources to draw on for information and financial professionals that understand SRI. Subsequent chapters will help you with the process of identifying investment candidates and financial professionals.

def•i•ni•tion

A **mutual fund** is a pool of investor money managed by professionals with stated investment goals and objectives. Investors leave the buying and selling decisions to professional managers. Investors own shares of the mutual fund and may cash them in at virtually any time. Fund managers are responsible for making buy and sell decisions and sticking to the fund's strategy.

Many socially responsible investors use mutual funds as their investment vehicle of choice. Mutual funds pool investors' money and hire professionals to manage the funds. For socially responsible investors, this is particularly important. SRI funds are structured to meet certain "values tests." Investors can find a fund that reflects almost any value they hold dear. The funds screen investment candidates before investing so owners of the mutual fund's shares know the portfolio of stocks and bonds is qualified to meet the values tests of the fund. SRI funds can be index funds or they can be actively managed. The difference between these two types of funds is explained in later chapters.

Socially active investors can also buy bonds issued by companies identified in their search for stock purchases. Bonds provide an important part of every portfolio and a balance against the volatility inherent in the stock market. Generally, the closer you are to retirement, the more heavily invested in bonds you should be. Corporate bonds of socially responsible companies can generally be as attractive as any other comparably rated bond.

One of the hybrid investments enjoyed by socially responsible investors is in community investment projects. Community investments are usually locally organized investment pools that provide capital for housing and small business loans to people in low-income areas of a community.

Contrasts with Traditional Investment Styles

Socially responsible investing can truly be classified as an investment style, just as value or growth investing are styles. The difference is that SRI contrasts with all other investment styles, while traditional investment styles are usually thought of as mirror images. For example, growth and value investing are two contrasting styles, as is small cap and large cap (investing in small companies or investing in large companies). SRI because of its extra layer of discernment is in contrast with all traditional investment styles. SRI investors may pursue a growth strategy or some other investment style, but only after identifying companies that meet their socially responsible requirements.

Success Stories

Socially responsible investors can make a difference by putting pressure on corporations to change policies and by advocating better labor and environmental policies. Many of SRI's successes come through discussions with corporate leaders behind closed doors, which have resulted in companies addressing issues of pollution, climate change, corporate governance, and so on.

Emphasis on Impact

Socially responsible investing has a history of making a difference, as we'll see in the next chapter. This sets it apart from traditional investing, which has no particular interest in influencing the actions of a corporation unless shareholders are upset with management's stewardship of their assets. Most individual shareholders do not have enough influence (don't own enough shares) to change the course of a company's policy. Shareholders, both individual and institutional, may get involved when it serves their interest, for example, in the case of an offer to buy the company by another company.

Socially responsible investors who want to encourage better corporate behavior will interject themselves in many issues that traditional investors avoid or ignore. Traditional investors leave it to management to work out details of environmental policies, labor issues, product mix and so on. SRI investors may use these same issues and others to exclude investments or they may lobby within the company as shareowners for more responsible behavior.

While some SRI investors are actively engaged in confrontation, others choose to open dialogues with corporate officers in an attempt to show them how policy changes are in the company and shareholders' best interest. A key component of this argument is making a financial case for socially responsible behavior. This is an important tactic in the SRI arsenal, since an improved financial picture is always an attention-getter in corporate circles.

This can be a tough sell, however, since some of the financial improvements advocated (better environmental controls, for example) may require an upfront investment that won't pay off until some point in the future. This rubs against the current market imperative to improve

Red Flag

Be aware that some companies appear to make socially responsible changes, but really are executing a public relation's policy. Such PR efforts put appearance before substance.

the financial picture from quarter to quarter. Long-term investments often have the opposite short-term effect of dragging down current earnings. The traditional market system rewards consistent growth in earnings and disruptions in this pattern are met with rejection by investors. Of course, many environmental improvements actually save money from day one. Others don't require any additional costs up front.

Other SRI advocated changes often cannot directly capture a dollar figure on the financial statement, but rather are best viewed as insurance against future problems with environmental, labor or product liability law. Whether it is dialogue with corporate leaders or shareholder resolutions, SRI investors push for change and that separates them from most traditional investors. We'll explore these in more detail through out the book, but be aware that socially responsible investing is about making a profit while making a difference.

Offers Many Opportunities for Expression

Socially responsible investing opportunities are abundant and come in many forms including traditional instruments such as individual stocks and bonds; mutual funds; managed accounts for wealthy or institutional investors; and exchange traded funds and closed-end mutual funds. In addition to these publicly traded investments, socially responsible investors may find satisfaction in community investments and accredited investors may find attractive opportunities in social venture capital.

Many of the same investment strategies, such a margin trading, options, and other sophisticated instruments and techniques are available to SRI investors for many of their selected investments. The SRI process does not necessarily preclude aggressive investment tactics, although some investors driven by religious values may avoid certain practices that conflict with their faith. Islam, for example, does not allow the paying or earning of interest (more about religious values in SRI in Chapter 6).

The SRI movement is not one of common interests or values, but of several clusters of values. Not everyone who is an SRI investor values the same characteristics in a company, nor do they need or want the same investment vehicle to express their values. (The majority of SRI funds utilize several common core screening criteria. There may be some difference in how they are used, but they do not necessarily "conflict.")

Socially responsible investors have a full range of investment vehicles (individual stocks, mutual funds, and so on) to use as fits their comfort and tolerance for risk. To be a successful SRI investor, you also have to be a successful traditional investor because you are using the same investments, markets, and investment tools. The only difference between SRI investors and traditional investors is that socially responsible investors want something more than an adequate financial return on their investment. They want to feel their money is also making a difference in the world, however they choose to define that difference.

Responsible Tip

Fitting into the SRI world is not difficult. The practice is broad enough so that most people can find a way to express their values through an investment program.

SRI Strategies

Socially responsible investing features three main strategies to express its values. SRI investors can use one or all of these strategies to express their values and priorities for society in their investments. The strategies focus on how the investor wants to be involved in the process—either active or in a more passive role. The purpose of the strategies is to define the investor's role in the process and/or to set up an investment for future financial gain. Screening is the most common strategy used by SRI investors, followed by shareholder advocacy and community investment. Each of these strategies has multiple variations and uses.

Screens and How They Are Used

Screens, which are discussed in much greater detail in later chapters, are simply ways to filter large amounts of information to find only what you seek. Investment screens look at thousands of possible investment candidates (stocks or mutual funds) and select only those that match the characteristics desired. If you only want companies with sales in excess of $10 billion per year as one of your screen elements, then only those companies that have sales over that amount will be included. Financial screening tools are common and SRI investors have adapted them to their needs.

Positive Screening

For the SRI investor, positive screening means looking for companies that meet her value requirements. Positive screens are sometimes more difficult then negative screens because they look for values that aren't as easily identified. For example, environmental policies, labor relations, inclusive corporate governance, and so on may be difficult to measure. We'll discuss this in more detail in Chapter 10, but consider how you would define your values in these areas so they could be expressed in a screen.

A positive screen may identify companies that will be positioned to avoid many of the negative effects of new environmental policies because it has already built the necessary systems before the require-ment became law (and, by definition, at a lower cost than competitors must now pay). This is an example of an SRI policy that is also a good business practice. Although it may have suffered temporarily lower earnings while preparing better environmental controls, the company is now in a better strategic position. Best practices in the realm of corpo-rate responsibility are often benefi-cial long-term business solutions.

Responsible Tip

Although our market system does not always reward long-term invest-ments by companies, SRI acknowledges that investing in many of the values it holds will pay off for companies in the future—an attractive prop-osition for long-term investors.

Negative Screening

Historically, SRI started with negative screens, and today is better known for negative screening than positive screening. These screens block out companies that make or sell certain goods or services. The most common exclusions include alcohol, tobacco, firearms, weapons systems manufacturer, nuclear power producers, and egregious polluters. Various groups use negative screens for religious, moral, or ethical reasons. Some of these reasons may conflict with each other, but that is the nature of SRI investing—your values are not necessarily my values. One group of SRI investors opposed to the sale of alcohol products might still invest in hotels, even though there are bars in many hotels because most of the revenue comes from room occupancy, not liquor sales. Another group opposing the sale of alcohol, however, might exclude hotels because although the sale of liquor is not a large percentage of revenue, it is normally very profitable.

Though relatively rare, some SRI investors will use negative screens to identify companies in violation of their values and will invest in them to advocate for change from within the organization (see the following description of shareholder advocacy). In this case, the negative screen is identifying targets of opportunity rather than investments to avoid.

Success Stories

Socially responsible investing actions against companies are often controversial, since there are usually two sides to every story. SRI efforts to discourage investment in certain countries where it is clear that companies operating there are supporting the heavy-handed behavior of dictatorships have, nonetheless, been blamed for lowering the standard of living of the population.

Another effective way negative screens work is identifying companies doing business in offending countries around the world. As we'll see in Chapter 3, socially responsible investors targeted companies investing in South Africa during the era of apartheid. More recently, SRI investors pushed companies doing business in Darfur to pull out of that African country because of the terrible human rights violations.

Many SRI investors rely on mutual funds to do the screening for them, since it can be quite complicated. Simple screen tools are also available to investors free on the Internet and some rather powerful ones cost only a small monthly subscription fee. If you want to do your own screening, many tools are available and we'll look at some of them in later chapters.

Shareholder Advocacy

For many SRI investors, simple investing or not investing is too passive. They want to effect change in a more direct manner. One of the most direct and sometimes confrontational methods is shareholder advocacy. This strategy generally involves buying stock in a company that is already a pretty good company and advocating for improvements. Owning stocks gives the SRI investor the right to present shareholder resolutions for a vote of all stockholders. As will see in Chapters 12 and 13, the act of shareholder advocacy has a long and interesting history. While there have been successes, there are mostly failures. Nevertheless, it remains a strong tool in the total SRI strategy. It is most successfully performed by socially responsible mutual funds, pension funds and asset managers that have the staff and expertise to research and advocate on behalf of many investors. Most of their successes come in conversations with management rather than in votes at annual meetings. Getting management to change policies or procedures is the end game and if it can be done in a negotiated manner, the results are usually better and permanent.

 Responsible Tip

Several companies assist SRI investment groups in preparing and filing shareholder resolutions. These professionals know the procedures and steps required by regulators and companies to be successful.

An SRI investor who wants to bring a shareholder resolution to the floor of a company's annual meeting can find resources to help him with the procedures that must be followed. The investor should consider securities' regulations and company rules. SRI shareholder advocates must be certain their resolutions are heard and not disallowed because of a technicality in procedure of filing the paperwork.

Community Investment

Community investment is possibly the closest to hands-on SRI investing of all the strategies. Community investing occurs in local communities and helps build stronger neighborhoods. There are several ways the process can work, but essentially it boils down to investing in a manner that creates opportunities locally. A community investment fund might be set up through a local bank that issues CDs or other instruments to SRI investors at going rates. [For many investors, the simplest option is to invest in a checking or saving account at a community development bank or credit union, many of which can take deposits from all over the country.] Investors purchase the CDs or other money market instruments and the community investment bank lends money at favorable rates to people in the designated investment area. Sometimes state and federal money is part of the package to extend the reach of locally generate capital.

These loans are seed or development money to fund new life in specific neighborhoods. Housing for low-income individuals is one of the primary focuses of community investment, since decent housing is required before any area can expect to redevelop economically. Along with housing, micro-loans to individuals start-

Responsible Tip

Community investment funds provide direct money, along with government programs to neighborhoods in your community. Housing for low-income residents is often the chief focus of these funds.

ing their own business is an area that many find promising. There are global efforts in the micro-loan area that have proved very successful.

Socially Responsible Venture Capital Funds

Socially responsible venture capital funds could be considered a part of community investment, but on a grander scale. Rather than focus on redeveloping communities, SRI venture capital funds approach the high-risk practice of funding start-up companies with a social or values approach (funding companies that make or market environmental solutions, for example). Like all venture capital funds, these are for investors that have a very high net worth ($1 million) and an annual salary of at least $250,000 ("accredited investors").

While they are not for every investor, these funds are illustrative of the broad appeal of SRI investing, since they are identical to traditional venture capital funds except in focus. Investments at this level, whether SRI or not, should be weighed very carefully. They carry a high degree of risk and are illiquid.

The Least You Need to Know

◆ Socially responsible investing focuses on values as well as return.

◆ SRI offers typical investment opportunities such as stocks, bonds, and mutual funds.

◆ SRI strategies include passive as well as active ways investors can be involved in the process.

◆ Community development and venture capital funds are more hands-on forms of SRI.

Chapter 2

What About SRI Performance?

In This Chapter

- ◆ The myth of poor returns from socially responsible investing
- ◆ The importance of financial return to SRI investors
- ◆ Why some forms of SRI produce superior returns
- ◆ Investors have many choices to meet financial goals

Traditional investors scoffed at an investment selection system that included the choosing or excluding an investment based on a personal value as one of the primary decision points. They reasoned that this value factor could easily exclude investments that were very attractive by every other standard. For example, if all the financial and economic factors pointed toward defense industry stocks as poised for significant growth, SRI investors opposed to these types of investment would miss a prime opportunity. Multiply all the potential missed opportunities (based on the many different types of SRI investors) and it would seem logical to conclude the socially responsible investing couldn't match the returns of traditional investing strategies. Fortunately, that thinking is wrong, and the conclusions are wrong.

Investing and Rate of Return

Before we go too far in our discussion of socially responsible investing and return, it is important to put it in a proper context. The most important context applies to all investing, both SRI and traditional, and that is there are no guarantees. Investing is about risk and anticipated reward—not guaranteed reward. If you want a guaranteed return on your investment (therefore, no risk), you should buy a U.S. Treasury Bond or a bank certificate of deposit. When you invest your money in the stock market, in either individual stocks or mutual funds, you are

Responsible Tip

Investment professionals are very fond of numbers, but before you assign too much importance to any they toss around, remember that the only numbers that matter are what your investment will earn in the future. And no one can tell you for certain what that might be.

taking a chance that you will earn a reward higher than what a no-risk choice will earn. Over a 70-plus year history, the stock market as a whole has returned an average of between 10 and 11 percent annually. This means if you owned a broad portfolio of stocks that represented the entire stock market and held it for 70 years; it would earn you on the average 10 to 11 percent annually. Some years it would do much better and some years it would do much worse.

As interesting as that is, you can't assume individual stocks will do the same. Drawing specific conclusions from broad general truths often leads to incorrect answers. Socially responsible investing does require an extra step in the analysis process, but that doesn't mean it results in inferior investment selections. Some SRI advocates argue that socially responsible investing has outperformed traditional investing because of these extra steps. We'll look as both sides of this issue.

Will My Retirement Fund Suffer?

Socially responsible investors may be concerned with social justice issues, the ecology, or any number of values or causes, but they are also pragmatic investors. Some SRI investors may not be concerned with the return they get on their investment and are more focused on the cause or issue that brought them to socially responsible investing. In the early days of SRI, there were few choices, especially for individuals, so you took what return you could get. But times have changed for the better. SRI is no longer a marginal part on the investment business. Over 200 mutual funds are available for investors to use. Many have similar social mandates and compete on return.

The net benefit to the investor (in mutual funds) is that if your fund is not performing to expectations, there is probably another fund in the market that reflects your social concerns that may offer a better return. More sophisticated screens now allow SRI investors to focus their investments with greater precision.

Success Stories
The success of SRI investing breeds more success. The more investors it attracts, the more mutual funds are created to compete for their investment dollars and the more choices investors have to place their investment dollars.

History of SRI Performance

Measuring the performance of an investment strategy—any investment strategy—is subjective at best. Not only must you examine the soundness of the strategy, but also its execution. A good investment strategy is no better than a bad strategy if the investor doesn't execute it correctly. You must also consider that a strategy may work better in certain market conditions, but not so well in other market conditions.

Critics of socially responsible investing note that most screens exclude the basic industries, which includes almost all "smoke-stack" manufacturing and some noncyclical companies like cigarette and alcohol products. Detractors point out that by avoiding certain sectors automatically, SRI misses many opportunities for significant gains. *Value investors*, who look for stocks selling below their true value, often find opportunity in these sectors of the economy. Traditional value investors look for opportunities (think stocks on sale) to buy a stock they believe will rise in price because it is currently undervalued by the market. Many of the most successful investors use this strategy.

def•i•ni•tion

Value investing is a strategy that seeks stocks that the market has priced lower than the companies' true value. The value investor counts on the market recognizing the company's true worth at some point and biding the stock's price up. Some of the most successful investors of all time have been value investors.

Growth investing is a strategy that attempts to identify companies with significant growth potential. Growth investors make money by knowing when to sell a growth stock before it reaches the limits of its growth. Growth stocks that fail to keep growing often fall sharply in price.

Socially responsible investor screens tend to favor technology and service sector companies because they have low ecological impacts. Many are also smaller, new companies managed and staffed by people more in-tune with some of the same issues important to SRI investors. Many of these so-called new economy companies fall into the *growth* category on the investing spectrum, meaning the company is expected to grow much more rapidly than the economy or other companies. Growth stocks led the stock market in the bull market of the late 1990s—the exact type of companies SRI investors buy, which explains why some SRI portfolios outperformed during that time.

The superior performance of the SRI strategy during this bull market was simply a matter of being at the right place with the right strategy at the right time, detractors argue. A legitimate investment strategy works in good markets and bad, the detractors state. Unfortunately, investors will find very few mutual funds that are successful in all types of markets, regardless of its investment strategy. This will be true for SRI funds as well as traditional funds. It is common knowledge in the investment community that many traditional mutual funds that go on a hot streak for a couple of years often fall hard and fast. The investment strategy the manager was using worked for a particular market condition, but

Red Flag

Although SRI investment success can be attributed to several factors, some of the most popular screens favor high-tech companies. When this sector is hot, SRI funds will likely do well. The challenge to the fund manager is to maintain performance when the high-tech sector is off.

when market and economic factors changed, his winning game plan fell apart.

In our discussion of mutual funds, we will examine what it takes to make a fund successful and how you can use that information to choose an SRI fund that meets your needs. The issue of return is important because you should not have to sacrifice your retirement fund to invest where you feel comfortable.

However, some SRI investors take up shareholder advocacy as a prime part of their socially responsible investing strategy. This may require you to invest without a thought to return in order to gain access to annual meetings and so on. In these situations, you aren't typically investing huge sums, so any loss should be minimal and something you can afford.

Community investing poses another situation where, because of the local nature of a project, you have limited choices about where to place your money. If you are going to participate in local projects, the money you deposit or invest may or may not be at market rates. We'll discuss this in more detail in Chapter 9.

Responsible Tip

Socially responsible investors have enough choices that there is no reason to settle for poor performance. The "mainstreaming" of SRI will continue, which will make it even easier for investors to shop for a good return.

What Comes First, Value or Values?

The beginnings of the socially responsible investing movement for individual investors came not from financial professionals, but from people involved in social justice issues. The Pax World Fund was the first mutual fund for individual investors interested in having their investment dollars reflect their personal values. Historically, personal values drove the growth of SRI investing. As the number of investment options grew and SRI became more sophisticated, investors found that they could achieve financial goals without violating personal values.

Recent studies by a mutual fund indicated that financial return is very important to SRI investors. Many SRI investors count on their socially responsible investment portfolios to achieve all of their financial goals.

As we'll discuss in the chapters on SRI investment products, socially responsible investors have all the tools they need to meet almost any financial goal. While it is obvious that socially responsible investors consider more than just the rate of return on their investments, a large and growing body of SRI investment options provides equal opportunity for SRI investors to meet all their financial needs while being consistent with their values.

Making a Statement and Making Money

Socially responsible investors initially found themselves in an odd position. Traditional, conservative investors scoffed at any investment strategy that considered anything but pure return on investment. Some liberals challenged SRI as selling out to the establishment. As socially responsible investing gained some success in shaping corporate policies and its growth spawned new investment opportunities, those criticisms faded. The reality of SRI is that you can make a statement about your values and earn a competitive return on your investment. Investing in socially responsible mutual funds or building your own portfolio of stocks and bonds that meet your social screens doesn't assure you of a profit, nor does it automatically mean a loss. Socially responsible investing then is just like traditional investing, there is risk involved and you may lose money. Some investments will earn a better return than other investments. Unless your social screens are extreme, there are ample choices to properly diversify an SRI portfolio. To these choices, you can apply traditional investment analysis tools to select the investments that best fit your portfolio needs and risk profile.

Responsible Tip

Despite the admonitions of some financial professionals in the early days of SRI, there are plenty of socially responsible investment vehicles to meet your social and financial goals.

The Truth About SRI Performance

The performance of socially responsible investments is a subject of much concern for its advocates. Early descriptions of SRI as underperforming traditional investments were inaccurate when applied to all funds, but have persisted as perceived truth for many years. SRI advo-cates can roll out stacks of performance data they claim not only shows that myth to be wrong, but also shows that socially responsible invest-ing outperforms traditional investing. Peter Camejo has written a book on the subject, *The SRI Advantage: Why Socially Responsible Investing has Outperformed Financially.* His arguments and those of other expert contributors are that SRI screens select companies that are financially strong, less likely to be sued or commit a crime, and are in tune with customers and society. The book was compiled in the 2001–2002 time-frame.

While it is interesting to note their arguments for the value of SRI screens and the performance history of SRI mutual funds, investors don't profit from the past. The author and contributors make the point that SRI screens can enhance performance, however, no investor buys large groups of mutual funds. Most of us buy fewer than 10 to balance our portfolios. Some investors may buy fewer than five. So, discussing the overall performance of SRI funds as a universe is not helpful. You want to know how to find a fund that matches your values and financial expectations for a return. If SRI funds as a group out perform a similar group of nonscreened funds (traditional mutual funds), but the fund you own is down, that's the only number that matters to you.

In the chapters on mutual funds, we'll discuss the factors that help drag down returns, such as expenses. One of the most popular forms of mutual fund investing is in index funds that mimic the performance of a selected group of stocks. The most famous stock index is the Dow Jones Industrial Average. Although it contains only 30 stocks, the Dow is considered one of the most impor-tant large company stock indexes in the world. Another popular index is the S&P 500, which includes 500 leading companies. This index is widely considered a proxy for the whole stock market because of its broad composition. The S&P 500 is commonly used by financial profes-sionals as a benchmark to measure performance. For example, invest-ments are said to "beat the market"

Success Stories

The development of socially responsible indexes was an important step in adding credibility to SRI investing. It gave practitioners a yardstick to measure how well they were doing and created the SRI "market" much like the S&P 500 is the traditional stock market proxy.

if they perform better than the S&P 500. Many traditional mutual funds measure their annual performance against the S&P 500. Several index mutual funds follow the S&P 500. These funds own the same stocks that comprise the S&P 500 and their goal is to match the performance of the index.

The Domini 400 Social Index compiled by KLD Research & Analytics is a comparable index for socially responsible stocks—that is, stocks screened for ecological and social issues. The Domini 400 is used in much the same way as the S&P 500. SRI mutual funds use it to measure performance and index funds exist to track its performance. We'll discuss the Domini 400 index and its importance more in the mutual fund chapters.

For now, let's look at the performance of the index relative to the S&P 500 to see how it informs our discussion of SRI and performance. The Domini 400 was formed in 1990, so it has a number of years of operating history. Has the Domini 400 consistently beaten the S&P 500? The answer is no. In some years, the S&P 500 has outperformed the Domini 400 and in other years, the Domini 400 was the better performer. This is not unexpected, despite the enthusiastic claims from SRI investing advocates. Unless you only invest in index funds, it doesn't really matter whether the Domini 400 was on top one year and the S&P 500 was the winner the next. The reality is that over the life of the Domini 400, the performance of the two indexes was very close. The Domini 400 had a slight edge with an annualized return of 11.87 percent compared to 11.31 percent for the S&P 500 (as of August 31, 2007). During the life of the Domini 400, there have been years when it performed several percentage points over the S&P 500 and years when it underperformed by several percentage points.

Another Reason SRI Is Mainstream

Socially responsible investing is no longer considered marginal by many investors and professionals in the financial community. The proven performance of some SRI investments has also contributed to the acceptance by the mainstream investment community. The history of socially responsible investing has shown, you are not automatically penalized by choosing to express your values in where you place your money. Not only that, but there are many large pension funds, university endowments, healthcare organizations, etc. that are SRI investors, which further demonstrates that SRI is quickly becoming a mainstream investment concept.

There are other reasons SRI is considered part of mainstream investing and we'll explore those in the chapters on issues. People considering socially responsible investing should understand that there is a broad range of opportunities under that umbrella. Finding one that matches your values and financial goals is a matter of doing your homework—just as you would do when examining any other investment opportunity.

Socially responsible investors have argued for years that offending industries and companies pass costs they should be responsible for to others, most often the public. The favorite example is tobacco companies. No tobacco company would be profitable—or even stay in business long—if it was responsible for the health costs associated with tobacco use. The massive national tobacco settlement of 1998 called for tobacco companies to make payments totaling about $246 billion over 25 years. While this sounds like a huge sum, the cost to the country in health care related to tobacco usage approaches $96 billion per year. Tobacco-related deaths top 400,000 per year. The settlement was a slap on the wrist.

> **Responsible Tip**
>
> Success in socially responsible investing requires the same skills and work as is required to succeed in traditional investing, especially if you are going to invest in individual stocks.

Screening out tobacco companies and polluters that often pass the cost of clean up to taxpayers, identifies financially stronger companies that are less likely to face large lawsuits or liability issues because they are better corporate citizens, SRI advocates say. In that sense, SRI proponents argue social screening reduces risk by eliminating companies that may be targets for lawsuits or government actions. Reducing risk while improving return is the ultimate goal of mainstream investing strategies. If socially responsible investing can help investors accomplish this, it can be argued that these strategies fall into mainstream investing.

Overview of Opportunities

Socially responsible investors have a full range of investment opportunities, just as traditional investors do. They can also measure the performance of their opportunities against both traditional and special SRI market yardsticks. SRI investment opportunities are best known by the 200 plus mutual funds that have been formed in response to market demand. Although some funds have been around for a number of years, as a group SRI funds are still relatively young and relatively small. Many of the funds will not have lengthy performance histories. Although a fund's past, performance is not an indicator of future performance it can give you an idea of how the fund might react in different market conditions. This is especially helpful if the same fund manager has been in charge of the fund for five or ten years. And this is true of any mutual fund—SRI or traditional—an investor may be considering.

Socially responsible investors should also consider which type(s) of investments you are most comfortable owning individual stocks, bond, or mutual funds. Most investors own more than one of these and many own all three, however, they may favor one over the others. Each has its strengths and weaknesses.

Responsible Tip

You can increase your chances for overall portfolio performance and reduce your risk if you spread your investments over several different products and types of investments. Diversification can be an effective risk reduction strategy.

Mutual Fund Performance

Mutual funds are the investment vehicles of choice for most socially responsible investors. We will spend Chapters 14–16 looking at mutual funds in detail. With over 200 SRI mutual funds on the market, it is impossible to generalize about their performance. Some have done very well, some have not done so well, and others have tracked about in the middle on performance relative to similar traditional mutual funds.

One of the common mistakes in looking at mutual fund performance is to compare dissimilar funds; that is funds with a different composition and different objectives. The fair and objective comparison is between funds with a common or similar composition and objective. For example, it is incorrect and misleading to compare a growth mutual fund that invests in large companies with a value mutual fund that invests in small companies.

To gain an understanding of how a fund performed, you need to compare it to similar funds and an overall market gauge of some type. This will give you a picture of whether the fund is a "best of class" fund or just another fund in the mix. More about this process will be included in the mutual fund chapters.

As noted earlier, most SRI investors are deeply concerned about financial return and expect their money to work hard while invested in funds that are supportive of their values. With all the SRI funds available to consumers, this is an entirely reasonable expectation. If, as SRI proponents have argued, socially screened stocks are stronger investments, there is no fundamental reason funds built around them should not perform as well if not better than traditional mutual funds.

Of course, some SRI funds don't perform well. In most cases, you can trace the reasons to faulty management, high expenses, market risk, or other factors. In other words, SRI funds generally underperform for the same reasons traditional mutual funds underperform.

The only factor that may be related to SRI investing is that ecology screens tend to be heavy in technology and service sector companies, while eliminating heavy industry and other traditional "smokestack" industries. When the market favors these companies as it did in the late 1990s tech bull market, SRI funds score impressive gains. When the market shifts away from those sectors, as it did in 2000–2002, some SRI funds can be hurt. The important point to remember is that you aren't automatically penalized by choosing to consider your values when you invest, however, you must do your homework. SRI funds should be analyzed like any traditional mutual fund. We'll look at how that works in the chapters on mutual funds.

> **Red Flag**
>
> If you want a financial advisor to help you with your SRI investing, be sure she understands socially responsible investing and is willing to listen to which social issues (values) are important to you. Expect a personal plan that meets your social as well as your financial needs.

Performance of Stocks

Many investors carry a number of individual stocks along with mutual funds in their portfolio. SRI investors are no different. Unlike mutual funds, however, there is no one to screen stocks for you, unless you work with a financial advisor. In Chapter 23, we'll explore this topic in detail. If you choose to do the research yourself, you'll find research ideas in Appendix A. Investing in individual SRI stocks, which is discussed in detail in Chapter 17, is potentially more rewarding, but carries more risk than investing in mutual funds. It is more risky because if an individual stock goes bad in a mutual fund, it is unlikely to have a huge effect on the fund's performance because it may be one of 75 stocks the fund owns. If you own the stock individually and it goes bad, you must sell quickly or watch your losses mount. If you are reluctant to sell, as many investors are, your losses may mount until you finally give up any chance of recovery. What should have been a small loss is now a big loss.

Owning individual stocks puts that responsibility on you to sell when the stock begins to turn. Knowing when to sell is a difficult skill to master, which is why so many people favor mutual funds over individual stocks. The fund manager makes all those decisions for you.

Responsible Tip

You don't need to own dozens of individual stocks to have a well-rounded portfolio. If you don't own any mutual funds, a careful selection of 10 to 12 individual stocks in diverse industries bought over time can provide you with enough diversification to create a reasonable level of exposure to market risk.

The flip side of that problem is the reward for taking the risk of owning an individual stock. It is possible to enjoy a greater percentage increase by taking the risk of owning individual shares. Your chances for greater share price appreciation are higher with an individual issue.

All of these risks and opportunities are generally true for any investor in individual stocks. The extra work comes in screening companies for your values.

Performance of Bonds

Bonds are legal debt obligations of corporations and governmental entities. Traditional bond investors use them to offset the volatility of the stock market and to provide a source of current income. U.S. Treasury Bonds, Notes, and Bills are among the best known, but are not the only bonds available by a long shot. States and municipalities issue them to fund projects from new roads to dams to other civic projects.

With the exception of U.S. Treasury issues, most bonds are sold by the issuer or are negotiated in an inter-dealer market. The costs are hidden, so it is difficult for individual investors to easily understand pricing and so on. Many SRI investors use bond mutual funds for this portion of their portfolio. While a bond mutual fund and an individual bond don't have the exact same characteristics, the funds are a convenient and easy way to add bonds to your portfolio. SRI bond funds come in many of the same formats as traditional bond funds. The only difference is the SRI bond funds screen the companies behind the bond on a social justice and ecology scale before investing. SRI advocates explain that these screens at the company level can help identify financially stronger companies and safer bonds.

Responsible Tip

Buying individual bonds is possible, but can be very complicated. Most individuals can buy bonds at the time of issue and pay no extra fees or commissions because the issuer usually pays the broker. You really need a broker competent in bonds to help you buy and sell bonds in the open market.

Returns on Community Investment

The other primary investment area associated with SRI is community investing. Socially responsible investors saw a need to provide capital to revitalize low-income areas, mainly in our larger cities. People in these communities were often trapped in a cycle of poverty. The early stages of community investing raised money from a variety of sources to help fund low-income housing projects and other programs. Most of the money to capitalize these efforts came from foundations, grants, generous individuals and so on. The return was below market rates because the goal was to provide capital where the private sector was not willing to risk lending.

More recently, community investing has added a sector of proponents who want to attract market-rate capital to fund projects in low-income communities. This is changing the nature of how community investing is structured and who participates. The area of community investing is one of the most exciting to many SRI participants because it allows them to invest in local projects rather than corporations. This local connection includes banks, credit unions, venture capital partnerships, and other financial organizations.

Investors in many of the newer forms of community investment projects can expect competitive rates of return as well as a sense of connection to their community. We'll explore the whole spectrum of community investment in Chapter 9.

The Least You Need to Know

◆ Socially responsible investing does not mean giving up a competitive rate of return.

◆ A solid financial return is very important to most SRI investors.

◆ Proponents argue that SRI can produce superior rates of return.

◆ Socially responsible investors have a full range of investment products at their disposal.

◆ Mutual funds are the most common investment vehicle for SRI investing.

Shareholder vs. Shareowner vs. Stakeholder

In This Chapter

◆ Profit, the only goal in traditional business models

◆ Individual shareholder passivity and their lack of power in corporate governance

◆ Shareowners are assertive of their rights and seek change from within

◆ Effect of corporate decisions on stakeholders

The myth that individual owners of stock in most corporations have any real say in the governance has been stripped away in the last 20 years. Many individual investors are happy to be passive as long as stock in the company provides a good return.

In recent years, however, more stockholders have become concerned with the way major corporate decisions and policies are made and how much influence management has in the process. As more scandals resulting from management wrongdoing surface, it is clear that some companies have no real accountability to stockholders. Even when there is no evidence of legal or civil misdeeds, a growing number of investors are becoming concerned about such issues as senior management compensation, labor practices, environmental policies, and other social issues. Many of these owners now refer to themselves as shareowners to indicate their active interest in how corporate decisions are made.

At the same time, investors are asking corporations to recognize that they do not operate in a vacuum. The decisions made in the boardroom affect not only shareowners, but employees, customers, suppliers, communities where the company operates, the environment and possibly other constituencies. These stakeholders have a vital interest in how the business does its business.

Responsible Tip

Socially responsible investing involves an understanding of the investor's connection between personal and corporate values.

The difference between shareholder, shareowner, and stakeholder may seem like semantics, but the terms can frame key distinctions in socially responsible investing.

Shareholder: Traditional View of Business Goals

The traditional view of the goal of any business is to maximize shareholder wealth—in other words, to make the owners as much money as possible. In many ways, this makes sense. It is not the purpose of a publicly held corporation to make its management wealthy, although that seems to be happening in too many companies.

Shareholders are the owners who have invested their capital in the corporation and should be rewarded if the company does well. When the first proponents of SRI suggested there might be additional goals besides shareholder wealth, some in the investment community reacted with shock and distain. The idea that a business would have any goal besides making as much money as possible for the owners was totally alien to the critics who went so far as to call SRI "un-American."

Maximizing Shareholder Wealth

The traditional approach to ownership seeks to maximize shareholder wealth. It is management's job to use the assets provided by shareholders to generate the greatest return possible for the owners. There is no doubt that this focus can achieve results if management is talented enough to use the assets wisely. The results are profits returned to shareholders in the form of dividends and ever-higher stock prices.

Pressure from large *institutional investors* such as pension funds, insurance companies, and such for constant growth is equally responsible for the short-term growth strategies that drive business plans. Every quarter, companies announce their earnings, after analysts have already predicted what the major companies will report. If a company falls short of estimated earnings for a quarter, the stock will probably be hammered by investors selling and driving the price down.

def•i•ni•tion

Pension funds, insurance companies, trust funds and other large pools of money are called **institutional investors.** These investors tend to be very conservative. As a group, they own the majority of outstanding shares of stock and can move the price of an individual stock or the whole market up or down, depending on whether they are buying or selling.

For many years, a small, but growing number of shareholders questioned the wisdom of focusing on short-term profits to the exclusion of other priorities. They wondered if the "profit at any price" was a responsible model and suggested that companies had a corporate citizen role that extended beyond making money for its owners and paying management well.

Changing Role of Individual Investors

The nature of individual ownership of stock has changed over the past 50 years. The biggest change has tracked with the growth of the mutual fund industry. The popularity of mutual funds has meant a shift from ownership of individual stocks to ownership in pools of stocks (and other investments). Many investors still own and trade individual stocks, but thanks to the ease of investing in mutual funds and their use in retirement programs such as 401(k) plans, mutual funds or institutional investors such as pension funds own the majority of the shares of individual stocks. For those investors who rely on mutual funds for most or all of their investments, the fund(s) place a barrier between them and what the stocks they own. Many *actively managed mutual funds* may turn over 100 percent of their holdings during the year so even keeping up with what you own through the fund may be difficult.

Concurrent with the growth of mutual funds has been the number of households directly or indirectly owning stocks. As companies eliminated traditional pensions and replaced them with 401(k) plans and other *defined contribution plans*, more families and households have come to rely on those investments to secure their financial futures.

def•i•ni•tion

An **actively managed mutual fund** is one that the manager uses aggressive stock picking strategies attempting to earn the highest return possible. This may mean a significant number of trades during the year.

A **defined contribution plan** is a retirement plan where the contributions to the plan are known, but the ultimate benefits paid in retirement are not. Benefits paid in retirement will depend on the performance of investments made in the defined contribution plan, such as 401(k) retirement plans.

Individual Shareholders as Passive Investors

If you own stock in a corporation, you have certain rights. Those rights include electing a board of directors to represent your interests and to oversee management of your investment. You also have the right to vote on important matters concerning the corporation (approving mergers, for example). And you can attend the annual stockholder's meeting.

Unless you own or control a large block of stock, however, your concerns will largely go unnoticed beyond a boilerplate investor relations letter (signed by a computer in many cases.) Your ability to bring meaningful change to the corporation is severely limited by the way corporations are organized and governed.

The unfortunate truth is that many investors are more than happy to let senior management and the board of directors run the business. As long as many investors get a dividend check every quarter and the stock does reasonably well, they are content to let the system work without them. Of course, the premise isn't wrong. Corporations are supposed to be run by management and the board of directors. It would be chaos if every stockholder tried to micro-manage the business. It becomes a problem when the corporation doesn't act in a manner that the owners (shareholders) feel is appropriate.

Shareholders are passive investors because the system makes it hard for them to be any other way or because they simply don't care how the corporation makes a profit, as long as it does make a profit. For those investors and potential investors who believe it is important how profits are made and do want a voice in matters of corporate social responsibility, being a passive investor is just not acceptable.

Responsible Tip

Shareholder activism is one of the hallmarks of SRI, despite the fact that corporate governance practices are stacked against the small investor. This is one of the reasons for the growth of SRI mutual funds—more clout because of more capital.

Shareowners as Active Owners

Shareholder or shareowner—the difference may not seem great, but for many investors it signals a break with the idea that, even those with only a very tiny piece of ownership, must surrender personal values to invest in stocks. The history of SRI was built around issues that attracted and continue to attract investors. Shareowners place issues that are important to them on the same scale with fundamental financial concerns about the health and future prospects of the company.

Shareowners may be active in selecting investments that meet their values or may carry their involvement a step further by pressing for change in business practices within a particular company or industry.

Shareowner Resolutions Face Mixed Results

Shareholders have a formal way to bring issues before the corporation for consideration. Shareholder resolutions, which are discussed in detail in Chapter 11, allow individuals and other stockowners (mutual funds, institutional investors, and so on) to push for changes that the board of directors and/or management may be reluctant to make.

Shareholder resolutions can be complicated to put together and must meet certain Securities and Exchange Commission guidelines. Some senior managers are reluctant to bring them forward and follow a strict interpretation of the regulations as a disincentive for shareholders to consider this action.

Socially responsible mutual funds and other interested institutional investors have a better chance at the process because they can afford the expertise required to produce resolutions that meet regulatory and company guidelines. Even with the expertise to craft and file the documents, most shareholder resolutions are either withdrawn or do not receive enough votes to pass. Many resolutions that make it to a vote do so with a board of directors' recommendation that stockholders defeat the resolution. If non-SRI institutional investors have any hint the resolution may negatively affect earnings, they will likely vote against it.

> **Success Stories**
>
> Although shareholder resolutions themselves seldom gather a majority of votes, engaging management and directors in dialogue can be much more beneficial. Many of the success stories are achieved behind closed doors through negotiations.

Hundreds of socially responsible shareholder resolutions are introduced each year. Many deal with environmental issues, although a significant number address other concerns such as the AIDS/HIV crisis. Other major issues addressed include:

- Sexual orientation discrimination
- Executive compensation
- Political contributions
- Global warming
- Sustainability reports
- Human rights
- Equal Employment Opportunity
- Annual board election

The reasons the vast majority of shareholder resolutions are either defeated or withdrawn are as varied as the groups presenting them and the companies being confronted. In some cases, management can report they are already addressing the concern raise through a plan or program not readily identified by stockholders. Often a resolution is withdrawn because the group initiating action has opened a dialogue with management on the issue and resolution is sought via that avenue. In other cases, management may discount the resolution as impractical, too costly, or possibly undoable. Management disapproval often sinks a resolution. For example, one of the big arguments against reducing greenhouse gasses for some companies is that it costs a lot of money with very little return as direct benefit.

A problem that is particularly confounding is a practice known as "green-washing." Green-washing is the appearance of doing some socially responsible practice or project, when the corporation is really performing a marketing or public relations exercise. The company can claim some socially responsible policy or action without really changing any existing policy or practice.

Growing Movement to Press for Change

Socially responsible investing covers a wide spectrum of interests and issues. In coming chapters, you'll see the breadth and depth of issues that bring socially responsible investors together. One of the methods you can use to categorize socially responsible investors is by their approach to problem companies. One group will exclude those companies whose products or corporate practices conflict with its values. Those conflicts could come from production of tobacco, alcohol, or firearms, for example. It could also be driven by policies and practices that were environmentally abusive.

Many SRI investors screen out the worst companies in a field, and then use dialogue and resolutions to encourage progress in the companies they hold. These companies are not the best or worst, rather they are in the middle in terms of corporate responsibility.

Responsible Tip

Many SRI investors find that simply avoiding a company is not enough. They prefer some type of action that engages the company and encourages positive change.

Although rare, some investors who object to these products and practices may invest in a company to establish a dialogue with management and the board of directors. This is usually done by a mutual fund that advocates on behalf of its shareholders who all share similar values. A socially responsible mutual fund can be in a better position to advocate for change. It usually represents a larger block of voting stock and has the resources to employ the professionals who can engage companies in informal dialogue as well as preparing more formal shareholder resolutions.

The SRI movement has not been an organized effort, but a collection of many groups of investors who share common values. As we have seen, some SRI movements have even been in conflict with other groups whose values were at odds. For example, religious groups might object to the use of condoms while groups advocating safe sex in countries where AIDS/HIV is a national crisis may push for massive condom distribution.

Responsible Tip

Socially responsible shareowners often consider it a success when a company chooses to act in a responsible manner even if it is slightly more costly or time-consuming to do so. Sometimes greater disclosure and transparency alone is also considered a success.

The combative role of SRI (no investments in offending companies, boycotts of products/companies, divesture of investments in countries with poor human rights or environmental records, and so on) is still part of the scene, but many proponents are opting for what they consider more constructive tactics.

The concept of shareowners, whether exercised by an SRI mutual fund or as an individual investor making ethical investment decisions, places importance on acting like the owner of the company wanting to impart your values to the company. A successful SRI strategy helps companies see how ethical decisions are good business as well. Many SRI strategies seek dialogue with companies rather than confrontation. If there is an environmental concern, for example, the dialogue may seek to keep the company moving toward a more environmentally friendly policy in incremental steps rather than insist it move to full "compliance" instantly.

One measure of the acceptance of the term and concept of "shareowner" is the number of corporations that now refer to shareholders as shareowners in annual reports and other correspondence. This may signal recognition of shareowners as more active participants in the governance of the corporation or it may just be an investor relations effort. Corporate actions will speak louder than language.

Stakeholder Recognition of Other Parties

The shareholder view of corporations suggests that its sole role is to increase the wealth of its owners. Under that operating basis, the corporation can focus on a narrow ban of inputs: customers, employees, suppliers, and investors. Some corporations now regard that view as limited and shortsighted. A broader view reveals that corporations operate in a wider context where they influence and are, in turn, influenced by a variety of different constituencies.

This broader view, often called the stakeholder theory, is the subject of academic research in the field of business ethics. The stakeholder concept has been explored longer in Europe and Great Britain in particular than here in America. The stakeholder theory doesn't abandon the notion of creating wealth for the shareholders, but takes a broader and longer-term view of a corporation's role in society. One stakeholder theory suggests that the corporation has an obligation of fairness to any stakeholder entity or group that adds value to the company.

> **Responsible Tip**
>
> The stakeholder theory is, at its simplest, a doctrine of fairness—a way of responding to those entities that positively affect the life of the corporation.

Corporate Responsibility Beyond Profit

A corporation that embraces the stakeholder concept makes a statement that it has a responsibility beyond making a profit for its owners. Before a company can consider the importance of stakeholders, it has to identify them. Not every company has exactly the same list of stakeholders, although most will share the same types. Some common stakeholders beyond the traditional employees and investors include:

- **Community or many communities**—Corporations operate in one or more communities and as such are citizens with responsibilities of citizenship. It receives all the benefits of being a citizen of the community and shares in the responsibilities. These responsibilities extend beyond the legal requirements of paying taxes, and so on. Most of the company's employees are probably citizens of the community who are concerned about schools, public safety, the arts, and all the other items that add to the quality of life. Corporate citizens have an obligation to play a role in the life of the community as a contributor to charitable organizations, as a provider of leadership in civic activities and possibly are a patron of the arts.

- **Suppliers**—Not all businesses include suppliers as stakeholders, but those that depend or want to depend on local sources or that set aside a certain amount of purchases for minority or women-owned businesses or small businesses, often see the need to work with suppliers on more than just a best-price basis. A good example of this is the number of coffee shops that use "Fair Trade" coffee, which is supplied with the understanding that the growers get a fair price for their coffee beans. With domestic suppliers, some companies may offer technical or managerial support to small businesses to help them succeed.

Responsible Tip

There is plenty of justification for a company wanting its suppliers to stay in business, especially if there aren't many that can supply critical pieces to a company's process. It is in a company's best interest to help them succeed if possible.

- **Unions**—The relationship between management and organized labor is often adversarial. But unions are true stakeholders in most businesses. This doesn't mean management rolls over to union demands, but it does mean that the legitimacy of the union to represent workers is recognized and respected. Working with labor in a forthright manner goes a long way toward treating them like the stakeholders they are. If that air of trust is established, it will be easier to deal with unpleasant situations such as layoffs or contract negotiations when they arise.

- **Government entities**—Local, state and federal governments are partners with just about every business to one extent or another.

Between taxes and various permitting processes, the tensions can run high. If a company can look beyond its own self-interests, a positive relationship can be beneficial to both parties. This is especially true on the local level, which may welcome a company's input on questions facing decision makers.

Examples of Recognizing Stakeholders

What role do corporations have as citizens? What responsibilities do corporations have to their various stakeholders? The stakeholder theory is one of the leading topics discussed and debated by business ethicists. Although not all corporations formally acknowledge the stakeholder concept, many companies understand they ignore those whose lives and fortunes they touch at their own peril. At its minimum, good stakeholder relations are good public relations. Unfortunately, some companies will only view the concept in that light—a way to help smooth over any problems before they happen.

Some corporations embrace an operational model that considers the rights and inputs of stakeholders as protection against pressure groups and as a more responsible way to manage the business. Companies that isolate themselves when times are good may find little goodwill to be had when fortunes are reversed.

Responsible Tip

Companies that don't need any relationships when times are prosperous may not feel that way if business turns sour.

An all-too unfortunate example of how a company might work with its stakeholders involves closing a facility that will result in workers losing their jobs, suppliers losing business and a community losing an asset.

A company with little concern for its stakeholders might give employees as little notice as legally possible as required by the state. That could be days or weeks notice that they are losing their jobs. In the case of manufacturing or assembly jobs, it is possible the work is being sent overseas to a cheap labor country, where the company can significantly reduce costs and avoid most of the worker protection laws in the United States. The company may offer (or may have to offer by law) the displaced workers positions at other facilities, but in most cases there aren't enough open positions and most workers don't want to move many miles away for a low-paying job.

If the facility was very old, the company may sell it for next to nothing leaving a potential environmental mess to be cleaned up.

The community loses jobs, a facility on the tax rolls and a source of business for other local businesses.

Corporations that consider their stakeholders are not immune from having to close facilities (they still have an obligation to make money for their shareholders). But they would approach the problem differently.

A company that considered its stakeholders in the closing of a facility would plan the transition to have the least impact possible. This might start by announcing their intentions several months in advance of the mandated state required notification. The company would work with local training facilities to help workers get additional training for other jobs. Other companies in the market, including competitors would be contacted and workers would be encouraged to apply for openings. Job fairs would be organized.

Responsible Tip

Stakeholders provide companies with real benefits and to ignore them is overlooking an obvious asset, especially when the company has a problem.

The company would work with the local government and real estate community to find a buyer for the facility. If a buyer was not found and the facility lent itself to this usage, the company might consider a low-cost lease to the city's economic development department to use the building as incubator space. New businesses could rent space at below market rates while they were getting started and move out to bigger spaces when ready.

If the facility was old and/or had environmental problems (asbestos, chemical spills, and so on), the company would clean up the problems before selling or demolishing the facility.

These are simple examples of things a company might do to acknowledge that stakeholders are important in a worst-case situation (plant closing). When contrasted with the first company that stole away in the night and left its employees and community without any attempt to ease a bad situation, these actions are notably better.

The Least You Need to Know

- The shareholder perspective is the sole purpose of the company is to create value for shareholders.

- Shareholders tend to be passive investors, letting the board of directors and management run the company.

- Shareowners want a more active role in the management of the company.

- Shareowners press for change using shareholder resolutions and SRI mutual funds

- Stakeholders provide a benefit to corporations in a tangible or intangible manner.

- More companies are recognizing the role of multiple stakeholder groups in their success.

Part 2

Important Issues to SRI Investors

Socially responsible investors address many issues. Most fall
into the broad categories of issues effecting the environment or
harming our society, concerns over corporate governance or the
economy, and community development. Scandals over corporate
governance and the lack of urgency on critical environmental
issues push investors to become involved in SRI.

Chapter 4

Environmental Issues

In This Chapter

- ◆ Ecology: a founding issue of the socially responsible investing movement
- ◆ Ecological concerns: once fringe now mainstream
- ◆ Environmental issues in production and packaging
- ◆ Global ecological issues gaining importance

The idea of making the environment a part of the socially responsible investing movement has always caused concern. In the early days, hot social issues such as Apartheid, the Vietnam War, and nuclear energy shared the spotlight. The business community found environmental issues more frightening and threatening, because any movement that caught on could lead to stricter regulatory controls. Though not every business was a polluter, some polluted without knowing how much damage they were doing. But there were too many ecological disasters for industry to hide from the consequences forever. Chemical waste, asbestos, toxins in lakes and streams, oil spills, air pollutants, and contaminated work areas led to a number of landmark regulatory steps.

The most significant regulatory step was the creation of the Environmental Protection Agency, which is charged with protecting the environment. The current controversy over global warming is a direct outgrowth of generations of concern for the environment finally achieving mainstream attention.

One of the Founding Issues

Concern for the environment is not a new issue for socially responsible investors. It was a founding issue of modern SRI. Like other socially responsible investing issues, environmental concerns span a wide spectrum from the very radical to more moderate. Some SRI investors practice absolute exclusion (as best as can be executed). They have a zero tolerance for environmental sins and want nothing to do with any company that has a hint of pollution in its products or operations. On the other end of the spectrum are SRI investors that acknowledge steps companies are taking to improve their ecological scorecard and work with them to improve their score.

Responsible Tip

Global warming is going to be a controversial and difficult issue for many years as society grasps the full implications of what changes will need to be made to halt the damage.

The issue that has attracted considerable interest from consumers, political leaders, scientists, and the business community is global warming. Many in the environment movement see global warming and the accompanying climatological disasters as the result of decades of environmental neglect. Others simply don't believe it is even happening.

The Green Movement

Former Vice President Al Gore's book and Academy-award winning documentary *An Inconvenient Truth*, brought the issue of global warming into sharp focus for many people. He was honored for years of work on global warming with the 2007 Noble Peace Prize. For a number of SRI investors, it was just another reason to invest their money in companies that take a commitment to ecology seriously. These investors commitment to ecology and "green investing" began in the 1960s and gained momentum as nuclear energy was spreading as the answer to a growing economy's need for more power. Early SRI investors who focused on the ecology excluded companies involved in nuclear energy.

The conflict over nuclear energy was heated (pardon the pun). It galvanized a core of environmental leaders in the SRI movement. Companies involved in nuclear energy were excluded from socially responsible investor's portfolios. A number of nuclear plants were built or licensed in the 1970s, but with much protest. More than a few communities objected to reactors being built near their populations. Environmentalists objected to the reactor's need for large volumes of water for cooling and to run the generators. Warm water discharge into lakes often created ecological problems. The danger of an accidental discharge of radiation worried people living close to the reactors.

> **Success Stories**
>
> Socially responsible investors avoided nuclear power companies in the 1970–1980s because of the dangers to the environment and the risky financial condition of the operators. They were right in avoiding those investments for the most part, as they proved poor returns.

One major environmental problem with nuclear energy is storage of spent energy rods. These fuel rods remain highly radioactive for hundreds of years, but are not suitable for use in the reactors any longer. Storage of these spent rods presents a present and future liability. This liability is not adequately reflected on the financial statements of nuclear energy companies, SRI investors contend. Even though the federal government has capped a company's liability in the event of a nuclear accident at $10 billion that has never been tested in court.

The interest in the ecology as a socially responsible investing focus is broader than nuclear energy. It has ranged from protesting timber companies that clear-cut old-growth forest to convincing companies to use recycled materials in their packaging to supporting steps to curb pollution through new technology.

> **Responsible Tip**
>
> Like other forms of socially responsible investing, environmental concerns take many forms from energy production, to manufacturing, to recycling, and to other policies that affect the environment.

Socially responsible investing screens for ecology look for specific exclusions (nuclear energy is on most lists), while others look for companies working to improve their impact on the ecology. In Chapter 11, we'll look at how some SRI investors prefer to work with companies to change behavior rather than exclude them from investment. This form of SRI has gained a strong following, particularly among those with an ecology agenda. Thanks for environmental laws and societal pressure, more companies are open to changes that make them environmentally friendly. SRI investors working with companies can help make those changes.

From Fringe to Mainline

The single event that turned the tide for the environmental movement was the creation of the Environmental Protection Agency (EPA) in 1970. Prior to that, enforcing laws protecting the environment was difficult and often bogged down in court. The EPA had the power of the federal government to take action against polluters. It could even force state and local governments to act. One of its strongest weapons was requiring developers to file an environmental impact statement before permits on certain projects could be granted. The EPA was no friend of business and remains a thorn in the side of many today. It has its critics who complain the agency has become bogged down in bureaucracy and too close to those it is suppose to regulate. For SRI investors, the EPA represents an agency that can enforce protections for the environment—something that was missing.

Success Stories

Along with creation of the EPA, Earth Day has done more to keep the environment and the importance of ecology in front of the public than any other single event. Socially responsible investors manifest the spirit of Earth Day by allowing ecologically based issues to guide their investments.

The same year the EPA was formed (1970) Sen. Gaylord Nelson of Wisconsin organized the first Earth Day to acknowledge the importance of ecology. Patterned after "teach-ins" he had observed during anti-war protests, Earth Day attracted 20 million people around the county—a number that astounded everyone involved with the ecology movement. Earth Day is now an international event celebrating the environment and is attended by hundreds of millions of people.

Clearly, many people feel strongly about ecology. Socially responsible investors who specifically wish to emphasize ecology will find a large number of opportunities. Since ecology is a core SRI issue, a number of funds with lengthy histories are available. Some use exclusion screens to avoid investing in companies that harm the environment, while others choose to work with companies to improve their environmental policies.

Environmental Issues on Two Fronts

For many people, environmental issues are about recycling, turning off the lights when not needed, and driving a fuel-efficient car. While these are important environmental concerns, they are not the ones specific to investors. SRI investors focus on two aspects of corporations: their operations and their products. Both have environmental impacts and SRI investors may exclude a company based on practices in either area. Those SRI investors who choose to lobby for change from within the corporation may focus on one or both of these issues as areas that need improvement from an environmental perspective. Operational issues include pollution, materials, and storage of components or finished products. Product issues might include packaging, materials, safety and other concerns. SRI investors realize that the manufacturing and distribution process is complicated and potentially threatening to the environment without some forethought by the company. The payoff for investors, SRI proponents argue, is in companies that have a much lower liability for environmental lawsuits or legal action by a regulatory body.

In recent years, more companies are adopting environmental statements and promoting their concern for the environment in marketing material. This is a reflection of ecology's importance to consumers and investors.

> **Red Flag**
>
> Environmental issues raised at annual meetings through shareholder resolutions are among the most contentious. Companies fear, with some justification, that raising these types of concerns may frighten investors and hurt stock prices.

Operational Environmental Issues

Operational environmental issues are the most obvious problems in many companies. The image of smoke belching out of tall smokestacks or pipes draining evil looking liquids into rivers is the iconic image of American industry for many in the early days of the environmental movement. Unfortunately, it was more than an image. Fouled air and polluted waterways are the legacy of that lack of concern for the environment. While some progress has been made in cleaning emissions, the damage remains, especially in many of the country's rivers and lakes. Sediment contaminated with chemicals makes many of our rivers so polluted it is unsafe to eat fish caught out of them.

Thanks to the EPA and aggressive action by civil courts, many of the worst polluters have cleaned up their emissions or gone out of business. SRI investors that exclude these industrial polluters still leave many off the list of approved investments because the companies haven't gone far enough to control the environmental damage they do in the making of their products. The companies might argue that they are within the letter of the law, but SRI investors are more concerned about the spirit of protecting our environment than whether a company has dotted every "i" and crossed every "t" on the regulatory checklist.

No company will get a perfect score on the environmental scorecard (nor would any family). All companies, even nonmanufacturing firms, directly or indirectly impact the environment. Screens exclude those whose environmental transgressions go beyond the norm. SRI investors believe, with justification, that companies scoring low on environmental issues are open to lawsuits and governmental actions that would probably impact the company financially. Management that dodges environmental issues (and perhaps law) is likely to dodge some other inconvenient rule or regulation that gets in the way of running the business. This type of attitude reveals a potential for trouble. SRI investors believe they are better off avoiding these companies.

Responsible Tip

Penalties for pollution violations are nothing compared to the civil lawsuits a company can face if their pollution is tied to some harm, such as illnesses of nearby citizens. This is one reason SRI investors avoid companies with a history of polluting.

Many environment screens exclude oil companies for a variety of concerns. When oil companies are posting record profits and their stocks are paying handsome returns, critics of socially responsible investing point out the terrific opportunities missed because of the screens. This will be an issue for anyone interested in SRI investing. Great short-term financial opportunities will be missed because excluded industries are on a hot streak. But SRI investors should look at the long-term and not measure success or failure on strictly short-term gains or losses.

Environmental issues lend themselves to long-term solutions. A company that might otherwise be a SRI investment candidate except for environmental problems could need several years to correct those problems. Long-term SRI investors that were willing to stick with the company while it corrected its environmental problems may be rewarded with a boost in the stock's price when the market recognizes the company's accomplishment.

Carbon Footprints

One major concern being addressed by companies is their "carbon footprint." As it relates to global warming, a carbon footprint is the amount of *carbon dioxide* given off during the consumption of fossil fuels (coal, oil, natural gas, and so on). The larger a company's footprint, the more greenhouse gasses it pushes into the atmosphere. These gases are directly related to the warming of the planet. While many gases dissipate harmlessly into the atmosphere, others, including carbon dioxide, do not. Scientists believe the build up of the so-called greenhouse gases is causing global warming.

def•i•ni•tion

> **Carbon dioxide** is a colorless, odorless gas produced from the combustion of fossil fuels. It occurs naturally in our atmosphere and acts as a blanket, among other things, to regulate the Earth's temperature. Global warming theorists say we are producing so much carbon dioxide (CO_2) that the percentage is changing and more heat than normal is being retained.

Carbon footprints are a way companies can measure their impact on global warming and are usually listed in tons of carbon dioxide released into the atmosphere. All companies (and families) have a carbon footprint, even service companies that don't manufacture anything. Any consumer of energy leaves a carbon footprint because of the electricity used for lights and heating/cooling, the fuel used for vehicles, and the energy needed to create anything. The more energy a company consumes, the larger its footprint.

Numerous calculators are available for figuring carbon footprints. Each makes assumptions about energy sources, types of equipment, and other factors. The better calculators allow entry of multiple variables. For example, you may be asked to enter the number of cars in your family, the approximate gas mileage, size of house, type of heating, your zip code, and so on. The calculator uses industry averages and standards for carbon emissions to calculate your carbon footprint. The theory behind the calculators is sound, even if the actual calculations may lack precision.

Carbon footprint calculators are important instruments for consumers and investors who wish to understand the impact of energy consumption. Some companies publish their carbon footprint information. In England and Europe, moves to make reporting mandatory, such as labeling consumer goods with some type of carbon footprint code, are on the horizon. Investors, like consumers who are concerned about the environment, will have more information available to them in the near future. Conscious consumers will require this type of reporting. Companies that get out front on this issue will be rewarded in the stock market and at the corner market.

Responsible Tip

Carbon trading, emissions offsets, and other means of reducing a company's carbon footprint through a free market solution are gaining acceptance. The key is to ensure the total carbon units keeps dropping so the total reflects an overall yearly drop.

Reducing a company's carbon footprint may not be easy—reducing power consumption through conservation measures can save some energy, but it will only take a company so far. Some companies address the issue by offsetting their carbon footprint with measures such as planting trees (trees absorb carbon dioxide from the atmosphere) or buying carbon offsets or renewable energy certificates. These market derivatives allow a company to offset

part of its carbon footprint. The system of trading carbon offsets is complicated. Basically trading allows companies that can easily reduce their
carbon footprint (for example, a service company) to take carbon units
from a company that can't easily reduce its output (for example, a manufacturer).

Socially responsible investors can track companies that are working
to reduce their carbon footprint. Many companies are reporting the
results of their efforts. In cases of emissions trading or the purchase of
energy offsets, the transactions sometimes show up on corporate financial statements. The idea of carbon footprints is still new and being
refined. It may be replaced by more sophisticated measurements or
the business community may settle on a general standard. Either way,
SRI investors concerned about the environment and particularly global
warming can look forward to having more information on companies
that are working to meet their standards. In the meantime, SRI investors rely on company reports and measures from third parties to verify
carbon reductions—either directly or through offsets.

The offsets and carbon trading programs are becoming more sophisticated with greater verification capabilities. SRI investors can rely on
their measurements to track how well companies are reducing their
carbon footprint.

Product Issues

Operational issues of businesses are not the only problem for the environment. Many companies produce products that may be harmful to
the environment or the packaging
of a product may be harmful. For
example, Americans use approximately 2.5 million plastic bottles
every hour, but very few are recycled. For SRI investors concerned
about the environment, this issue
troubles them greatly. In some cases,
socially responsible investors work
with companies to change the way
they do business so they have a less
harmful impact on the environment.

Success Stories

Small steps can make a big
difference. For example, a
computer manufacturer commits to reducing the packing
material in each product it
ships. This company ships
well over a million products a
year, so even a small reduction per shipment adds up to
much less packing material
going into landfills.

Many companies that use excessive packaging or packaging that is not environmentally friendly believe they have no responsibility for their product or packaging after the sale is made. Someone else, they argue, should solve the problem of disposing of the packaging. This is an example of how companies can push off costs on to others and make themselves more profitable. By not concerning themselves with the disposal of the packaging, the company forces taxpayers to pay for a collection and retention system for the accumulated trash the product creates (trash collectors and landfills). It is incorrect to think that companies don't have a responsibility after the sale of their product. The use of materials in products or packaging that can't be recycled, or that present a hazard during disposal, forces taxpayers to pay for a company's irresponsible action. This is, in effect, a government subsidy to the business, since the company is escaping an expense and passing that cost along to the government. To counter this, some states use deposits, notably on glass or plastic bottles, to encourage recycling.

When companies are trying to reduce their contribution to pollution and overflowing landfills, SRI investors look at scorecards that include policies on packaging, recycling, energy conservation in product distribution, and paper reduction plans. For product-oriented companies, reducing and/or changing product packaging can make a significant difference to the environment. For example, if a company changes its packaging to either a recyclable material or one that is biodegradable, it lowers the cost for future generations who will have to pay for new landfills or other means of dealing with garbage that can't be recycled and won't go away. Companies that adopt materials that can be recycled or are biodegradable may pay a higher price today, but SRI investors believe they will eventually financially pass rivals that ignore long-term solutions in favor of short-term gains. It is not inconceivable that the government might some day soon begin enforcing mandatory changes in packaging beyond what is already in place. Companies that make the switch to new environmentally safe materials and processes ahead of the game will likely be positioned for successful compliance.

Success Stories

Many recycling steps have been voluntary. But that is changing in some areas where compliance is no longer a matter of individual company decision, but community necessity. This is particularly true in some areas of the water-starved west where consumption is closely regulated.

Recycling is already the law in some locations—companies and individuals are not allowed to discard recyclable materials with other trash. But the payoff for SRI investors is in reducing the strain on the environment by using recycled materials in production, packaging, and other areas of the company. For companies to score high on recycling their effort must be more than tying a few collection bags by the gate and asking people to drop off recycled goods.

Environmental Impact of China and India

Two of the fastest growing economies in the world are China and India. Between the two countries, approximately one-third of the world's population struggles to better themselves. Both countries have their own economic barriers, but each has managed to develop roaring economies built primarily on cheap labor. Indeed, most of the socially responsible investing complaints against the two—China in particular—are in the area of human rights abuses. But environmental concerns are also high on the list because of the relative lack of controls on industry. China, for example, produces much of its power by coal-fired generators with few pollution controls. Manufacturing facilities have almost no government restraints and may be among the worse polluters on the planet. Both India and China have push policies of exporting manufactured goods—China to a greater degree than India. This emphasis has been without controls on manufacturing or power generation. Among the biggest customers in both China and India for manufactured goods are American companies. In many ways, U.S. companies have outsourced their pollution to China and India.

> **Responsible Tip**
>
> China's pollution problems are so bad that there have been riots because of contaminated water and food supplies. China consistently has several towns in the list of the top 10 most polluted cities in the world.

U.S. Companies Outsourcing Pollution

China is the fastest growing large economy in the world. Although it is not a "free market" economy, it operates with the government's encouragement to produce goods to export. Exporting manufactured goods brings hard currency from countries like the United States into the Chinese economy. China has a stock market, entrepreneurs, and many of the trappings of a free market economy. It is growing at a tremendous rate, fueled in part by government policy that makes doing business with Chinese companies very inexpensive for western companies. There have been numerous allegations of human rights violations, such as forced child labor, prison labor, and slave labor used in Chinese plants to keep costs down.

Socially responsible investors look with skepticism on U.S. companies that outsource work to China and India (or other cheap labor countries). More about this in Chapter 5 when we look at human rights issues, labor concerns, and other societal issues.

In addition to outsourcing manufacturing to a cheap labor country, U.S. companies are outsourcing potential environmental problems to that country. If a product would have an environmental impact and require special equipment or processing to prevent pollution, a manufacturer only has to send the work overseas and labor costs drop dramatically and any potential environmental problems go away.

Socially responsible investors can't ignore environmental problems just because a company has outsourced them to China or India. Polluting the air and water in China or India is just as bad as polluting the air and water here—in fact it is worse because citizens in those countries have fewer rights and avenues for seeking damages caused by polluters than we do. SRI investors will be cautious about investing in companies that have outsourced much of their production. Avoiding U.S. pollution laws is not a sign of good management.

Responsible Tip

Sending pollution overseas is not a solution socially responsible investors support. Companies that practice this type of outsourcing are excluded from most SRI investing screens.

Pollution in the Supply Chain

Companies, especially manufacturing concerns, must buy parts from multiple vendors. China and India are big players in this business also with China in the lead. Parts and components that U.S. firms once bought domestically are now being made in China and to a lesser extent in India. For some U.S. companies, it is a matter of the lowest bidder and no questions asked. There is no concern about the vendor's pollution controls or any other factor. The only important items are price and delivery time. This type of thinking is not characteristic of socially responsible firms. They insist on each link in the supply chain complying with a minimum environmental standard that is probably over what the vendor would do on their own.

It would be a sham to invest in a company that claimed a great environmental policy only to discover that several of its vendors were big polluters in another country. Socially responsible businesses insist that vendors comply with minimally acceptable environmental policies and verify that compliance. SRI investors find that information in company literature and from various socially responsible investing information resources (see Appendix A).

The Least You Need to Know

◆ The environment is a fundamental socially responsible investing issue that attracts many to this style of investing.

◆ SRI investors may exclude companies for environmental issues or choose to work for change.

◆ Companies may have pollution issues in the production and distribution of its products.

◆ Environmental issues in foreign countries like China and India impact socially responsible investors.

Chapter 5

Societal Issues

In This Chapter

- ◆ Socially responsible investors are concerned with social justice issues and work for political change
- ◆ Human rights concerns have been a focus of SRI investors from the early days of the movement
- ◆ As socially responsible investing grew, a subset often called faith-based investing addressed concerns of particular religious communities
- ◆ Product safety as an issue for SRI investors is an extension of environmental concerns

Social justice issues drove the founders of the socially responsible investing concept. The Quakers, Christians, and others spoke out against slavery and war when it was not popular to do so. They backed their words with admonitions against investing in slavery and war efforts. Churches built the first schools for children of slaves and the first public hospitals that took charity cases. Later, religious organizations fought for women's right to vote, temperance, and many other major social issues.

In modern times, groups that supported socially responsible investing also backed the civil rights movement, and continue to promote equal employment opportunities. For many SRI investors, the human rights fight has moved offshore, much the same way some environmental issues have been outsourced. SRI investors interested in societal issues come from a variety of perspectives and with differing agendas. Some of these agendas may conflict with other SRI investors, as we'll see in this chapter. The socially responsible investing world that focuses on societal issues is diverse and passionate. If you have a concern about human rights, social or political change, or investing in accordance with religious values, socially responsible investing has a place for you.

def•i•ni•tion

Social justice is the concept that everyone in society deserves fair treatment. It goes beyond what the law prescribes and asks what is right and just. But different groups may define "justice" differently.

SRI for Social/Political Change

For many socially responsible investors, making the world a better place for everyone to live means changing social and political structures to be more responsive to the needs of all people, not just those with power. This is a radical concept for many investors who have grown up in an economic system that rewards power and punishes weakness. Corporate America is a powerful force for change and it is through this venue that SRI investors act. Socially responsible investors concerned with human rights take their charge from religious directions or a more humanistic sense of fair play. Regardless of the motivation, societal issues figure prominently in why many people turn to socially responsible investing. Many SRI investors interested in social and/or political change are inclined to be involved in advocacy as opposed to passive investing (more about shareholder rights in Chapter 11).

Major companies can have a direct affect on social issues, both at home and aboard. They employ thousands of people and through connections to suppliers, distributors and others can influence tens of thousands more. Changing the policies or encouraging a major company to establish a new policy that supports a social or political goal is a major step in gaining broader acceptance of the goal.

Racism, Diversity, Social Justice

Although great strides have been made since the civil rights movement of the 1950s and 1960s, much remains to be done. Minorities still are under-represented in many corporate executive ranks. When systematic discrimination in hiring and promotion can be proved, the results are painful for companies in terms of public relations and fines. In 1998, Texaco settled a hiring discrimination suit for $175 million and a court-ordered change in the way it recruited, hired and promoted its employees. To its credit, Texaco changed its culture over a period of years and went beyond the court-ordered steps to improve minority hiring and promoting.

Socially responsible investors note that examples such as Texaco that verify the business soundness of having strong policies of minority recruiting, hiring, and promotion. Companies with those policies in place are unlikely targets for huge discrimination settlements. Not only are those policies right from a moral point of view, they are also smart business because they prevent potential problems.

Success Stories
While it is common to think of large corporations as soulless and unchanging, that is simply not true. Corporations are made up of people who can act in an enlightened manner, even if it is enlightened self-interest.

Along with racial and ethnic minorities, women have lagged behind white males in successfully climbing the corporate ladder. Wages for women are rising, but are still around 80 percent of what men earn for the same job. There can be some argument that the statistics don't factor in the time many women take off to have children. When they re-enter the workforce, they may not have as much experience as a male counterpart who did not leave to have a child. Socially responsible investors will advocate for workers rights as shareholders. Some of their positions include extended family leave, paternal leave, programs to re-integrate women returning after maternity leave, onsite day care, and other programs that make it easier for women and men to raise a family and pursue a career.

Diversity of the workforce is very important to many SRI investors. Diversity provides for a richer work experience where different ideas and perspectives can be explored. It is also important because our culture is becoming more diverse each year. Companies that reflect the diversity of the marketplace in their workforce relate to their customers more easily and naturally.

A number of SRI investors believe that the idea of diversity as expressed by ethnic and racial minorities and women is too limited. They argue that it does not accurately reflect the world and marketplace where a company must operate and compete. True diversity includes a workplace that hires, trains, and promotes without regard to race, ethnic origin, religion, age, sexual orientation, mental or physical abilities, or AIDS/HIV status. Each year, a large number of shareholder resolutions are filed concerning employment policies for people with HIV/AIDS. Employment discrimination in this area is seen as significant by SRI investors.

Responsible Tip

Companies that hang on to 1950s management structures do not do well in today's diversified employment marketplace. Understanding the value of a diversified workforce is to also understand the consumer marketplace.

Equal Employment Opportunities

Equal employment opportunities span a wide variety of SRI concerns including the ingrained types of discrimination found in some companies. It is broader in scope including employees' lawful right to organize into labor unions and negotiate for better wages and working conditions. Some of the earliest institutional investors to practice socially responsible investing were labor unions. SRI investors recognize that even if unions are not represented in a company's labor force, there is still an obligation to treat workers and potential workers with respect and dignity. For example, if a company must close a facility, SRI investors would advocate a policy that called for as much advanced warning as practical and benefits for workers losing their jobs that exceeded any minimums required by the state where the facility was located.

Equal employment opportunities also relate to various discriminatory situations discussed in the previous section where certain categories of employees or potential employees were denied the same opportunities as other employees.

Unsafe Working Conditions

Companies that promote fair employment conditions usually follow through with policies that make the work environment safe and as pleasant as possible. The other side of this issue is those companies that maintain unsafe and/or uncomfortable working conditions. When workers are treated badly, through unfair employment practices and unsafe working conditions, lawsuits and other legal proceedings often follow. Employees that work for companies that treat their workers with respect and maintain safe working environments and fair employment policies are more likely to stay with the company. Retaining valuable employees is an important step in the financial success of a company. Companies that disregard their employee's safety and have high turnover are often less productive and profitable over the long term.

Socially responsible investors believe companies with strong worker safety records tend to also be stronger financially. Part of rationale for this is that financially weak companies sometimes cut corners and expenses not directly related to producing revenue, such as safety measures. Weaker and poorly managed companies focus only on short-term financial results, which can lead to low worker morale and

Responsible Tip

Companies that preach worker safety and insist that safety rules be followed send a message to employees that they are valuable and worth protecting. That helps employee morale and leads to employees valuing and respecting each other.

high turnover. These companies tend to be low-skill producers that don't mind high turnover because it keeps wages low. A relentless focus on the bottom line, however, can fail to provide for minimal employee needs. Eventually, an employee could be seriously injured or turnover could become so high that even at low skill levels it is costing the company money to recruit and train workers.

Companies that follow strict worker safety protocols and provide proper training and equipment usually have higher productivity. Higher productivity means the company achieves more results per employee than other comparable situations. This means that the company's per/unit cost will continually drop as experienced workers get better at their jobs and incorporate on-the-job suggestions for improving how things are done. When a company takes pride in its workers by taking care of them, it is not unusual to see the work force return that attention with innovative suggestions for improvements in products or production. It is unlikely employees will step forward with suggestions to improve the company in environments where they are treated as expendable components in the work process.

Responsible Tip

Thanks to the Internet and open records, most government agencies reports are available online. SRI investors can find safety and labor reports on a company by searching various federal databases or by simply "Googling" the company.

Socially responsible investors can track a company's work safety and grievance proceeding through several government agencies including the National Labor Relations Board, the Occupational Health and Safety Administration, the Securities and Exchange Commission, and state labor relations agencies. Find contact information for these agencies in Appendix A.

Human Rights

Globalization has spread U.S. products and production around the world. Large multinational companies may have more sales overseas than domestically, and more production in other countries than in the United States. Globalization has even brought foreign companies to the United States to produce their goods—Toyota, for example, has several production facilities here. Economists can argue the merits of this reality, but it is unlikely to reverse itself short of some cataclysmic economic or political event.

As U.S. companies have moved or expanded production capacity overseas, some difficult ethical questions have arisen. Whether a U.S. company opens a plant in a foreign country or contracts out the work to a domestic supplier (the more common solution), the labor laws, and practices of the country are applicable. Because the incentive for moving production out of the United States is lowering costs, the work often goes to developing countries or countries with few labor laws. In some cases, local laws can easily be avoided by paying off the proper officials. The result is workers who are exploited for their labor and paid almost nothing in many cases. They work long hours, often

without breaks and without days off. The conditions may be dangerous, especially if there are toxic chemicals or fumes involved. There is
much concern that workers in
these developing countries are
being exploited in violation of the
country's own labor laws and in
violation of basic human rights.
Socially responsible investors
reject "profit at any cost." They
are concerned about working
conditions up and down the supply chain, not just for workers
in the United States. Although
abuse is harder to track overseas,
SRI investors know that's where
it is most likely to occur.

 Red Flag

Some companies that
contract work overseas
go to great lengths to hide
sources and vendors. Some
do it in the name of trade
secrets, but others know
they are violating human
rights standards and want to
avoid unpleasant publicity.
SRI researchers are wary of
supply chains that disappear
when they leave our shores.

Investment in Foreign Countries

As we discussed in Chapter 4, U.S. companies have been outsourcing production to foreign partners for many years. In some cases, U.S.
companies establish overseas operations that they manage. However,
it is more common for companies to outsource production to existing
companies in foreign countries. This is done to lower costs and keep
the product competitive on the world market. Foreign companies can
often produce the company's product for a fraction of when it would
cost the company to make it domestically.

Foreign producers are often found in less developed countries that are
hungry for exports. Exports help these countries by bringing in hard
currency from stable countries into their economy. This capital helps
grow the economy and stabilize the inflation rate. In exchange, foreign
producers offer rock-bottom prices for their work, often because they
can pay extremely low wages and demand long hours from workers. In
many cases, the concepts of overtime or holiday pay are unheard of and
workers who argue otherwise are soon without a job. The labor pool
in these countries is usually very deep with plenty of workers eager to
replace any who balk at working conditions. In some countries, child
labor, indentured workers, and penal laborers are used to cut wages even
more. All of these cases are considered violations of basic human rights.

An even more insidious role played by some companies with foreign investments makes them complicit in human rights violations by governments. Companies may secretly support government policies that create terrible working conditions for their citizens in order to keep wages low. Bribes, political contributions and other questionable policies promote the status quo, which is often a violation of basic human rights. This was the case in South Africa during Apartheid, although not all companies doing business in this period were guilty of these acts. SRI investors often avoid companies with questionable connections to foreign governments that may contribute to human rights violations.

Countries that do most of the outsourced manufacturing need the work to raise their standard of living. But SRI investors must be concerned about the benefits of globalization reaching the workers. The danger is that money pouring into a country without a structure of checks and balances will find its way in the pockets of only a few, while the general population will not benefit to the extent it should.

Responsible Tip

Not only manufacturers have overseas connections with foreign governments. Some large financial service companies have been found doing business with repressive governments and, in effect, helping despots loot their own country.

Sweatshops, Fair Trade

A number of high-profile media exposés in recent years have uncovered the use of *sweatshops* and child labor in foreign countries to produce popular wearing apparel label products. Most of the clothes we wear are made overseas where labor costs are low. In some cases, workers were being paid one dollar a day for 12 hours of work and producing designer label goods selling for more than they could earn in two or three months or more. While it is not practical to compare wages in a developing country with wages in the United States, SRI investors hold companies accountable for paying living wages to people in their own country.

The global supply chain refers to all the steps in the process of producing a product, from procuring raw materials to fabricating the final product. A number of industries, clothing in particular, accomplish the whole supply chain, except for some or all of the actual sales outside of the United States. This puts U.S. companies in arrangements with many companies around the world to gather material and parts and do the final assembly. Companies with the attitude that price and delivery are all that matters encourage abuse of contract workers. In countries where no effective laws protect workers, some companies meet competition by abusing workers. (In recent years, we've also discovered they meet competition by cutting corner with food safety and other dangerous practices.)

def•i•ni•tion

A **sweatshop** is a derogatory term for a place where workers are treated badly and paid poorly. It is used to describe foreign operations today, but had its roots in England and the United States in the middle 1800s. Ironically, the term had nothing to do with perspiring. Rather it was a system where tailors would piece out work to a "sweater" who would have isolated groups of workers doing per piece labor. Because the laborers were kept isolated and never knew when more work was coming, sweaters kept their per piece wages very low. Thus, the term sweatshop. Sweatshops mostly disappeared with the invention of the pedal-powered sewing machine.

Thanks to mounting public pressure and pressure from socially responsible, a number of U.S. companies have taken steps to ensure foreign contractors meet minimum standards of conduct. When evaluating companies for their use of foreign contractors, SRI investors look for published standards the company expects each vendor to meet regarding working conditions and human rights. Does the company have a monitoring system in place to verify that vendors in foreign countries are complying with its standards? Does the company report to the shareholders findings and steps taken to correct any failings?

Transparency in the company's relationship with foreign vendors and how it is setting and monitoring standards goes a long way in instilling confidence in SRI investors. Companies that are forthright about problems with vendors, but report on efforts to correct those problems receive higher marks from SRI investors than companies that gloss over problems or attempt to spin them away. Companies that use celebrity spokespersons are particularly vulnerable to the bad publicity of being accused of supporting a sweatshop labor force in foreign countries.

Celebrities are becoming more cautious about linking their names with companies that may have human rights problems. SRI investors are concerned that foreign vendors pay a living wage in their country, treat workers with respect, and provide a safe working environment. Socially responsible investing advocacy is this area is very strong since the focus is on change. Mutual funds and institutional investors take the lead in working with companies to improve their relationships with vendors, help set standards for worker treatment, and suggest monitoring programs. These advocacy programs often take years of negotiations to work through and implement. This is one of the greatest success stories of socially responsible investing. As more companies adopt codes of conduct for foreign contractors and see that they are enforced, it raises the standard of working conditions in those countries and improves the well-being of workers and their families. Without some intervention by U.S. companies, many of the benefits of globalization would never find their way to the citizens of developing countries.

Success Stories
More U.S. companies are setting standards and monitoring foreign vendors. As a result, many more workers for these suppliers earn a living wage in their country and have decent working conditions.

Religious Issues

Religious organizations and institutions have been at the lead of the socially responsible investing movement from the beginning. Although most SRI mutual funds are not organized on "religious" principles, faith-based groups back a number of funds. We'll discuss these in more detail in Chapter 9. SRI mutual funds have a code of ethics that many religious groups would support, but may not include all the issues that a faith-based group finds important. In some cases, faith-based groups may take exception with some positions of more progressive SRI funds. For example, some religious groups have financial restrictions that might prevent them from investing in companies that earn or charge interest. Other religious faiths have strong beliefs about the sanctity of life and would be guided in their investment decisions regarding companies that made birth control pills or prophylactic devices.

The differences between traditional socially responsible investors and faith-based investors are not large. Most faith-based investors share the same concerns as traditional SRI investors: the environment, labor practices, product safety issues and so on. Faith-based investors are likely to avoid investing in companies that have documented ethical problems, much the same as traditional SRI investors. Faith-based investors, however, are more likely than traditional SRI investors to avoid companies involved in the "sin" businesses of alcohol, gambling, and tobacco. Faith-based investors have at least as much interest, if not more, in coupling their beliefs with investment decisions. The growth of faith-based mutual funds and industry studies indicates that mainstream investors share many of the same values even if they may not be a part of the faith community.

One of the faster growing segments of religious funds is the conservative Christian funds. Proponents of these funds often refer to it as values-based investing. A key component is the understanding that investors will not be profiting from the sins of others. How the funds interpret "sins" is driven by the organizers' understanding of conservative Christian values. As we'll see in Chapter 9, a number of different faith communities offer mutual funds that interpret their values through investment choices.

 Responsible Tip

Faith-based investors look very much like traditional investors, but come at the investing process from their religious beliefs. While they would agree with many of the values in most socially responsible funds, they may not support them all. A faith-based fund may be more comfortable for those investors who feel strongly about their religious beliefs.

Product Liability/Responsibility

A company's responsibility for its product after the sale is a huge issue with socially responsible investors. It is also a huge issue with trial lawyers who sue for damages and the government that can impose fines and other measures against companies. Socially responsible investors avoid companies with histories of producing products that become liabilities after they are sold. There are cases where unforeseen problems can arise, but in the most egregious cases companies become aware of a problem with a product and choose to do nothing about it, and even worse, some attempt to cover up or deny the problem.

The tobacco industry is the worst offender and the classic case of a whole industry that knew its products were addictive and caused cancer, but denied any liability for many years. There are many other examples such as asbestos, pharmaceuticals, and defective automotive equipment. Any company that produces any type of product is a potential target for a liability suit, whether it is justified or not. SRI investors avoid industries with patterns of lawsuits by consumers and governmental agencies. The worst offenders shift what should be their expense to the public for correcting. This distorts the true value of the company and creates a drain on public resources. Eventually, many of these worst offenders face a bill for their irresponsible behavior.

Responsible Tip

Companies that avoid or shift product liability are not good investments for SRI investors. They attract lawsuits and may face serious legal action for hazardous products.

Safety and Product Liability

Dangerous products can create liability issues for companies that socially responsible investors want to avoid. The danger may come because of poor design or workmanship or because the product is inherently dangerous, such as tobacco products. Although there are specific industries that SRI investors avoid because of obvious dangers (tobacco, alcohol, weapons, and such), almost any industry can have problems. Pharmaceutical companies, for example, face potential liabilities if drugs they bring to market are discovered to have serious side effects, especially if the company knew or suspected there was a problem. The drug industry is highly regulated, however, that has not prevented some major problems in medicines reaching the market that had serious, unreported side effects. In recent years, a number of major drugs have been pulled from the market when problems, and sometimes fatal consequences, were reported. Socially responsible investors look for companies with good records of product testing and meeting or exceeding government standards for safety. For example, food producers are questioned about the use of pesticides on the crops they either grow or buy. Pesticide management programs can reduce the amount of chemicals used on food crops. Companies that follow these principles and require growers to do the same receive endorsements from SRI investors. These companies exhibit an understanding that their responsibility doesn't end when they sell the product.

Socially responsible investors exclude companies that make dangerous or socially irresponsible products, such as tobacco, alcohol, pornography, and weapons. Many of the SRI funds exclude companies that derive a major portion of their revenue from work with the Department of Defense or are connected with war efforts in other ways. They also are concerned about companies that make products that are marketed to children in a way that glorifies violence or promotes stereotypes of any group. A number of food producers that make "kid food" such as cereal or snacks are beginning to address the health crisis of overweight children by marketing products that are more nutritious.

On the positive side, SRI investors encourage companies to exercise honesty and integrity in advertising and marketing their products. It is important that consumers be able to make informed decisions about what a product will and will not do, and that will only come with truth in labeling and advertising. Companies that respond quickly and forthrightly to product safety or other issues and move to correct the situation in a manner that puts the consumer's interest first are highly regarded by SRI investors.

Responsible Tip

Animal testing is another area of concern for SRI investors. Companies should avoid it if possible and follow strict guidelines if it is not possible. Some socially responsible investors will not support any animal testing for any reason.

Environmental Concerns

Poor environmental practices are among the worst offenses that SRI investors find when screening companies. In addition to the concerns expressed in Chapter 4, the question of who pays for cleaning up the mess is a major concern for SRI investors. The tobacco and asbestos industries reached major settlements over liability for their products. Other major industries have also face product liability suits and others will in the coming years. The issue of greenhouse gases is a potentially huge product liability issue if courts rule that producers of these gases have a responsibility for fixing the problem. With the controversy over the role of greenhouse gases in climate change, it may seem unlikely that this will happen. However, if the scientists who believe that humans are changing the climate of the world are correct, what may now seem as unlikely may become a reality. Socially responsible investors look at current potential liabilities, but they are also concerned about those companies that shift liabilities to the future or to some other source. For example, the nuclear industry is an example of shifting liability to the future. Spent nuclear fuel must be stored in a secure, contained environment for hundreds of years to prevent it from polluting the air or water. Who will pay for this storage? Most of the cost will undoubtedly be borne by taxpayers. Many industries that used chemicals, which ended up in rivers and lakes, now are defunct or unable to clean up their mess. Virtually, every waterway, river, and lake anywhere near a coal-fire generating plant is contaminated with mercury, which falls out of the sky from the plant's discharge. If the mercury could be cleaned up, who would pay? Socially responsible investors screen companies based on the potential for current and future liabilities. Companies that passed represent safer long-term investments, and they are generally better corporate citizens.

The Least You Need to Know

- Socially responsible investors are interested in social and political change.
- SRI investors advocate for equal employment rights for all workers.
- Human rights issues for foreign workers contracting to U.S. companies are important to SRI investors.
- Faith-based investors have much in common with socially responsible investors.
- Product liability issues are screened by SRI investors.

Chapter 6

Corporate Governance

In This Chapter

- ◆ The correct and distorted roles of boards of directors
- ◆ The role of socially responsible shareholders in corporate governance
- ◆ The problems shareholders have of voicing concerns to management
- ◆ The problems of disproportionate executive compensation

Some may find the issue of corporate governance a strange inclusion in socially responsible investing, however, the link is direct and well-connected. To jump to the conclusion, companies that practice polices of responsible governance—putting the shareholder first—are most likely to also practice responsible stewardship of the environment and other important SRI issues.

How companies are managed makes a difference beyond social issues. The news reports of unethical and illegal practices by corporate managers never seem to stop. These practices not only cost shareholders, but they often lead to employees suffering, too. In some cases, companies are forced into bankruptcy or sold off and employees lose their jobs and pensions. Poor conduct by managers is a real problem. The board of directors should represent the stockholders' interests, but too often it rubber-stamps management's plans. The issue of executive compensation, where some top managers of failing companies receive huge salary and retirement packages despite poor performance of the company's stock illustrates this point perfectly. Socially responsible investors want shareholder interests fairly represented and the company managed in an ethical and legal manner.

Role of Board of Directors

In theory, the board of directors represents the shareholders, who own the company. The board is usually made up of senior business executives—sometimes retired—who can help management make sound decisions and provide the benefit of their experience. Management is hired to run the company for the shareholders' benefit. Shareholders elect the board of directors, which in turn hires the top manager, usually the president of the corporation. The president hires a team of people to help her run the company. The president reports to the board of directors.

Although it should work this way, the reality is something different. In reality, the president handpicks most members of the board of directors It is much like being able to pick your own boss, but better. Not only do you pick some or all of the board members, you can often arrange to get rid of them if they cause you trouble. While the shareholders may vote on the slate of board members, your handpicked candidates are often the only ones on the ballot. Other candidates must usually be added by special means. Guess who wins most of these elections?

Responsible Tip

The top management position in a company is often the president, but sometimes it might carry another title. Chief Executive Officer can be a real title or it is often used as a catchall term for the senior manager of a company, whatever his title.

Represent Owners of Corporation

The role of the board of directors as representing shareholders in the governance of the company is well-established and makes good sense. Thousands of owners (shareholders) can't effectively oversee management of a company. A small group that represents the owners makes the oversight role manageable.

The board of directors hires senior management and makes major decisions for the shareholders. Some decisions must go the owners for their direct vote (for example, the shareholders, not the board of directors or management must approve the question of merging with another company). The board of directors on behalf of the shareholders can handle other matters.

Problems arise when the interests of the board and management are more closely aligned than the interests of the board and shareholders. Board members are often handpicked by management and often are senior managers (or retired senior managers) at other companies.

They represent an exclusive club of sorts that has little incentive of reforming management practices—if they did, the boards of directors of their own companies might get similar ideas. The status quo is closely guarded. It is rare to see boards of directors challenge senior management unless the company is in serious financial or legal trouble. Even if the company is not doing well financially, and the president is asked to leave, he still might receive a fat separation package that appears to reward him for poor performance.

More difficult problems for board members are the all too frequent ethical and legal lapses when the head of the company is caught in serious breach of the law. Recent scandals have pushed boards to be more vigilant about rubber-stamping anything management puts in front of them. Socially responsible investors have pushed for accountability from the board for its role in letting serious legal or ethical problems create liabilities for the company and its employees.

Responsible Tip

Despite numerous scandals triggered by outright fraud, stock manipulation, and other crimes, very few members of boards have been held legally accountable for actions by management they were supposed to be supervising.

Board Independent of Management

The concept of a board of directors that exists independently of the company's management is theoretical at best. The reality is that some companies have financial structures that make any true independence impossible or unlikely. For example, most companies began as small, privately owned corporations and grew to a point where the owner(s) decided to offer shares of stock to the public. At this point, the stock is made available to buy and sell on stock exchanges. But the owner(s) may retain enough of the stock to control the board of directors by holding enough votes to elect whomever they choose. Another way owners retain control is by issuing two classes of stock. Class A shares get one vote for each share owned, and Class B shares get ten votes for each share owned. Either of these methods allows management to retain control of the board of directors and may be the reason a corporate executive holds the dual title of president and chairman of the board of directors.

Another problem that challenges SRI investors is the use of classified boards of directors. Not every corporation uses a classified board system, but a number do. A classified board is a system where board members serve different length terms. Each board has its own classification system, but it is often built on seniority, with more senior board members serving longer terms. This is a staggered board system, but not all staggered board systems are classified boards. A staggered board could have seats that were two-year, three-year, and four-year terms, so each year one-third of the board would be up for re-election. The classified board doesn't necessarily split the board evenly. In any year, there may be several board slots to fill or none, depending on the classification system.

Supporters of classified boards claim the system provides continuity and keeps experienced board members in key positions longer. Classified boards are also seen as barriers to unfriendly takeovers, since it is difficult to remove a majority of members at once.

 Red Flag

Companies where the control rests in the hands of a few original owners are not truly publicly held companies, since the founders still control how the company will be run. Shareholder resolutions will not work unless the founders want them to.

Critics cite several research studies that show that classified boards don't perform as well as firms with more open board election processes. The conclusions indicate classified boards foster an unhealthy closeness to management. Board members become even more aligned with the interests of management leaving investors as adversaries to the company they own. In response to initiatives by SRI investors, a number of companies have dropped previous board election procedures and adopted an annual election of members.

Socially responsible investors prefer annual elections of board members because they believe the elections hold members more accountable to shareholders. Except in the cases noted above, where management controls significant voting blocks of stock, this is certainly true and it doesn't prevent board members who are doing a good job of representing shareholder interests from being re-elected to multiple terms. Each year, multiple shareholder resolutions have been introduced at annual meetings asking shareholders to approve this form of annual election of board members. Some are successful, while others fall on less responsive ears.

Corporate Policies Unchallenged

Because of many boards of directors' election processes, there are seldom any viable alternative candidates other than those put forth with management's blessing. This process ensures that the almost incestuous relationship between management and boards of directors continues. Board members understand how they come to serve on the board and who they really owe allegiance to (it isn't the shareholders). Because of this stacked deck, it isn't often that the board openly challenges management's policies or decisions. Without this check, management does whatever it pleases, whether or not it is in the stockholders' best interests.

Socially responsible investors advocate issues they find important and honest. Transparent corporate governance is high on the list of social issues. SRI investors often use public records to track a company's actions and do some sleuthing to discover other actions that do not make the public record. As long as the company stays within the letter of the law, it is unlikely any agency would call them on policies that might appear on public records. Even when companies go too far and are caught, usually the underlings take the brunt of any penalties.

A company may choose some of its executives to serve on the board of directors, and other directors elected from outside the company. These outside directors should be more inclined, in theory, to question management practices. That works in some companies, but not in others. Outside directors are compensated for their service on the board. Depending on the size of the company and any committees the member serves on, compensation can be in the form of cash and stock options or some other granting of equity compensation.

Board of Directors Relates to Management

The board of directors, both inside and outside directors, looks more like management than stockholders in most cases. Directors are often former or active management of other corporations. They use their business experience to help make broad policy decisions about the future of the company. If directors fulfill their role, they are valuable resources to the company and serve the shareholders well by adding their experience and wisdom to the decision-making process. Unfortunately, in some cases, directors are on the board merely for appearance sake—to sign off on whatever management brings to the table. In these cases, the directors have aligned their interests with management and not with shareholders. Socially responsible investors advocate that outside directors should receive most of their compensation in stock or *stock options* rather than cash. If the board of directors' compensation is tied to the share price, they become more likely to hold management accountable for growing shareholder value. Directors compensated primarily with cash may not feel aligned with shareholder interest. SRI investors see the board of directors as a valuable ally or significant barrier in moving a company toward transparency in governance.

Fortunately, thanks in part to the many corporate scandals that have shaken investor confidence, boards of directors are being held more accountable for the actions of management. Pleas of ignorance concerning illegal or unethical activities will not go well for boards of directors in the future. It is the board's job to oversee what is happening, but if it is simply rubber-stamping management plans, it is failing in its role.

Board members are usually partially protected by insurance, but regulators and the investing public are becoming tired of the "we didn't know what was happening" excuse. Board members may face civil and criminal penalties in the future if they knowingly passed on illegal activities or even if they should have known an action was illegal. Reform is coming and SRI investors have been in the forefront pushing industry to clean up its act.

def•i•ni•tion

Stock options are contracts giving the holder the right, but not the obligation, to buy a certain number of shares of stock at a fixed price before the expiration date. Stock options are used as incentives to encourage directors and management to grow the company and raise the stock price. The option holders exercise their options, buy the shares at a lower price than the current market price, and then sell the shares for a profit if they wish.

Shareholders Lack Effective Voice

Unless you own a significant block of voting stock, it is difficult for an individual to have any influence on the decisions of a corporation. The only opportunity shareholders have to exercise their voice is voting on major issues before the company, either by mail or at the annual meeting. Shareholders have the right to bring resolutions before the annual meeting. There is a process to follow and steps that are outlined by the Securities and Exchange Commission. We'll look at shareholder resolutions in detail in Chapter 11. Filing and pursuing shareholder resolutions is the major task of many groups involved in socially responsible investing. Hundreds of these resolutions are filed each year, but very few are passed. Those that do pass often have management's public blessing. Without management's open support, most shareholder resolutions are doomed. Socially responsible investing advocacy groups are often more effective working with companies behind closed doors than challenging management at annual meetings. This process may take a long time, but as we'll see in Chapter 11, it can pay off in accomplishing some significant goals.

Most SRI investors (and traditional investors, for that matter), however, can do little to make their voices heard by management. Of course, companies with thousands of shareowners can't effectively listen to every idea about running the company in a different manner. If boards of directors functioned more in the interests of shareholders and less for the convenience of management, however, there would be less need to hear individual shareholders.

A large number of investors interested in socially responsible investing choose mutual funds as their investment vehicle. These mutual funds carry much more weight than individual investors and have the staff and expertise to address concerns. We'll see this in action as we look at the role of mutual funds in advocating on issues such as corporate governance in Chapter 11.

Responsible Tip

Socially responsible investors that choose to use individual stocks for some or all of their investments are at a disadvantage if they are interested in advocating for corporate governance or other issues. Unless you hold a large block of stock, it will be difficult to get the serious attention of most companies.

The Role of SRI Investors in Corporate Governance

Socially responsible investors have advocated for transparency in corporate governance for many years. Advocates have pushed for more detailed disclosure especially where there is or may be the appearance of a conflict of interest between management and vendors or other cases of potentially unethical behavior. SRI investors have insisted on more openness in committee meeting records and clarity in how policy and procedures are decided. The over-arching goal for many SRI investors involved in corporate governance has been to move companies toward a more stakeholder-oriented point of view—that is to understand the company's goals extend beyond the single-minded pursuit of short-term profits.

Success Stories

While scandals grab the headlines, it should be noted that a number of companies are voluntarily moving toward more openness and transparency in all their activities. An environment of openness builds a corporate culture of accountability and leads to fewer problems with ethical and legal lapses.

Investors of all types are more aware that significant ethical, moral, and legal lapses by companies are much more common than previously thought. These lapses can result in significant losses for shareholders and, in extreme cases, cause a company to fail (think Enron). Regulators have put stricter controls in place, but investors still should be aware of potential problems. SRI advocates monitor corporate activity and help investors make decisions regarding potential problem companies. Companies with histories of civil or criminal violations are prime candidates for financial trouble and selective SRI stock screens will eliminate them from consideration. We'll look at screens in more detail in Chapter 9.

Major Corporate Governance Issues

Socially responsible investors differ on which corporate governance issues are the most important (much as they disagree on the importance of other issues). Executive compensation and corporate political contributions, however, are close to the top of most lists. These two issues create much discussion in the press, especially executive compensation. The issue really hits the front page when a CEO is fired or retires with a huge multi-million dollar package, even though the company has done poorly under his stewardship. These "golden parachutes," as they are sometimes called, outrage shareholders and baffle the public. While several million dollars is not much to a company with revenues in the billions, it still represents a significant sum of money to most investors and employees.

Political contributions by executives and corporations (basically, the same thing) are another area of great concern. Complicated campaign finance laws place limits on what can and can't be done at the corporate level. Nevertheless, sharp political action officers at corporations figure out ways around the limits or come up with some other strategy that will work. The influence that money buys through political contributions may be viewed by some as the cost of doing business. But excesses in this area, which includes lobbying for legislative favors has gone to excess in some cases and evolved into bribery. The dangers of buying political influence are especially acute in some foreign countries where U.S. companies have sought to influence the politics of a country.

CEO Compensation Issues

The issue of executive compensation has been clouded by recent scandals and inappropriate packages that reward the chief executive officer regardless of how the company performed. CEOs who manage large corporations and make or keep them profitable during trying economic times are true business superstars. Operating a business in this era of globalization and accelerated demands requires a person of exceptional skill—not everyone can do their job. CEOs who can produce value for the shareholders and grow the company deserve to be compensated in a manner relative to their impact on the company's success. This type of compensation puts the CEO's interests in alignment with the shareholders. Some compensation packages reward the CEO regardless of how the company does, through either ample cash salary, or a combination of stock options and stock grants.

Responsible Tip

Feeble attempts have been made to control excessive compensation through the tax code. For example, companies are not allowed to deduct as an expense compensation in excess of $1 million per year unless it is tied to performance in some manner. Companies can set easily obtainable goals that meet the tax code requirements, but don't necessarily add real value to the shareholder.

CEO Compensation Out of Synch with Performance

What is the right compensation for a CEO? Boards of directors grapple with that challenging question on a regular basis. A suitable solution should be attractive enough to recruit and retain the quality of senior managers needed for the success of the company, yet put the bulk of the compensation in an incentive formula. This creates a relationship with the shareholder that is logical and natural—if the executive can grow the company and add value to the shareholder; he should share in that growth in the form of a bonus or some other incentive. But if the company doesn't grow and the shareholder doesn't gain value, the executive would miss the incentive compensation.

In theory, most SRI investors don't have a problem with this type of compensation arrangement as long as the incentive can be directly tied to the executive's decisions and not growth that would have happened naturally. SRI investors are also concerned by the fact that the CEO is at most a team leader and could not accomplish much without the hard work of the company's other employees. Huge salaries and bonuses for senior management, but nothing for the workers sends a message that can damage employee morale. Also, some CEOs use means to boost profits—some of which are clearly unethical or even illegal—in order to boost their compensation. The scandals of the past decade were in part caused by this problem.

CEOs that are richly rewarded for slashing jobs, outsourcing, and moving production overseas may find that SRI investors have lost their taste for the company with so little regard for its stakeholders. This is one of the problems with tying executive compensation to performance. One of the classic ways to improve performance of a company is to drastically reduce expenses and, for many industries, that means laying-off people. If the work still needs to be done, the CEO can move it to a low-labor cost country, outsource it, or contract it out to a foreign company that is not concerned with human rights, but can deliver the goods at a rock-bottom price.

In this way, performance can be increased in the short term, but at a terrific cost to the employees and the communities where the company has facilities. SRI investors often temper performance requirements with a more holistic approach to management that considered how the CEO improved not only the financial performance, but also issues such as environmental policy, labor policies, employment practices, and other social concerns.

 Responsible Tip

How to measure company performance is a major difference between socially responsible investing and traditional investors. For example, traditional investors might reward an executive for slashing costs even if it meant compromising environmental standards. SRI investors would view such actions as a negative.

The classic "bad boys" of the executive compensation issue are executives who work deals with their boards for fat packages regardless of what happens to the company. This type of excess led the Securities and Exchange Commission to adopt regulations in 2006 requiring companies to disclose their executive compensation practices. The requirement shines some light on what has been a closed-door process. But many don't think it goes far enough. At the urging of SRI investors and consumer advocates, other measures requiring a nonbinding shareholder vote on executive compensation packages are being considered. Similar rules are on the books in other countries. Several U.S. companies have voluntarily adopted the nonbinding vote on their own. Shareholder resolutions on this issue are drawing significant numbers of votes. The proposed rules don't set any caps on executive compensation, but establish a system for shareholders to vote on compensation packages. This will require investors, particularly institutional investors, to learn about the packages and what the implications are for the executive and the company.

Disparity Between CEO Compensation and Workers' Pay

The gap between CEO compensation and workers' pay has been growing. Personal income has largely been flat (when you factor in inflation and other cost of living expenses) for a number of years. Until 2007, the minimum wage, which is often used as a benchmark for other wages had not been increased in seven years. Yet, CEO compensation kept rising. Depending on how you want to measure it, the ratio can be anywhere from 300:1 to 400:1. What is the right ratio? That's difficult to say. When CEOs earn tens of millions of dollars each year, it creates morale problems for the company workers whose wages have been flat for years. When huge numbers of workers are laid off or jobs outsourced in the name of cutting costs, how does it look to workers when the CEO receives a bonus?

Several SRI funds look at executive compensation on a case-by-case basis to determine where companies have been overzealous in rewarding executives, but have not recognized the contributions of employees. An excessive disparity between CEO compensation and employee wages can also signal that the board of directors is more aligned with the interests of management than with stockholders.

Political Contributions

Corporations have a legitimate interest in the political and legislative processes. Regulations and laws can help or hinder an industry, especially when competing in a global marketplace. But the issue is not one of interest in the process, but of undue interest. Scandals of excessive and sometimes illegal contributions to candidates, political action committees, lobbying or trade groups, and such, have suggested that some companies buy favorable influence in the political process. Limits have been put on amounts corporations can directly contribute to candidates, but these have been circumvented by groups organized to air "issue" ads during campaigns that don't name any candidate, but clearly support one. These "soft money" groups are free to raise millions of dollars and most of it will come from corporate sponsors. Political reformers note that more than $1 billion will be spent on the 2008 presidential election.

Socially responsible investors have multiple problems with political contributions by companies. The first concern is a practical one and traditional investors share it: are shareholders receiving any value for the money contributed. Of course, they are not looking for payoffs that suggest companies are buying a particular piece of legislation. But there needs to be some accountability and expectations for money spent for any purpose.

> ### Success Stories
>
> Limits on corporate spending have been in place for several years, however, some are being challenged in court and the future of controls on how much influence companies have in the political process is in doubt.

Secondly, are the contributions ethical and legal? Influence pedaling is an old business in politics, but there is a line between retaining a lobbyist who can help get a company's message to the right people in Washington and writing checks to re-election campaigns in exchange for getting a problem fixed. A third area of concern is the lack of oversight and transparency of political contributions. Who decides which candidates or causes to back? What is the process? Are goals set and monitored? Companies with a presence in a foreign country may be active in local politics, which has the potential for abuse. U.S. companies have bought considerable influence in foreign countries through "contributions" and outright bribes of government officials, although it is illegal under U.S. law. This illegal involvement in foreign political matters has often been at the expense of native workers and citizens.

Socially responsible investors who monitor political contributions look for patterns of contributions to particular groups and any civil or criminal charges against the company or its officers. Short of actual violations, it's a judgment call on the part of the person doing the screening as to whether the company is flagrantly violating the spirit of campaign contribution laws and whether the company is receiving any benefit from the contributions.

The Least You Need to Know

◆ Boards of directors help management grow the business and represent the interests of the shareholders.

◆ The relationship between the board and management is sometimes too close and leaves the shareholder unrepresented.

◆ Compensation of senior executives is a concern to SRI investors because it may not be tied to creating value.

◆ The disparity between CEO compensation and worker pay can be a morale issue.

◆ Political contributions can be excessive and even illegal.

Chapter 7

Economic Issues

In This Chapter

- ◆ Importance of economic and wage justice issues
- ◆ Concerns over health insurance
- ◆ Moral and ethical obligations in other countries
- ◆ Corruption at home and abroad follows political contributions

The plight of workers has always been a concern of socially responsible investors, whether the workers were slaves, child laborers, women in textile mills and sweatshops, or foreign workers in substandard conditions. Labor organizations, including unions, have fought for workers' rights and benefits for years with varying degrees of success. As the industrial age ended and the service/information/technology age began (in roughly the 1960s), jobs shifted out of the manufacturing sector and into what can be called the knowledge sector. With this shift, many manufacturing jobs either disappeared or went offshore to cheap labor countries.

Those jobs were replaced by many more jobs in businesses that required fewer physical skills and more mental work. Knowledge workers and service personnel were fast growing job areas, but many positions did not pay as well as manufacturing jobs did. Retail and other service sector jobs are traditionally on the low end of the pay scale. With expenses rising faster than personal income, it became necessary for most families to have two wage earners whenever possible to afford a good house and college for the kids. Unfortunately, people with limited educations and skills often found themselves in very low paying jobs with little chance for advancement. No matter how well the economy did, they never did much better than hold their own.

The idea of a "living wage" may seem contrary to some, but it reflects the status of our nation's working poor—the employed who make so little, they can't make ends meet. Added to the plight of the working poor is the concern for health care insurance coverage, which is a national crisis. Unpaid medical bills were cited in over 50 percent of the personal bankruptcy filings in recent years.

Responsible Tip

As jobs changed, some workers were able to adapt to the new knowledge-based industries, while others weren't. This has created a class of workers who are struggling to find a place in the new economy.

As the world has become not only a global marketplace, but also a resource for inexpensive labor, the United States has not done a good job in monitoring working conditions in facilities on foreign soil. Whether it is a plant owned by a U.S. company or a foreign company contracting work for an American client, worker abuse is the focus of SRI investor attention. Poor labor practices are not the only problem spread by U.S. companies. Influence pedaling both at home and abroad can only lead to problems. SRI investors avoid those companies with poor records on ethical and moral grounds and because they are generally not quality investments.

Living Wage Issues

The idea of paying workers a *living wage* is a controversial issue. First, what is a "living wage?" The term is not widely understood by all. Secondly, the traditional concept of wages is that they are a function of supply and demand. When the labor market is tight (too few workers), wages rise as employers compete for their services. When the labor market is loose, wages remain flat because more potential employees exist than jobs to be filled. Most Americans accept this explanation of how wages are set as valid. But nothing is quite that pure.

Thanks to technology, it takes fewer employees to do more work than just a few years ago. The increasing productivity tends to keep the labor market at the low end of the skills set full of potential employees, including recent high school graduates or dropouts, retired people, workers laid off from manufacturing jobs, and so on. Many of these people come into the service sector portion of the labor market (think Wal-Mart) at the lowest level. While they may not earn minimum wage, what they do earn may not be enough for a person, much less a family to live on.

> **def•i•ni•tion**
>
> **Living wage** is defined several ways, but it is often thought of as what a family of four needs to earn to reach 100 percent or 150 percent of the federal poverty level. It is then adjusted for the geographic area's cost of living.

Employee Compensation

In defined Chapter 6, we discussed CEO compensation and how it has grown out of proportion to worker wages in some companies. We noted that this was the source of poor morale. Low wages may make good economic sense in the short run, but they don't work for socially responsible investors. Workers who can't survive on one job are under tremendous stress. If they have dependents, the stress of surviving from paycheck to paycheck can take its toll on the physical and mental health of workers. Millions of people in this situation know that it only takes one problem, even a small problem, and they face a financial crisis. An illness in the family, car problems, and so on can shatter a fragile budget.

Socially responsible investors are concerned that employees working under these conditions can't possibly do their best. Moreover, as a matter of simple social justice, companies and senior executives shouldn't take in hundreds of millions (if not billions) in profits on the backs of the majority of the employees who can't afford to go to the doctor or eat out once a week because the company's wages are so low. This is an area where the idea of a living wage takes root.

One way a living wage is defined, although not always by SRI investors, is through "living wage ordinances" enacted by governmental entities. These ordinances in general say if a company is going to do business with the city or county that enacts the ordinance, it must pay a living wage that is equal to some percentage over the federal poverty level for a family of four. The amount is set with consideration to the cost of living in the community, so the living wage may be lower in a southern community than it is in a northeastern one. This is a tangible expression of what a living wage can actually be. While a living wage mandated by law may not be what all SRI investors advocate, it does address the issue.

Responsible Tip

More than 70 communities and government agencies have enacted living wage ordinances. Critics say they drive up the cost of government projects, while proponents say it is a way to advance the wage issue locally.

Some SRI investors are less concerned about a specific number and more interested in companies that have comprehensive compensation policies recognize employees' contributions and ensures that they share in the success of the company.

Health Insurance Accessibility

Health care costs have been rising at rates three times faster than the growth of personal income. Unpaid medical bills are cited in over 50 percent of all personal bankruptcy filings. Families with health problems that don't belong to a group policy may find it impossible to get health insurance at any cost. Millions of Americans work for smaller companies that don't offer health insurance to employees.

Our country is in a health care crisis and it is families who suffer the most. Health care insurance is almost unaffordable to all except the largest companies and governmental units who can still negotiate with insurance companies. Providing affordable access to health insurance is a high priority for many SRI investors. While it is understandable that small companies may not be able to afford this benefit for their employees, there is no reason larger companies can't make it available at a reasonable cost to their employees. The stress of health problems and the added danger of putting off seeing a doctor because of money is reason enough for SRI investors to advocate the availability of basic "affordable" health insurance coverage for all employees. The key term here is affordable and it ties back to the living wage issue. If an employee makes barely enough to cover food and housing, but not enough to pay insurance premiums, it does not just cost the employee. Several big employers such as Wal-Mart were criticized for having a large number of its employees of welfare-sponsored health care plans.

Socially responsible investors advocate for health care insurance plans that don't push all of the rising cost of premiums off on the employees. Every increase in premium that employees must pay means their real income (what their take home pay is actually worth) is diminished. At some point, the expense becomes too much for employees in the lower pay grades or part-time employees and they must choose between health insurance and food. SRI investors advocate with companies so employees are not forced into this decision.

> **Red Flag**
>
> As companies look to unburden themselves from health care responsibilities more will find ways to push them on employees much like they abandoned traditional pensions for employee-directed retirement plans such as 401(k)s.

Globalization

Globalization is a word thrown around with such abandon that it has become meaningless—that is, it means everything. For economists and businesses, it means competing in a global market that operates 24/7. For many companies, it has opened vast new markets for its products and abundant sources of inexpensive labor or contractors to produce the products. These markets have existed for many years and U.S. companies have been in them. In the years following World War II, however, the personal incomes in many "developing" countries mushroomed creating new markets for American goods and services. Americans have eagerly embraced foreign produced goods such as electronics and clothing. A number of America's largest consumer goods companies sell the majority of their products in foreign markets. In the process, the mix of our economy and job base has changed dramatically. The supply of manufacturing jobs has declined for decades. They are being replaced by service, retail, and knowledge-based jobs. Companies can outsource manufacturing to low-cost labor countries, which accounts for the decline in personal income among people who have lost good-paying jobs as factories have shuttered.

Jobs and goods are not the only things that have gone overseas with globalization. The United States has also exported parts of its culture to almost every country in the world. You would be hard pressed to find a country that doesn't have a McDonalds or Starbucks. American cigarettes are widely exported and are major brands in many foreign countries. Even our television shows, movies, and popular music spreads around the world. While there are many good aspects to the "Americanization" of the rest of the world, it is particularly problematic in very poor countries where American lifestyles clash with the basic needs of daily survival. In too many cases, we have assumed that our values and ideals should be those of everyone else. This attitude doesn't win us friends.

Responsible Tip

Nationalists in more than one country have resented the intrusion of American cultural icons such as Coke, McDonalds, and our rock music. Yet, things American continue to spread. It works the other way also. Japanese video games, European fashions, and other international influences are spreading thanks to the Internet and television.

The Scope of Globalization

It would be wrong to understand globalization in just U.S. terms because the very word implies a scope far beyond our borders. The term can be defined as a convergence of economies, cultures, information technologies, political interests, and ecological concerns. Geographical borders still matter (and wars will be fought over them), but as other barriers drop, the world is moving toward interdependence. For example, it took years to put together the European Common Market because of all the nationalistic suspicions, especially surrounding the common currency—the euro. Now, economists are seeing the benefits that were promised come to fruition. Interest rates are lower in many of the countries than they have been in years. As a result, businesses invest in expansion, and so on. It is not perfect, but countries are trying to get in because they see the benefits.

The world's financial markets, especially those in Japan, London, China, and the United States are moving toward cooperative agreements or partnerships that will allow investors access 24/7. Thanks to technology, there is no real barrier to the flow of information other than the human capacity to distill and digest it. SRI investors are concerned that powerful institutions, which already own most of the stocks and almost all of the outstanding bonds in the U.S. markets will be able to manipulate world markets in a manner to the detriment of individual investors.

Despite the obvious interdependence developing among countries of the world, arms sales continue at an uncomfortable pace. Many SRI mutual funds exclude companies involved in the production and sale of weapons or other materials deems exclusively made for war efforts. Despite the fact that some of these companies have been very profitable at times, SRI investors have an ethical problem with profiting from the production of goods designed to kill other humans.

Red Flag

Huge corporations have so many subsidiaries and divisions operating under different names it is difficult to keep up with who owns what. A company that is well known for an innocuous line of products may also have a division or subsidiary that produces weapons of war.

The Impact of Globalization on Local/Native People

Socially responsible investors realize how easily a company can take advantage of people in developing countries either directly through its plants or indirectly through its vendors. Operating a manufacturing or assembly plant in a desperately poor country is an opportunity to exploit its citizens. When companies have thought only of profit, they have chosen to pay much less, than they could have and still made a substantial profit in favor of making an even larger profit. This exploitation recognizes that poor people willingly work in substandard conditions for poor pay just to have some income. It is all the more terrible because officials in some foreign countries are party to the exploitation of their own people.

The United States has laws and regulations against bribery and corruption in foreign countries, however, they are not easy to enforce. Exported through globalization is the corruption of the political process with money. SRI investors do not accept the argument that corrupt practices are the norm in many countries, and they want companies to export higher standards of corporate behavior. It is bad enough to pay off a local official to look the other way on wage or work condition violations in a foreign community. But it is something completely different when a company or industry controls or influences a national government. In the sordid history of American companies doing business in less developed countries, influence pedaling on a national scale is not unheard of. The countries are often stripped of natural resources with none of the wealth returning to the people. Dictators and despots have become incredibly wealthy because they made choices that favored huge corporations rather than their citizens. In all fairness, U.S. corporations are not the only entities guilty of manipulating foreign governments. Some major players today are state-sponsored oil companies, which take "whatever-it-takes" views of acquiring mineral rights in foreign countries.

Responsible Tip

Discoveries of mineral assets are often bad news for native peoples because their property is taken, their way of life disrupted, and very little of the riches are ever returned to improve their way of life.

At particular risk are native or indigenous peoples. These populations descended from the original inhabitants often live in very fragile environments and circumstances. Development of their traditional lands, such as farms, or watersheds behind dams, threaten their way of life. In many countries, indigenous peoples have little to no political representation. Their cultures, which are usually different from the dominant population, are endangered and they often face discrimination.

Socially responsible investors, particularly through the use of some mutual funds, support companies that honor indigenous peoples and work with them to secure their place in the social and economic structure of their country. This means protecting against exploitation of workers and theft of rightful property. SRI investors also strive to return fair market prices for produce marketable goods and open distribution channels to direct markets.

The United States has a terrible record of treatment of its indigenous peoples, the Native Americans. After taking their land, breaking every treaty signed with them, and ghettoizing them on reservations, the United States is in an awkward position when attempting to tell any other country how to treat its native population. Several SRI mutual funds work with U.S. groups for the rights of Native Americans, both economic and cultural. One battle that seems to be mostly won, at least with large companies, is the use of Native American images in advertising. Over the years, Native Americans have been portrayed (along with other minorities) in a cartoonish manner for all types of advertising and in sports logos. There is still work to be done, but SRI investors have worked closely with Native American advocacy groups to successfully limit the exploitation of images that degrade their history and heritage. Many SRI screens would exclude companies that perpetuate use of inappropriate Native American logos or images.

Responsible Tip

Younger investors may have a hard time understanding that not long ago minorities were depicted in the most demeaning and stereotypical ways throughout advertising. Thanks to the hard work of a number of groups, most of that type of humiliation is gone.

Impact of Globalization on Foreign Cultures

Despite what some may think, many good things about American culture are exported with globalization. Does it change foreign cultures? Yes, it does, but all cultures are subject to outside influences and they either accept and incorporate those influences or they reject them. That is the way countries grow and change. It is arrogant of the United States to insist that a country in Southeast Asia shouldn't adopt some of our culture because some of theirs will be lost. Those are not our decisions. On the other hand, we shouldn't insist on thrusting American values on countries that are not ready for them or don't want them— that's also arrogant.

Globalization will continue to happen. SRI investors should be concerned that U.S. companies not insist that foreign countries bend to our will as a price for doing business with us. We must recognize the values of the host country and work to accommodate their way of doing

business. Companies open to working with foreign business environments may find they have something to learn as opposed to telling a
whole country what it is doing wrong.

The Impact of Globalization on the United States

Depending on who you ask, globalization has been the greatest thing
for U.S. businesses or a complete disaster that is destroying our economy. One theory is that globalization is resulting in more efficient use
of resources (humans are included in this definition of resources). For
example, manufacturing and assembly jobs can be done much cheaper
in many developing countries where a day's wage would not cover a
coffee break for many wage earners in U.S. manufacturing plants.
The more efficient decision is to move those jobs offshore, and that is
what has been happening for several decades. The result has been an
upheaval in many American towns that relied on the factories to provide good-paying jobs for years. When plants close, displaced workers
have a difficult time replacing income. Going from a $20 an hour job
in a factory to $8 an hour at a convenience store is a difficult transi-
tion. Companies have not universally trained displaced workers for job
positions above clerk. After the factories close, young people that finish
school leave their communities because there are no good paying jobs.
The community loses its best and brightest to other areas where jobs
pay higher wages.

On the other hand, some businesses have prospered because markets
for their products have opened around the world and they have found
places to manufacture at a fraction of the cost. Major companies have
been marketing their products overseas for years, but thanks to globalization the barriers for smaller companies have lowered in some
foreign markets making it possible for them to export—something the
U.S. Government strongly encourages. While the opportunity to sell
and produce overseas is attractive, it
doesn't make for as many U.S. jobs
as once was the case. SRI investors
are concerned about displaced U.S.
workers and how companies help
the transition when this occurs. Is
retraining help offered? Are other
jobs at other facilities made available?

Responsible Tip

Like many social and
economic changes, glo-
balization has advanced
some segments of society,
while setting others back.

How much notice do displaced workers receive? What type of separation package do workers receive? All of these questions point toward a company that either takes its role in the community seriously or sheds workers like dead weight.

Money and Political Influence

Many people argue that the political process, especially on the national level, has been corrupted by the influence of special interest money. The reality is that politicians in the U.S. House of Representatives or Senate face the almost constant need to raise money for re-election or old campaign debts. Those who seek national office must raise staggering sums to mount effective campaigns. The Federal Government provides matching dollars for people seeking the office of president, but the money carries limits on spending. No serious candidate accepts the free money because of the limits on spending. It is estimated that expenditures in the 2008 presidential campaign will top $1 billion. Is it any wonder that candidates spend as much, if not more time, at fundraisers as they do with voters?

The question then is what influence does all of this money buy? What do politicians owe those who have funded their re-election? SRI investor ask: Has money donated to political campaigns, either directly or indirectly through trade groups, been in the company's best interest? Has it always been legal? Have other, not as closely regulated, avenues been used for political contribution?

Campaign finance laws leave room for transactions that push the ethical boundaries, and opportunities exist both at home and abroad for outright bribery and corruption. SRI investors monitor companies for their contributions to political campaigns and consultants or lobbyists that stray over the line. Companies are pushed for more disclosure. Transparency in political contributions is an antidote to the natural suspicion that surrounds big business and politics. Businesses have a poor record resisting the temptation to quickly adopt local customs of

Responsible Tip

A consistent theme with SRI investors is transparency. An open and honest accounting of political contributions means it will all be done within the spirit and letter of the law.

bribery in foreign countries where they do business. This acquiescence to criminal behavior because everyone else does it is wrong and illegal in the United States.

Political Donations

Federal campaign laws limit how much corporations can donate to political candidates and campaigns. The whole campaign finance process is subject to ongoing reform and revision by legislation and court decisions. Recent scandals of influence pedaling for campaign donations are only newer versions of an ongoing problem. The perception and, to a very real extent, the reality is that individuals have very little influence in the political process unless they bring substantial sums of money or guarantee large blocks of votes. Socially responsible investors recognize this perception corrupts the political process and alienates individuals from the process. At the same time, companies should support candidates and issues that will favor their business. But where is the line drawn between supporting a candidate or issue and seeking undue influence through excessive political contributions or fundraising efforts?

While limits exist on directly supporting a candidate, a whole industry has emerged that offers companies the opportunity to contribute virtually unlimited amounts without facing legal problems. The so-called soft money organizations allow companies and executives to contribute large sums for "issue" ads. These campaigns don't mention candidates by name, but it is clear whom they appeal to and whom they support. These organizations are called "527" groups after the section of the IRS code that allows them to raise funds and sponsor issue ads. Corporations and individuals can contribute to these organizations at much higher levels than they can in directly supporting candidates. Federal election laws do not allow these special interest groups to coordinate their campaigns with candidate campaigns (although in the 2004 presidential election, both sides accused the other of this behavior).

Virtually all corporations belong to one or more trade associations. These groups are often active politically. SRI investors have expressed concern that as shareholder dollars are farther removed from the control of management, the chance increases that the money will be used to support issues and candidates that don't represent the company's best interests. This lack of control raises concerns about oversight and transparency of political donations. Management should be held accountable for the effectiveness of money spent on political action projects. Companies that adopt policies of more openness and transparency in matters of political campaigns have better records of consistent and ethical application of those funds.

Responsible Tip

Soft money groups will likely be the target of campaign finance reform, but probably not until the 2008 presidential election is past. Their influence grows each year, which has reformers in both parties concerned.

Bribery and Corruption

Money and power are the great corrupters of the political process—and you could say the same for the business process. Cynics say the national political is the best money can buy. While that is an exaggeration, the ongoing scandals that seem endemic to Washington alienate people from the process. Even the majority of honest political leaders are forced to spend too much time raising money if they wish to be re-elected. With money comes obligations, often unspoken ones.

Given that some bad eggs are always going to find a way to enrich themselves at the public's expense, SRI investors hold out for companies that use political contributions as part of a strategy to help elect people who will do the right thing for the country and economy. There is nothing illegal or immoral about asking your congressional representative for help with a problem, whether you are an individual or a company. The problem comes when you ask for special consideration over your competitors or to avoid some rule that others must abide by. If a promise of a large campaign donation accompanies the request, the company has crossed from asking for help to offering a bribe.

While this activity occurs in the United States, it is much more common in some foreign countries where American companies do business. Paying off local officials to look the other way may be considered the cost of doing business, but it also can be illegal in the United States. Corrupting a local political system, even one that may be somewhat corrupt already, is not right.

The Least You Need to Know

♦ The living wage issue centers on paying workers enough for a family to get by in the community.

♦ Access to health care is a national crisis and one that companies can help fix.

♦ Globalization has created a worldwide market for goods and services, but has also created some problems.

♦ Jobs have changed thanks to globalization and some workers have not adapted to the new reality.

♦ The political process may not return much for the shareholder dollars that companies contribute.

Chapter 8

Community Investment Issues

In This Chapter

◆ Community investment focuses on poverty issues through investing in local neighborhoods

◆ Community banks and credit unions provide financial services in underserved areas

◆ Programs fund low-income housing and small businesses in targeted neighborhoods

◆ Microloans fund very small businesses in the United States and women in foreign countries

Poverty is a growth industry around the world. The income gap between the rich and poor is a serious problem that is only getting worse. Poverty contributes a number of other social problems, such as school dropout rates, teen pregnancy, and crime.

Community investment is a broad term that describes one of the major components of socially responsible investing. SRI investors seek to help people break the cycle of poverty by providing capital in areas where people generally don't have access to it through conventional sources. By investing in community development institutions, SRI investors help provide a source of capital for a variety of projects including affordable housing, small business and microloans, and community services.

Socially responsible investors have several means of accomplishing community investing ranging from deposits in community development banks to participation in community development funds through either direct investment or via a number of mutual funds. Community investing differs from the other investing component of socially responsible investing in the directness of the effort. Your investment, in many cases, results in projects and progress you can actually go visit. Revitalized neighborhoods, thriving community services, and small businesses are the tangible results of community investing. Some mutual funds offer SRI investors the opportunity to participate in community investing projects at work in foreign countries where a small amount of capital can make a significant difference.

Responsible Tip

Much of community investing focuses on affordable housing because it helps keep people in their neighborhoods and revitalizes communities.

Local, Hands-On Approach

Community investing appeals to many SRI investors by addresses a real need in every community. It helps real people directly and in tangible ways not available from other sources. Parts of community investing can be as simple as switching your bank account, while others may choose more aggressive forms of participation. A number of nonprofit groups exist to facilitate community investing and many SRI mutual funds offer opportunities also. You can find listings of various resources in Appendix A. A specific term for some of these institutions is Community Development Financial Institutions (CDFI) . This umbrella term includes community investment banks and credit unions, along with loan funds, *microloan* or microcredit funds, and some venture capital funds. CDFIs are certified by the U.S. Treasury and must meet certain qualifications in exchange for assistance from the federal government. Community Development Corporations are owned by members of the community and focus on housing needs and revitalizing neighborhoods.

def•i•ni•tion

Microloans are very small loans granted to small businesses for expansion or working capital. In the United States, they follow fairly traditional application procedures, but may have looser credit requirements. Overseas, microloans are often less than $100 and most often go to women so they can help feed their family through running a business.

While socially responsible investors want a return on their investment, many find community investing as satisfying if not more so than earning dividends or compound interest. SRI investors who engage in community investing often feel more connected to the people and neighborhoods where their money is making a difference and that has great appeal for some investors.

Community Development Financial Institutions

Community Development Financial Institutions (CDFIs) are financial institutions certified by the U.S. Treasury. They serve neighborhoods ignored by traditional financial service companies with banking services, loans, including microcredit, and venture capital funds. The CDFI program supports affordable housing, job creation, community facilities, and other neighborhood building services. Some CDFIs receive technical assistance from the government for staff training and other resources. The Treasury's CDFI fund provides loans, grants, deposits, and other forms of financial assistance to the community organizations. In most cases, the local community bank or loan fund must match the award dollar-for-dollar with nonfederal money from private investors. This is where SRI investors play an important role. SRI investments or deposits in community development institutions can be leveraged with the federal money to have a greater impact on the community. Many mutual funds that contribute to community investing limit their investments to CDFIs for this reason. Frequently, SRI mutual funds will deposits assets from money market funds and bond funds in community invest banks. Individual investors can also open deposit accounts at CDFI banks and credit unions.

Basic Financial Services

Community investing starts with the premise that the path to self-sufficiency is through investment in people and the community infrastructures that bond neighborhoods. Bringing basic financial services including banking and loans to small businesses to a neighborhood can be the spark that helps people break the cycle of poverty. Many economically disadvantaged neighborhoods have no easy access to basic banking services and little chance of securing even small loans to improve housing or open a small business. Community investments banks and credit unions provide basic financial services where none existed before. Although many of these are CDFIs, not all are.

> **Responsible Tip**
>
> One of the primary differences between community investment banks and credit unions is the banks are for profit and credit unions are nonprofit.

Capital Pools for Local Investment

Community investment banks and credit unions focus on lending money to community development projects, local businesses, and residents of targeted neighborhoods. They function much like your bank, offering checking and deposit accounts. The major difference is that community banks work hard to reinvest in the community. They provide financing in areas where traditional banks and other financial institutions have not had a strong presence. Community banks let depositors pool their capital for use in community projects. Your deposits are federally insured and earn interest just like accounts at a regular bank. Although not every community has one, you can still participate in community investing by moving some of your money into a deposit account (a certificate of deposit, for example) at a community investment bank in another city.

Community investment credit unions often serve as a beginning point for economically disadvantage people to enter the financial services world. A large number of people don't have checking accounts at traditional banks and often pay exorbitant fees at check-cashing services to convert paychecks to cash. They may also pay fees for money orders they use to pay bills. Community investment credit unions can provide a full range of financial services to people who have never had access to them before. In addition to checking accounts and credit counseling, when necessary, community credit unions, along with community investment banks, make loans and investments to help redevelop neighborhoods.

Responsible Tip

Banks and credit unions are typically the only parts of the community investing financial system where your deposits are insured by the federal government. Most of the other organizations may offer insurance or other protections, but not the federal insurance that comes with banks and credit unions.

Investing in Community Projects

In addition to providing financial services and capital to individuals, community banks and credit unions invest in projects that add value to neighborhoods, such as health clinics, day care facilities, and other services. These investments create value in the community by adding to the quality of life and helping to raise the overall standard of living.

When a community has adequate day care facilities, children receive better care and working mothers are less stressed. In some communities, community banks and credit unions have provided financing for opening day care centers—not handouts, but real loans for people in the area with all expectations of repayment that come with borrowing. Community banks and credit unions listen to and work with people in disadvantaged neighborhoods. Community banking works because there is capital to lend, provided by depositors.

Investing in Affordable Housing

One big challenge in community redevelopment is finding decent, affordable housing. Rebuilding neighborhoods depends on people having an emotional and financial stake in making the community work. Nothing accomplishes those two goals better than home ownership. Community investing has a primary goal of providing the capital necessary to rehabilitate or create affordable housing. This means affordable mortgages, loans to remodel existing housing, and funds to acquire and renovate multi-tenet housing from absentee property owners.

This is a particularly strong area for community investing to have a real impact. A number of socially responsible mutual funds that participate in community investing have success stories on their websites of blighted areas transformed when community development banks provided the access to capital. Many communities realize that bulldozing blighted neighborhoods and putting up high-rise public housing projects, the urban renewal of the 1950s and 1970s, is a tragic mistake.

 Red Flag _____

> Investments in disadvantaged neighborhoods often are eligible for government assistance, such as low interest loans. Some unscrupulous developers take advantage of communities by promising development in exchange for assistance in acquiring favorable financing. The developments were either sub-standard or never happened as promised.

Community Development Through Loan Funds

While banking services are the lifeblood of a community, more capital is needed if residents are going to open or expand businesses in the community. Most traditional lenders avoid economically disadvantaged areas for business loans because of the perceived high risk involved. That's where Community Development Loan Funds play an important role. CDLFs provide much needed capital to small businesses, nonprofits, and other community resources, including affordable housing. The loan funds are formal organizations that offer investors the opportunity to participate in community development activities. Investors are paid market to below market interest rates. You should not invest money you'll need for the next one to three years.

How CDLFs Work

Community Development Loan Funds are pools of money that provide a variety of loans to higher risk clients in disadvantaged areas. The loans can be for a wide variety of uses, including small business loans, affordable housing, community resources, and others. CDLFs are open to individuals, foundations, nonprofits, investment companies, and others. Individuals should obtain a prospectus before investing any money.

CDLFs have some eligibility requirements and you should know all the risks before investing any money. Most funds have at least a $1,000 minimum for investing.

CDLFs have a process for reviewing loans just like any financial institution. Applicants are carefully chosen based on character and capacity to make the business successful. Unlike traditional lenders, credit scores are less important. The funds do, however, provide technical assistance to help borrowers with aspects of running a business that they may not know. The loan funds are backed by reserves and, in some cases, grant money against loan loses. However, the federal government does not insure them, so you could lose money. In fact, some investors volunteer to step in if loss reserves are ever breached and forfeit their principal first.

CDLFs often let investors set their own interest rates between zero and a maximum percent. Obviously, the lower you set the interest rate, the lower the cost of capital to the CDLF for its lending programs. In most cases, you should consider that your money will be tied up from one to three years in the fund. It is important

Responsible Tip

Loan funds provide the needed capital where traditional lenders will not do business. The programs are not give-aways and are run with underwriting guidelines for investors' protection.

you understand the risks and are sure you will not need the money you invest before the time set by the fund. You can donate your loan principal or any amount to the loan fund if you wish.

Who Should Invest in CDLFs

Although some eligibility requirements for investing in CDLFs exist, most individuals who can afford to tie up $1,000 (on average) minimum for one to three years can consider investing. Typically, you receive interest payments quarterly, but that is determined by the individual CDLF. At the end of the commitment period, you will receive your principal back. The interest earned on CDLF investments is not tax deductible. When your commitment matures, the CDLF will give you the opportunity to donate the principal to the fund. If you do donate the principal, that contribution is tax deductible. Not every CDLF actively solicits individual contributions.

Rather than invest directly in CDLFs, many investors choose to do so through SRI mutual funds. The funds provide the expertise and oversight for individual investors without the time or experience to do it themselves. Funds can also pool dollars and invest in a number of CDLFs by creating investment notes. The pooling and spreading of your investment dollars over a number of CDLFs provides a degree of geographic diversification that reduces your risk.

Loan Funds for Local Projects

CDLFs provide loans and credit services that are unavailable through traditional lending services. For most CDLFs, the priority is job creation and small businesses that are struggling because they have no access to traditional capital markets with loans for expansion and working capital. The funds also provide loans for community-based nonprofit health care facilities, day care centers, educational and community centers, and other community-based services.

Success Stories

Community centers are often the pride of the neighborhood and provide a focal point for gatherings, both formal and informal. Social and educational activities bring the community together with a sense of purpose.

Microenterprise Loan Funds

An important offering of some CDLFs is microloans. These very small loans to an individual have proven very effective, for example, by helping get a home-based business started. In some cases, the loans are funded in an entirely separate organization called a microenterprise loan fund. These loan funds are Community Development Financial Institutions just like the others mentioned above. Whether the microloan offering comes as part of a larger loan fund or from an organization that specializes in these small loans, they have been very effective in providing capital to individuals and small businesses who could not qualify for traditional loans. Important services that often accompany microloans are technical help in setting up a business and managing the financial aspects of a business. Some programs require applicants to complete a course in small business management before the loan is funded. Many of the microenterprise loan programs work with city and state economic development agencies—some are even managed by these departments.

Many SRI mutual funds offer access to microloan programs through their community investing programs. It should be noted that two different types of microloan programs exist and many funds are active in both. The domestic programs described above focus on small businesses and may make loans up to $5,000. In the United States, this is a very small loan. But microloans in developing countries target a different market with a different hope for the outcome.

Microloans in very poor countries are often targeted at women with the goal of helping them become more self-sufficient and better able to feed their families. For example, the loans may allow the women to buy a cow or some chickens. The woman can feed her family with some of the milk or eggs and sell the rest. Other loans may help a woman acquire raw materials to produce crafts or garments that she can sell.

 Responsible Tip

Microloans in the United States can be administered through or in partnership with a city or other governmental entity. These funds have been available for over 20 years in many communities and, when managed correctly, have a low default rate.

By U.S. standards, the loans truly are micro, but they have proven so successful that microfinance pioneer Muhammad Yunus, founder of Grameen Bank in Bangladesh in 1974, was awarded the Nobel Peace Prize in 2006. Yunus discovered that very small loans could make a difference in changing a family's standard of living. He also discovered that women were much better risks than men were, so the bank lends almost exclusively to women. His first loan was for $27 and it came out of his own pocket. The bank has now issued over $5 billion in loans.

Community Development Corporations

Community Development Corporations are similar to CDLFs, but are owned by members of the community. These nonprofit companies mostly focus on affordable housing and neighborhood redevelopment. Some CDCs have loan funds and many have access to various government programs.

Venture Capital Funds

Many people wouldn't think of disadvantaged neighborhoods as targets for venture capital firms—and for the traditional firms in the industry, that would be correct. But the same seeds of entrepreneurship take root in these communities as elsewhere, they just don't have access to the capital needed to make them grow. Community Venture Capital Funds fill this need by providing high-risk seed money to get innovative business ideas off the ground. These funds are not for every investor. They often have very high minimums ($50,000) and require a ten-year commitment. Although they may not be for everyone, the funds do provide a vital service in redeveloping neighborhoods. A number of SRI mutual funds participate in venture capital funds and that is often the best and easiest way for most investors to participate.

Responsible Tip

Community development venture capital funds tied to community investing are a small part of total community investments. But it is one of the areas where wealthy investors or institutional investors could potentially make a significant return on their investment. Of course, there is also a chance for significant loss.

Savings, family, and friends finance most business startups. In economically disadvantaged neighborhoods, those resources may not be available and, as noted above, it is unlikely traditions venture capital firms would do deals in these areas.

What Should You Expect

Community investing is not like investing in mutual funds, bonds, or stocks. Community investing is the fastest growing segment of socially responsible investing and it's easy to see why. Investing in screened portfolios of stocks or mutual funds with the goal of effecting changes in corporate behavior continues to be an important part of socially responsible investing. Shareholder advocacy, which offers corporations different ways of thinking about policies that effect the environment, workers, and other stakeholders, continues to push for positive change from within corporations. However important both these efforts are, they remain at least one step removed from any change they actually produce.

Community investing, on the other hand, is very much a personal commitment to your community—a commitment you can see and take pride in. The benefit to the investor may not be measured completely in dollars, but in a social reward that gives the investor satisfaction that comes from being a part of improving a neighborhood or giving someone a chance at a better life through their hard work and some of your lent capital. While community investing is not necessarily the best financial decision in many cases, socially responsible investors are finding it connects them with their community in a way the simply writing a check to a mutual fund does not. Through domestic and international community investment programs, investors can choose to invest outside their community in support of a particular issue such as women's development in poor countries.

Economic Justice Through Community Investment

Economic justice is a controversial topic, because it implies to some a redistribution of wealth that disregards ability and willingness to work. The fact is poverty is a disability that hurts the whole community. When people are given the tools to improve their neighborhood and way of life, most will leap at the opportunity. Community investing will not eliminate all the problems of urban decay or poverty, but it will make a difference for some people and neighborhoods. The success stories are too numerous to think otherwise. In addition to immediate results such as renovated housing and community resources, the long-term benefits may be even more significant. A disproportionate percentage of children growing up in poverty are minorities. Growing up in a household with a stable income can mean the difference between repeating a cycle of poverty and advancing to higher education or technical training.

The economic justice of community investing is providing families the opportunity to raise their children in a financially stable environment and a crime-free neighborhood. That is an investment that will pay benefits to the community for years to come.

The Least You Need to Know

◆ Community investing is about providing capital for loans and investment to financially under-served neighborhoods.

◆ Community Development Financial Institutions are the organizations that do community investing.

◆ Investors can participate in Community Loan Funds that do loans for affordable housing and small businesses.

◆ Microloans come in two varieties: those targeting very small domestic businesses and those aimed at helping women in developing countries become more self-sufficient.

Part 3

SRI Strategies

Socially responsible investing uses several key strategies, including positive and negative screening and advocating through shareholder resolutions. Screening out certain companies for social or environmental records is one approach, while another is using screens to identify companies to target for shareholder activism.

Chapter **9**

Screening Investments

In This Chapter

- ◆ Screens and how they work
- ◆ How socially responsible investors use screens
- ◆ Different types of screens
- ◆ Social, environment, religious screens

Screens are tools investors and financial professionals use to reduce the number of potential investment candidates. There are screening tools that work on just about any investment, but the most common are for individual stocks and mutual funds. The concept is simple, although the technique is much more complicated. A screen works to filter out stocks or mutual funds that do not meet the investor's criteria. There are thousands of stocks to invest in, so how does an investor begin the process of picking the few that he wants to own? A stock screen will narrow the choices dramatically by eliminating all stocks that do not match the investor's criteria.

For the socially responsible investor, screens are used to eliminate companies involved in certain businesses. Once the investor has eliminated all companies that are involved in offending industries or have poor environmental records, for example, she can begin to look for good investment prospects among the remaining stocks. SRI investors use screens to exclude companies more frequently than for any other reason. This process saves investors time and money. It also lets individuals do basic research that was once only possible for investment companies with large staffs. This puts the power in individuals' hands to decide what is important to their principles and values.

Responsible Tip

Screening tools were once exclusive to full service stockbrokers, however, thanks to the Internet and powerful personal computers, that technology is now available to just about anyone who has the time to investigate.

Socially responsible investors also use screens for positive criteria. These screens help investors identify companies that are doing the right things that match the investor's values. In depth research, is still difficult for most individual investors. This is why many SRI investors rely on mutual funds to do the screening work for them. In this situation, mutual funds use powerful screen tools to eliminate those companies that do not fits the standards of the fund.

Screens and How They Work

Screens are one of the most helpful and important tools investors use to evaluate stocks and mutual funds. Screens let investors determine what characteristics they want investment candidates to have (or not have). By setting the screen parameters in a certain manner, investors filter out all investments that are not potential candidates. The investor may run several screens, each more narrow in its criteria than the previous one. Screens cannot and should not do all the work. Investors simply use them to get to a short list of potential investment candidates. Working with the short list, an investor can then do a thorough job of analyzing each company for strengths and weaknesses before making a decision. Basic screens are available to individual investors over the Internet, while professional money managers have access to much more powerful tools. Screens that look at social characteristics in addition to financial results are very complicated and are based on detailed research of thousands of stocks.

Screens Filter Based on Criteria

Screens filter based on a set of expectations. The investor decides what items are most important and builds those into the screen, which is really a mathematical model of how the investment is supposed to act. In its simplest form, an investor factors in those elements that he wants excluded from the companies to be considered for investment. The screen filters a database containing information on all stocks and passes it (figuratively speaking) through the screen. Traditional investors use screens to look for companies with a certain profile—for example, a history of earnings growth or companies in a certain industry. You can find free screens online at a number of websites. Some of the better ones are listed in Appendix A. Most of these screens allow you to set multiple criteria on your screen. Investors can play "what if" games with the screens to see what results they get by altering some or all of the inputs. These screens use financial or numerical inputs found on financial statements almost exclusively. For example, your screen might look for companies whose earnings have grown by 15 percent or more for the past three years. Other questions of the screen might look at sales, dividends, stock price, and so on. Each of these is expressed in a numerical form, so the screen can check the information stored on the company to see if it meets the investor's requirement (15 percent growth for three years, four quarters of accelerating sales, and so on).

When investors use screens for the socially responsible concerns, the inputs aren't always expressed in a financial manner and they may not show up on a financial statement. The screens required for SRI investing are more sophisticated than those used by most investors for traditional investing. For example, many SRI screens need to know from which industry or industries a company derives revenue.

> **Responsible Tip**
>
> The screens use the most current data available on each company based on filings to the SEC. Some lag time exists between the filing and posting the information to the databases, however, it isn't much. In most cases, you are using very current information.

It is not too difficult to determine if a company is involved in a particular industry. That information is found in several places on a number of filings companies must make with various government agencies. All companies fall into a major sector. These major sectors are divided into industries within each sector. Although several methods can define sectors, the most widely accepted method assigns all companies to one of 13 sectors. Within each sector are a number of industries. Of interest to socially responsible investors, is the noncyclical consumer goods sector because within this sector are the alcohol and tobacco industries.

If the investor wanted to exclude companies involved in the tobacco industry, screening for this business sector and industry would eliminate all tobacco industry companies from your consideration. However, what about companies that are not in the tobacco industry, but profit from the sale of tobacco products (grocery and convenience stores, for example)? Should they also be excluded from your consideration? Each investor must answer this question for herself. Some SRI investors want total exclusion, while others look at how much revenue or profit the company makes from the product they would normally exclude. Tobacco sales might amount to a very small percentage of total revenue in a grocery store chain and many SRI investors may find this acceptable.

Red Flag _____

When selecting socially responsible mutual funds, be careful to understand its screening parameters—are they total exclusion screens, or do they allow for partial exclusion? The difference may be important to investors with strongly held principles.

Screens Can Exclude or Include Based on Choices

Depending on how you use screens, the same screening tool can include or exclude. If you want to exclude companies involved in the manufacture and sale of alcohol, a screen can eliminate those from further consideration. Likewise, if you are interested in following companies that produce solar energy products, a screen can pick out companies involved in this type of business. This specific type of business screening may require looking at company data by its North American Industry Classification System (NAICS). This numeric system replaced the old Standard Industrial Classification system some years ago. It is designed to assign a six-digit (in most cases) number to every type of business. Once a researcher has the correct NAICS, he can track down similar businesses. (For more information on NAICS, see Appendix A).

Not All Screens Are the Same

One investor's screen may not work for other socially responsible investor. Well over 200 SRI mutual funds support many differing opinions about what is socially responsible and what is not. Where those differences stand out most is over religious issues. Almost all major faith communities have some type of representation in socially responsible investing through a fund or funds—and they all feel strongly about the importance of their values.
Conservative Christians, Jews, Muslims, progressive or liberal Christians, Mennonites, Quakers, Catholics, and many other faith communities are able to express their values in ways that are meaningful to them without conflicting with others. Even among secular funds alcohol, tobacco, gambling, and the environment are common factors in the various screens.

Responsible Tip

Some funds associated with religions or religious groups do not categorize themselves as "socially responsible." Some may feel this term is politically charged. They prefer a term that reflects their religious or theological values.

SRI Use of Negative Screens

Negative screens are the most common in socially responsible investing and have the longest history with the movement. As we noted in earlier chapters, the founders of SRI can be found among the religious groups that would not invest in certain "sin" investments, including tobacco, alcohol, and slavery. These negative screens (also called avoidance screens) simply exclude from investment consideration any company involved in a particular product or line of business. The early days focused on just a few "sins" and many SRI mutual funds and individual investors still resist investing in companies involved in these businesses. A modern consideration is environmental issues. Companies with serious pollution problems and bad environmental records don't make it through environmental screens. As other social, economic, and environmental issues arise, new screens are constructed and tweaked to work for different concerns. It is important to note that not every screened mutual fund screens for the same characteristics. One fund may be especially sensitive to environmental issues and less concerned with alcohol sales. Others may focus on social justice issues and not concern themselves with problems that do not fall under its umbrella.

Success Stories

The original sin investments, tobacco and alcohol, remain on most SRI lists. Has decades of excluding them from SRI investing hurt these industries? That is difficult to say, but it is certain that generations of people have made the commitment to not profit from these two "sin" industries and to raise concerns about these companies' business practices.

Absolute Exclusion or Partial Screens

In subsequent chapters on mutual funds, we'll discuss the different approaches and philosophies to socially responsible investing. One of the key differences is how funds that use negative screening approach exclusion. In some cases, funds may choose what is known as absolute exclusion. This means that if the company is connected in any way to an excluded product or activity, the company is excluded. This is the strictest interpretation, but for some investors who feel passionately about a product or issue, there is no partial acceptance or middle ground. Investors associated with some SRI funds affiliated with religions may fall into this category. Many religions have certain prohibitions that do not have provisions for exceptions. Critics of absolute exclusion (for reasons other than religious beliefs) point out that to exclude a company because it receives less than five percent of its revenue from a prohibited product may mean missing a fine investment opportunity.

Partial screens or exclusions set thresholds for excluding a company for receiving revenue from a prohibited product. This threshold varies from fund to fund, but the idea is that investors should not lose the opportunity to invest in a good company simply because a very small part of their revenue comes from

Responsible Tip

Socially responsible investors balance their interest in investing according to principles and a need for financial return. SRI investors recognize and embrace the healthy tension between achieving a market return on their investments and holding tight to their principles.

prohibited products. A frequently cited example is excluding airlines because they sell alcohol on their flights. Alcohol sales amount to such a tiny part of an airlines revenue that some would argue it is wrong to exclude them on that basis. Where you draw the line is a matter of conscience for you to decide. Some national restaurant/bar chains make a substantial amount of revenue from alcohol sales, although some still make more from the straight sales of food. Do you only exclude manufacturers of alcohol? Or, should you draw the line at some percentage of revenue? At what point does a company go from being acceptable to not acceptable?

Negative Screens May Produce Better Results

Negative screens are simpler to run that positive screens, as we'll see later in this chapter and in more detail in Chapter 10. Some SRI money managers find that negative screens, in particular partial screens, give them the greatest flexibility to select winning stocks for the fund's portfolio. Setting up exclusions is a simpler matter than the more subjective positive screens. Generally, it costs less to run a fund on a negative screen than using a positive screen. It is particularly less expensive than funds where staff is advocating for change either through shareholder meetings and elections or through negotiations with the company's management. These take more time and staff, which increase the fund's expenses and consequently reduces the return to investors. Many religious funds are examples of negative screened funds. The fund managers exclude stocks based on the principles important the religious sponsors.

Does this conclusively mean that negatively screened funds outperform positively screened funds? Not necessarily. In fact, the opposite may be true in some cases and under certain market conditions. While negatively screened funds may have lower expenses, their exclusions may eliminate market leaders at certain times. This can reduce the potential return of the funds

Responsible Tip

Investing success, whether it is traditional or socially responsible investing, is greatly influenced by the expenses you pay to invest. The higher the expenses, the less likely you will achieve a market return on your investment.

when compared to positively screened funds that allow market leaders that are making progress toward their SRI goals.

The more important question for socially responsible investors concerns the relationship between your investments and your values. If you begin choosing return first, then you have placed that value above those socially responsible values that brought you to this area of investing in the first place.

The Big Four of Negative Screens

You can find negative exclusions for a variety of reasons among socially responsible funds, however, most negative screens eliminate four main categories:

- ◆ Tobacco
- ◆ Alcohol
- ◆ War/Military
- ◆ Environment

Tobacco companies have fought for their right to sell and market their products for years and have consistently won, despite a multi-billion settlement with most of the states. Many critics thought the settlement was too little and, in many cases, states are using the money to balance budgets rather than for smoking education programs and offsetting Medicaid costs attributed to smoking-related health issues. While some forms of tobacco advertising have been banned, the industry still finds ways to spend billions of dollars marketing their products each year. As the U.S. market began shrinking, tobacco companies started exporting their products around the world. Tobacco-related deaths number in the millions worldwide each year. Companies that produce tobacco, tobacco products, and that sell tobacco products are major targets of negative screens.

Alcohol, once banned in the United States, is the legal drug of choice for Americans. Although it is legal, ample proof shows causes more harm to society than all the illegal drugs combined. Its public misuse is a crime and drunken drivers are a leading cause of wrecks and fatalities. Negative screens can focus only on the companies that make and distribute alcohol products or broaden the scope to include companies on the retail end of the supply chain. Another issue is how to account for the sale of alcohol on a company's finances. In many cases, the actual revenue may not be a large percentage of the total, but earnings from alcohol sales can be significant because of the large profit margins in selling alcoholic drinks in bars and restaurants.

Success Stories

Socially responsible investors were active in the campaign to remove the advertising of hard liquor (high alcohol content) products from television. The move was voluntary on the part of the industry, which self-regulates its advertising. But pressure from SRI groups on media outlets and alcohol producers has not been entirely effective in curbing beer advertising.

War/military is a broad category that can include weapons, supplies, materials, and much more. Depending on how the negative screen is constructed, it could exclude all defense contractors or just those involved in supplying war-related goods and supplies. If an aircraft company makes commercial planes and military aircraft, too, some screens will exclude them automatically, while others may apply a revenue test of some kind. What about the company that makes food rations for troops or boots or radios or vehicles? This category is a good example of how partial or absolute screens achieve different results. Absolute screens would significantly reduce the number of potential investment candidates because the military requires so many different items and contracts for all of its supplies.

The environment screen can be as basic as avoiding any company that has ever been cited for a pollution violation, or as complicated as taking each on a case-by-case basis. What about a company that had a problem, but is working hard to fix it? Many environmental screens would exclude nuclear plants because of spent fuel storage issues and the potential for ecological disaster if there were a leak. The discharge of warm water into lakes and rivers can also be an environmental problem. Other issues include companies that have major pollution clean ups facing them in the near future, along with companies that have no *greenhouse gas* policy. Other issues that may be more specific to a particular industry are also considered.

def•i•ni•tion

Greenhouse gases are released when fossil fuels (oil, natural gas, coals, gasoline, diesel, and so on) are burned, also deforestation and unsustainable agricultural practices are an important issue. Some of these gases are thought to be changing the composition of our atmosphere making it denser so it retains more heat. This heating, known a global warming, is a major ecological challenge for the future and companies should have a plan to deal with it.

Criticism: Negative Screens Do No Good

Negative screens and socially responsible investors are criticized as naïve and perhaps irresponsible, but certainly ineffectual by many in the traditional investing community. Their criticism, which has basis in fact, is that not buying a company's stock because you don't like what it sells or you believe it is a polluter does nothing to the company. Except for an initial public offering, the stock you buy or refused to buy is not coming from the company, but from another investor. Another individual or institution, not the company itself, owns stock you buy on the stock market so you are not denying the company a source of capital.

If everyone refused to buy the stock, the price would go down and ultimately this would affect the company. The reality, however, is that there is usually a buyer. For a number of years, even while being pounded by the media and in the courtroom, tobacco companies did quite well for their stockholders. We can assume that a large percentage of SRI investors sold all their tobacco stock and refused to buy more. The companies you choose to exclude from your portfolio may not suffer immediately, but over time, as new SRI investors are introduced to the concept and practices, their stock may decline. Companies also suffer bad public relations when SRI investors go public with their reasons for not buying the stock.

For many SRI investors, the idea of not investing in companies has less to do with punishing the company and more to do with refusing to profit from a business that violates a personal principle. If you are

Responsible Tip

Negative screens accomplish their main purpose, which is to prevent the investor from profiting from a company involved in business practices that violate the investor's principles.

strongly antiwar, does it make sense to profit from investments in military suppliers and defense contractors? If you are as green as Kermit the Frog, is it consistent to own major polluters? This is the dilemma investors face when they buy traditional mutual funds, which invest by the numbers only. You do not know where your money is going or what you own—many managed stock mutual funds turnover a large percentage of their holdings each year.

Positive Screens for a Change

Some SRI investors are content with the negative screens and the stocks and mutual funds that come out of those exercises. Another group of SRI investors, however, looks at their investment dollars as a way to reward companies that make significant progress toward an important socially responsible goal. In this situation, the screen is looking for positive change in a company that has committed to improvement. SRI investors may reward progress with investment in the company and encouragement to senior management.

In some cases, these are new companies starting with a clean record that are involved in socially responsible industries such as alternative energy. These small companies often need capital infusions, such as secondary stock offerings, which can be an opportunity for SRI investors to step in if the situation looks right. Some SRI investors seek these types of investments as a way to feel a part of change for the better through our existing economic system. There is comfort in knowing that our market system is creative and innovative enough to tackle social and environmental issues. Not all of these companies are small. There are opportunities for investments in larger companies that give investors the sense that they own solutions to problems rather than creations of problems.

Socially responsible investors may also find these situations with larger, more mature companies. In these situations, investors may observe it is more difficult for the company to make progress toward SRI goals due to its size and other operating considerations. Older companies may need time to move toward more acceptable SRI practices. Along with shareholder advocacy, encouraging senior management to move in the direction of SRI goals is a way positive screening can advance socially responsible goals. The benefits of this type of approach however can be significant, especially if the company is a leader in its industry. As the leader of its industry, adopting more socially responsible business practices will have an important influence on all other firms in that category. Some in the socially responsible investing movement avoid many of the negative or exclusionary screens and focus on positive screens and encouraging shareholder activism. There is not universal agreement on the exact definition of all of these terms and some mutual funds use their own particular language as part of their marketing to set themselves apart from other SRI funds. Functionally most of the activities are very similar.

> **Success Stories**
>
> Industry leaders that adopt positive SRI principles such as strong environmental programs, excellent employee programs, and so on, can establish "best practices" for the whole industry and have a strong influence on moving a number of companies forward.

Positive Screening for Investments

Positive screening advocates suggest that investors want to do more with their money and negative screening is mostly focused on what they shouldn't do. By simply excluding certain companies based on a set of guidelines, you are making a statement about what you are not supporting, but not necessarily what you are supporting with your investments. Positive screening is not just the opposite of negative screening. It is an active approach to placing your investing dollars where your values are. Positive screening or as some call it, pro-active screening, gives you companies that are solving or trying to solve social problems.

> **Success Stories**
>
> Positive screening for SRI investments lets you express your principles by directly investing in companies that are making a difference today and will make a difference tomorrow.

These fall into two groups. The first group contains companies that are working to resolve issues such as environmental problems, worker relations, and other concerns that would make the company a more socially responsible member of society. The second group includes companies whose business is solving social or environmental problems. These are usually younger and smaller companies that are working in groundbreaking technology or social experiments. For example, companies involved in developing energy-efficient homebuilding techniques or companies that work with communities to develop green spaces in urban design projects or companies that build solar energy systems are all examples of companies that positive screens might extract. We'll discuss positive screening in more detail in Chapter 10.

Shareholder Activism Screening

Shareholder activism is one of the key strategies for many socially responsible investors. As we saw in Chapter 3 and will learn more about in Chapter 11, shareholder activism is the process of working with and advocating with companies to convince them to change some aspect of corporate behavior. Most shareholder activism is cordial and done through dialogue and shareholder resolutions at annual meetings. In other circumstances, shareholder activism can be confrontational, especially when participants feel their concerns are not getting a reasonable hearing from corporate officials.

Role of Screening

Screening is the starting point for many investors, whether individual or institutional. It is a fast and convenient way to reduce mounds of information down to a manageable amount. It can do much of the searching and eliminating (or including) for you before you begin your analysis in earnest. Screens offer many benefits, but they are only the first step in selecting an investment. Once you have narrowed down your list to a manageable number, it is time to do a through analysis of each one to determine which are closest to meeting your social and financial goals. If you invest in mutual funds, the fund manager will perform this analysis for you.

The Least You Need to Know

- Screens help SRI investors identify investment candidates.
- Negative screens filter out those companies involved in unacceptable businesses or activities.

- Negative screens can be absolute so nothing gets through or partial with an acceptable limit on excluded items.

- Screens are a starting point for investors to begin their analysis of investments.

Chapter 10

Positive Screening

In This Chapter

- ◆ The use of positive screens
- ◆ Selecting areas for positive screening
- ◆ Social activism screening
- ◆ Screening for management practices

Positive screens for socially responsible investors identify companies that are making or have made the decision to practice those philosophies of environmental sustainability, stakeholder partnership, and community involvement that set them apart. It is unlikely that too many companies—especially larger, more mature companies—will get 100 percent on all the SRI score-cards. Some companies come with a checkered past that may include gross violations of SRI standards. Positive screening can be a consideration of how the company is moving to change or rectify past problems rather than expecting an absolutely clean slate. This strategy looks to encourage movement by companies toward SRI goals by acknowledging ongoing efforts and pushing for further progress. In addition, positive screens are used to identify companies that work in socially responsible areas, such as environmental firms, alternative energy developers, and others.

Using Positive Screens to Identify Investments

As we noted in the previous chapter, building screens that identify financial parameters can be easier than picking out socially responsible criteria. You won't find environmental violations listed on balance sheets as a specific number, and repressive management practices don't show up on the income statement as a line item (although both of these issues have a direct impact on a company's finances). Pulling together the information for social screens is much more difficult than simply culling key numbers off financial statements. Environmental violations and any other fines or civil or criminal actions must be reported in filings to the SEC and made available to shareholders. Researchers comb documents for this information and add it to a database. Depending on how a SRI mutual fund sets up its screens, its researchers will dig into the companies it considers for investment.

Responsible Tip

Positive screens don't require companies to hit 100 percent on all points for inclusion; however, minimal levels of accomplishment must be met to satisfy most screens.

The Purposes of Positive Screens

Positive socially responsible screens serve several purposes, but all point toward identifying and monitoring companies that are candidates for investment. Positive screens differ from negative screens in that the objective is to find investment candidates rather than eliminate non-candidates. You could argue that you arrive at the same place, with a universe of companies to consider for an investment. But that misses the point of positive screening, which is to identify specific investment opportunities. SRI investors focus on situations where they invest to achieve a socially responsible result. This intentional matching of SRI values with companies is the most important aspect of positive screening.

As you will see in this chapter and others throughout this book, positive screening doesn't necessarily mean finding the perfect company. It can mean finding companies that are receptive to socially responsible initiatives or companies that have problems such as environmental issues, but are trying to reform. Positive screening can also identify those companies that are leaders in their industry and help SRI investors target them for improvement through activism and advocacy programs.

How Mutual Funds Use the Data

SRI mutual funds use information from a database (either their own or through a contractor) to screen investment choices. If a fund is negatively screened for tobacco and alcohol only, the process is quite simple. Of course, most funds are more demanding than this example. The fund may exclude these two sin investments, but be positively screened with all of its other choices. The fund may want to consider, for example, companies that have significant family leave policies. This would require a much more extensive search through a database than simply excluding tobacco and alcohol companies. Unlike bad news, companies often display their progressive policies as long as they can assure more traditional investors that the bottom line isn't taking a hit. Companies may selectively advertise their SRI good name by picking media and publications where that message would be well-received. For example, some companies advertise their environmentally friendly policies on their sponsorship spots for public radio. The assumption is that the audience for public radio might be more receptive to that message.

How simple or complicated a fund's criteria are may also impact the expenses investors pay in connection with the fund, which can affect potential returns. The more complicated the screen, the more expenses are usually involved. In addition, very strict screens may limit the money manager's ability to choose potential investment candidates, resulting in potentially lower returns.

> **Responsible Tip**
>
> Social screens are more complicated and more subjective than financial screens. SRI mutual funds use proprietary data or contract with others for the information.

Includes Companies Needing Change

Although this may seem incongruous, positive screens also can be used to identify companies that are offenders of SRI principles. These companies are often high profile or leaders in their industry and socially responsible investors target them for social activism. The strategy is to acquire shares of the company's stock, which buys you access to annual meetings and allows you to introduce shareholder resolutions. Many of these companies may not be in violation of many SRI standards, but if they could be turned on a particular issue, it would send a message to others in their industry. We'll discuss shareholder rights and social advocacy in Chapter 11.

Investment value is, to a large extent, based on a company's future earnings. This forward-looking mindset has some value to the SRI investor in working with companies that have tarnished records in socially responsible areas. A solid approach is to consider where the company has been and where it is today and what strategies are in place for changes in the future. It is usually unrealistic to expect instant changes, especially in large companies with lengthy histories. SRI investors, however, are concerned with direction and progress. Has the company made moves to solve the problems? Are these steps likely to be successful? If so, when will the changes manifest themselves? These benchmarks can be quantified, measured, and encouraged by SRI investors.

Responsible Tip

A company's history in social and environmental areas is important, but many SRI investors are more concerned about what the company is doing now and what they are doing to prepare for the future. Valuing a company's social responsibility in this manner is similar to the way its financial prospects are valued.

Choosing Companies That Do SRI

Positive screening also identifies companies involved in socially responsible activities as a business model. Most of these targets will fall into the environmental segment of SRI. For example, alternative energy and renewable energy are just two of the business models that SRI investors might embrace. These companies, which tend to be smaller and younger, are focusing on ways to capitalize on the perceived growing demand for environmentally friendly energy resources. Many other examples exist of companies filling or anticipating new needs ahead of the market. SRI investors may be attracted to these investments for their socially responsible focus, but also for the potential of significant rewards. Smaller companies that are carving out niches in the energy and environmental industries may have bright futures. Investing in small companies, however, whether they have a traditional or socially responsible focus, is riskier than investing in more established companies. Investors should weigh the risks and potential rewards of this investment strategy.

Individual Investors vs. Mutual Funds

Measuring social parameters such as environmental factors and social and workplace justice issues can be difficult and time consuming. Sophisticated tools are not readily available to the average individual investor. Mutual funds and other institutional investors (pension funds, life insurance companies, and so on) invest millions of dollars and can afford robust technology and staff (employees or consultants) to tackle these questions. Some answers are more subjective than objective, which makes coming up with a fair and balanced look across the spectrum of possible investments difficult.

Some individual investors take a shortcut and simply buy stocks that SRI mutual funds own. They conclude that the homework has been done and it is a matter picking the best of the best. This strategy has merit, however, what it lacks is the rationale behind choosing that particular stock. It is possible that the mutual fund manager was marginal on the stock, but felt it had short-term potential. If it does not show some quick growth, she will dump it and move on to a more certain return from another stock. If you cherry-pick stocks off a list of those owned by your mutual fund, you may pick the ones the fund is ready to dump.

Individuals can also limit their consideration to a much smaller universe of stocks so that the examination is manageable given the tools they possess. There is a downside to this: because of your limited universe you may miss opportunities you didn't have time to consider. The other possibility is that the universe of stocks you pick to examine may not have a winner in the bunch. You may spend a lot of time with nothing to show for it. We will examine the process of picking individual stocks in Chapter 16.

Success Stories
Despite the fact that individuals can only manage a small number of individual stocks, it is possible to have a relatively safe portfolio provided you have diversified across a number of different industry sectors. If your portfolio has high exposure to a particular industry, like those who owned only tech stocks in 2000, your risk increases dramatically.

Where Investors Can Find Bad News

Companies are, for obvious reasons, not excited about promoting bad news such as a big fine for violating environmental regulations. Yet we read about such fines almost every day, if not for fractures of environmental law, then for discrimination in employment or hiring practices or some other reason. As much as they would like to, companies are compelled by law to disclose this information. It is often published in the news media and if it is big enough, it will find its way to the front page or magazine cover. In addition, companies are required to report significant fines, settlements, and such on the documents they routinely file with the SEC. These include their *10-Q, 10-K*, and *annual report*. All of these reports are available to shareholders and the public. You can access them through the SEC's EDGAR website. See Appendix A for details.

Even though this information is contained in these reports, don't expect it to be highlighted for you. Most of the bad news is reported in a matter-of-fact manner and in some documents can be found in footnotes. Digging through this information is time-consuming work, which is why many SRI investors turn to mutual funds that have staff and expertise to do this type of research.

def•i•ni•tion

> **10-K** reports are detailed annual reports filed with the SEC. They are like annual reports, but contain much more detailed financial and narrative information.
>
> **10-Q** reports are detailed quarterly financial statements that must be filed with the SEC within 35 days of the close of the first three quarters of the company's fiscal year. The 10-K is due at the end of the year. The reports must include any relevant information about the state of the company's financial affairs.
>
> **Annual reports** are submitted to shareholders at the close of each fiscal year. The year's financial performance is reported along with significant details about the year's activities. The first part of the report is usually given to dramatic photographs, stunning graphics, and inspiring messages from the president. The backend of the report contains the important information on finances, operations, and the auditor's report.

Improvement in Areas Is Tracked

It is a given in investing that circumstances change. You should be monitoring your investments on a regular basis to determine if there have been any fundamental changes in the company that would make you rethink the original decision to buy the stock. Yesterday's industry leader is today's also-ran. The same is true when monitoring a company for social criteria. A company that had a good environmental record last year, for example, suffers a major ecological disaster this year and fails to respond properly. New management disassembles progressive workplace policies and ships thousands of jobs overseas to bolster his annual bonus. The SRI selection process is not a one-time event, but an ongoing process. For those investors who practice social activism and advocacy, buying stock in a company is just the beginning of their involvement. It may be difficult for an individual investor to manage more than eight to ten stocks and review them on a timely basis for changes—both of fundamental and socially responsible criteria. Mutual funds are better suited to perform an ongoing analysis, which, depending on the fund, may include weekly contact with the company.

Screens Monitor Progress

Mutual funds employ both technological and human screening processes to stay on top of companies in their portfolios. These can be very sophisticated tools, however, there is one tool that individual investors can and should use to help them keep track of stocks they own. The search engine Google offers a free service that allows you to receive e-mail notices if a subject you are interested in appears in the news. You can enter the name of a company you want to follow and Google will send you an e-mail alert every time this company makes the news. For some companies, this may produce more e-mails than you want to receive, but try the free service and see if it works for you—you can always turn it off if it generates too many notices.

Red Flag

Be careful of "green washing." Companies practice green washing when they generate more press coverage for their socially responsible efforts than the actual effort itself. Green washing is using public relations to create the appearance of being socially responsible without any real substance behind the claim.

Traditional financial managers track a company's financial progress continually. Companies must report financial summaries at least quarterly and more often if there is a significant event that investors should know about. Financial money managers also stay in contact with companies to determine how sales of new products are progressing, for example, or to get updates on holiday sales. There is no specific requirement to report or update socially responsible indicators. As noted earlier, if the company is hit with a fine or judgment, that information must be made public and it is considered public when filed with regulatory authorities. Investors who want to follow the progress of socially responsible goals need a different strategy. Mutual funds have more leverage with companies because they often own significant blocks of stock.

Company managers open to socially responsible overtures when the business is doing well may face significant pressure from the investment community if those actions are seen as a drag on earnings. While socially responsible investors advocate that their principles of environmental and stakeholder responsibility are also good business, they may put short-term strains on earnings. Corporate managers are often judged in the stock market by quarter-to-quarter performance. If key financial indicators begin slipping, the stock price may very well slip also. SRI investors may view this as an investment in the future and take a long-term perspective of the stock. Unfortunately, that's not the mentality of the stock market, especially for stocks placed in the growth column. Any stumble in revenue and earnings may send the stock price falling as traditional growth investors look for a better and more immediate return on their investment.

Progress of Activism and Advocacy

Positive screening of stocks leads SRI investors to companies that have the potential to change or improve on certain practices. Some SRI mutual funds are very active in this area and work with other advocacy groups to bring change to key companies. In many cases, mutual funds do not act alone but partner with other groups who have an interest in advocating with companies on a particular issue or set of issues. This leverages the resources of all that are involved in working for social, economic, and environmental change.

Socially responsible advocates, whether representing mutual funds or other groups, frequently meet with the management of companies to discuss issues of concern. These meetings can range from unproductive, to changes in corporate policy, and everything in between. Most agree that they are more productive than confrontational tactics.

Responsible Tip

One benefit of SRI investing through mutual funds is the funds' advocacy efforts on behalf of investors who may not have the time or expertise to do it on their own. Another benefit is professional portfolio management.

Identifies Management Practices

One key area of interest and concern to socially responsible investors that is somewhat difficult to monitor is management practices as they relate to employees and other stakeholders. Progressive companies recognize employees, including those represented by labor unions, as priority assets and structure policies to nurture and retain workers. As the economy continues its shift away from manufacturing and toward a knowledge-based economy, it is more important than ever to retain and encourage a skilled workforce. Human resource policies that are supportive of a diverse workforce acknowledge the changing demographics of our society and the global nature of our economy. Companies consistently in trouble with employment laws and regulations for discrimination or other violations are prime candidates for socially responsible advocacy. These companies may be easier to spot than others who benignly keep women and minorities out of key management positions or hold employment practices that put a ceiling on advancement.

Policies Toward Women, Minorities

Despite numerous laws and the simple idea of what's right, women and minorities still lag behind white males in pay for the same work. Equally disturbing is the smaller percentage of women and minorities in management positions relative to their numbers in the population and the workforce. Some mitigating circumstances can be cited that could explain small variations, however, no logic explains the large gaps other than years of repressive hiring and promoting practices. SRI investors know these shortfalls can't be made up immediately, but companies that show no real intention to fix the problem are hiding behind excuses that more progressive companies dismissed years ago.

Besides being morally, ethically, and perhaps legally wrong, this narrow attitude misses an important business opportunity. As noted in Chapter 7 and elsewhere, the demographic mix of the U.S. market is changing and will continue to change as minorities become a larger percentage of the population. This is a population fact, not racial or ethnic stereotyping. Lower birth rates among whites combined with immigration patterns are changing the mix of the U.S. population. Companies that do not reflect these changes in their workforce will not relate well to consumers. It is not a matter of having minority clerks to serve minority customers—that is patronizing. The idea is to bring a wealth of ideas, attitudes, and customs to a business at all levels so that they are a part of the business, not a "minority services" division. When a company designs products and services with input from a workforce that reflects the market it serves, it is more likely to find itself in tune with its customers. The opposite of this is doing business like it has always been done and wondering why market share is shrinking. When companies that insolate themselves from diverse employees in key decision-making roles produce products that flounder with minority customers, they can't understand why. This is why SRI investors view companies with progressive employment and hiring practices as good potential investment candidates. They believe that these practices will lead to a greater understanding of the market and more fertile ideas for growth of products and services.

Not only is the U.S. population changing, but also the marketplace for U.S. goods and services is now global. Our products are made and sold in hundreds of foreign markets. While there are some definite negatives about globalization, it is here to stay. Companies that employ a diverse workforce from senior managers on down will relate better to the challenges of operating in foreign markets.

Responsible Tip

Companies that recruit and nurture a diverse workforce understand the world is changing, and staying connected with current and future customers requires a number of different perspectives.

The additional benefit of a diverse workforce is an often more loyal and productive employee base. If senior managers set the tone for racial, ethnic, and sexual tolerance and follow through with their actions, it sets a standard in the company that will be emulated down the corporate ladder. Racial or sexual intolerance must be dealt with swiftly and decisively to send a message to other workers that this type of behavior is unacceptable. If management faithfully takes all the correct steps to prevent racial, ethnic, and sexual discrimination, it reduces the possibility of huge damage judgments by demonstrating that problems represent isolated incidents and are not representative of corporate policy or neglect.

For SRI investors, progressive hiring and promoting policies often mean lower employee turnover, higher productivity, and fewer employee discrimination lawsuits. All of this translates into less risk to the investor and the potential for greater returns. Where a traditional investor might see progressive employee policies as an expense, the SRI investor sees them as an investment in the employees and as insurance against huge damage claims from lawsuits.

Progressive Union Relationships

Labor unions have been losing membership for decades. In 1983, 20.1 percent of the workforce belonged to labor unions. By 2006, that number had dropped to 12 percent. There are many reasons for the decline, including a continuing transition away from manufacturing, which had a strong union presence, to service sector and knowledge-based jobs. As manufacturing declined, so did union membership. In some cases, the unions, through greed and corruption at the top, have been their own worst enemy. Regardless, many unions still perform a valuable service in representing the needs of workers to management.

Rather than fight unions, progressive companies embrace them and work with them to improve relations with employees. Unions that work with management to find the best solution for the workers they represent that doesn't bankrupt the company provide a valuable service to both their members and management. Managers that resent unions devise ways to skirt work rules and are more concerned with production than with their workers. Companies like this often ship jobs overseas when possible to avoid unions and high U.S. wages.

> **Success Stories**
>
> Management and labor unions don't have to be enemies. They can work together to build an environment that helps the company secure as many jobs as possible, while acknowledging that competitive forces challenge the best business models.

Socially responsible investors understand the value of a good working relationship with labor unions and reward companies that go out of their way to make the arrangement work.

Best of Class Models

No company is going to be the perfect model for all positive screens. This is especially true for larger, older firms. Many mutual funds and money managers employ a "best of class" approach to portfolio design. This model picks the best company in an industry group—one that is closest to making all the numbers work. This company is held up as the Best of Class model of how to act in a socially responsible manner. The inclusion of this company (in SRI mutual fund portfolios) is as an industry leader in socially responsible areas, not a necessarily financial leader. Progressive management teams that are open to talking about social and/or environmental issues can be leaders in their industry. SRI mutual funds that selectively invest in best of class companies, even in industries with negative histories (such as ongoing problems with pollution or other environmental concerns), help point the way for other companies in the industry to follow suit. Some SRI investors find these arrangements somewhat distasteful because they are asked to invest in companies and industries that would normally not pass many negative SRI screens. But if some companies can be persuaded to change legacy business patterns by investments from SRI mutual funds, much good can come of the effort.

The Least You Need to Know

◆ Positive screens help SRI investors identify potential investments.

◆ Screens evaluate companies in socially responsible areas such as environmental policies and employee relations.

◆ Screening helps identify companies that are targets for activism and advocacy.

◆ Screening identifies positive and negative management practices.

Chapter 11

Your Shareholder Rights

In This Chapter

- ◆ Your rights as a shareholder
- ◆ Socially responsible investors and shareholder rights
- ◆ How shareholder advocacy works
- ◆ Annual meetings and proxy voting

Corporations are unique legal entities. This is a fairly modern concept, but it is important to the discussion of shareholder rights and responsibilities. In broad terms, corporations are recognized as having legal rights and obligations the same as people have. This is why a corporation (not the owners or managers) can be sued and can sue in court to satisfy legal claims. When large corporations commit to repayment of a loan or other obligation, the individual owners are generally not obligated. (It's different for very small corporations, since most lenders require a personal guarantee from the owner(s) on any debt.) For publicly traded companies, the owners (shareholders) are not personally liable for any action by the corporation, which means if the company commits a violation of the law, you won't go to jail. As a shareholder, you get to vote on important issues before the corporation such as mergers, new members of the board of directors, and other matters. In most cases, one share of stock allows you one vote in these matters. You can cast your vote at the annual meeting or let someone else vote your shares.

Many socially responsible investors believe in the importance of advocating their principles to corporations. Shareholders can introduce resolutions that address areas of concern such as environmental policies, employment practices, and others. But the way annual meetings and the voting process are structured make it difficult for investors to succeed in bringing and passing a shareholder resolution. Most SRI mutual funds support shareholder advocacy and use it to help change corporate policies.

> **Responsible Tip**
>
> Being a socially responsible investor means taking your voting rights as a shareholder seriously and understanding the role of shareholder advocacy.

You're the Owner

Shareholders, not management, own corporations, unless managers are also major shareholders. Major corporations such as IBM or Microsoft can have shareholders numbering in the hundreds of thousands, because they have billions of *outstanding shares*. While major institutional investors such as mutual funds, pension funds, life insurance companies, and so on may own the majority of shares, individual shareholders have the same rights. As a practical matter, the power is where the votes are, so institutional investors can exert the most influence over corporations. Still, individual investors can participate in the governance of the corporation, including introducing resolutions for the other shareholders to vote on. Individual shareholders can attend annual meetings and vote their shares on important issues, although very few small investors do this. Shareholders do not get a voice in the day-to-day operations of the corporation.

> **def•i•ni•tion**
>
> **Outstanding shares** of common stock refer to the shares owned by the public, including individuals, mutual funds, and institutional investors. A company may retain unissued shares of its stock, but these are not considered outstanding.

Socially responsible investors use shareholder resolutions and negotiations with management to change and improve corporate practices that conflict with SRI principles, such as environmental concerns, executive compensation, employment practices, and so on. You can be an active participant in that part of corporate governance if you choose, however, the system is such that it responds more quickly to larger shareholders.

Corporations Organized to Give Management Power

Shareholders elect a board of directors, which hires the president or chief executive officer. The top management person is charged with operating the company for the benefit of the shareholders. Over the years, management has assumed more and more authority to act on its own. Many shareholders believe this is the way the system should work—hire professional managers to run the business and make the largest profit possible. By many standards, the only function of a corporation is to earn as much money as possible for the owners. (This is why some traditional investors have a difficult time accepting the concept of socially responsible investing, because it says there are additional priorities that are important for corporations.) Hiring professional managers to run the company makes good sense. A small group of experts can operate the business more efficiently than a board of directors or the shareholders.

The emphasis on earnings and short-term performance has resulted in management assuming more power and authority over the years. This has led to moves that reduce the participation in company affairs by stockholders. In many ways, this makes sense considering how large some companies have become in revenue and outstanding shares. The more owners, the less responsive a corporation can be to these shareholders. People who are very strong and accustomed to making major decisions run most publicly traded companies.

As management has been given (or taken) more power, the role of shareholders has diminished somewhat. Large corporations are extremely complex undertakings, and not just everyone can run one with any efficiency. CEOs who can make corporations hum with coordinated activity are paid large sums of money. (In some cases, opponents argue, too much money.) To make the system work, some CEOs have taken on extraordinary powers. In many cases, this has meant stacking the board of directors with people sympathetic to the CEO. This provides the CEO with a friendly authoritative body to approve his plans. Thanks to some major scandals, the SEC and other regulatory bodies have pushed corporations to do a better job with board oversight of management plans. Part of that push is to have more "outside" directors on the board. Theoretically, these directors would not have personal ties to the CEO and should act in a manner more representative of all the shareholders.

Responsible Tip

The issue of appropriate executive authority is a difficult one. Scandals such as Enron demonstrated that board members were either complicit in the scandals or incompetent in their oversight of management.

Board of Directors Should Represent Shareholders

In theory, the board of directors should represent all the stockholders of a corporation. The board is the connection between management and the owners, providing the oversight and guidance for the individual owners. Board members, in addition to representing the owners, should have expertise in some area of business or a related field that will help management formulate long-range strategies or make connections for the company with other centers of influence. Despite our high-tech world, a great deal of business is still done through personal relations and contacts.

Red Flag

Companies that have members of management on the board of directors raise a caution with SRI investors. The relationship suggests those board members are more concerned with representing management and cannot represent shareholders in matters that may be contrary to management's interests.

The reality is that boards are often stacked with friendly faces and people who are sympathetic to management. Board members are often asked to serve because of who they know or previous positions as CEOs of other companies. This may provide management with a board of directors that is more obligated to the CEO than to shareholders. When there is not sufficient oversight of management, the potential for abuse exists. The issue of executive compensation is directly tied to boards that have stronger links to management than they have to shareholders. Reform in this area could assure shareholders that their interests were well represented.

SRI Position on Boards of Directors

Socially responsible investors do not universally accept a position on how a board of directors should be constituted and function. But many SRI mutual funds do have positions on how they will vote their prox- ies (see next section for more on proxy voting) regarding the board of directors. Here are the major items most funds consider when looking at board of director issues:

- ◆ **Independence**—Most SRI firms agree that the majority of board members should be independent of financial ties to the corporation or management. In some companies, officers of the corporation sit on the board of directors. SRI investors believe this is a conflict of interest, since the board's first obligation is to shareholders, not management. Independent directors should head important board committees.

- ◆ **Diversity**—Boards should be representative of many different backgrounds and points of view. Just as diversity is important in the workforce and executive ranks, it is important also on the board to have representation that is reflective of the world and marketplace.

- ◆ **Member terms**—Staggered board terms are often used to help thwart takeover bids, which are sometimes in the shareholders' best interests. This system of staggering (also known as board classes) has members elected for different terms so that only a few are up for re-election each year. SRI investors generally support an annual re-election of the board.

- ◆ **Director compensation**—Directors are entitled to compensation for the time they spend at board and committee meetings. But some companies award directors excessive stock options or grants. SRI investors believe excessive compensation is wrong for direc- tors just as it is wrong for executives.

Most SRI firms go into much greater detail on what they will and won't support, but these are the broad topics. They represent the view that the board of directors has an obligation to shareholders first, and that may not be reflected in how many are organized.

Effect on SRI Investors

If the board of directors is stacked in favor of management, it makes change more difficult. Shareholder resolutions proposed under these conditions have limited success. SRI mutual funds have better success affecting change by negotiating with management and resorting to shareholder resolutions as a last choice. A major problem in some cases is the disconnect between the traditional role of corporations, to make as much money as possible, and the expanded set of expectations SRI investors have for corporations as citizens with obligations to society just like the rest of us. SRI proponents suggest that most of the changes they would like to see will ultimately be good for businesses.

Responsible Tip

SRI mutual funds that take on the shareholder advocacy role frequently partner with other interested organizations such as foundations or pension funds when their interests areas are complimentary. This combining of resources gives the effort more clout with companies because it usually represents a larger block of stock and/or group of shareholders.

SRI Shareholder Advocacy

The shareholder advocacy process allows owners to bring issues before other shareholders for a vote. Many SRI mutual funds take an active role in shareholder advocacy as a way to bring about change in corporate policies. The funds have the staff and resources to evaluate practices of corporations, although individuals can bring shareholder votes. In most cases, funds would rather settle the issue through negotiation rather than push it to a shareholder resolution. Funds that practice this form of shareholder advocacy may use the shareholder resolution as leverage in talks with the company to reach a settlement. Many of the shareholder resolution issues involve requiring management to report to shareholders on certain information important to socially responsible investors. This could include employment hiring practices, executive compensation, environmental issues, and so on. Not surprisingly, in many companies management is reluctant to share information, especially if it does not put them in a good light.

Responsible Tip

Shareholder advocacy is one of the pillars of socially responsible investing. Affecting change in major corporations can have a huge impact on others in the industry and help move a socially responsible idea into the mainstream of investor thinking.

The Process of Filing Shareholder Resolutions

Any shareholder, individual, or mutual fund can sponsor a shareholder resolution. The Securities & Exchange Commission governs the process. The basic requirement is that the shareholder own at least $2,000 of company stock for at least one year prior to filing the resolution. The proposed resolution must reach the corporation before the proxy statement materials are prepared, usually six months before the annual meeting. It cannot be longer than 500 words. The person or organization proposing the resolution must be present at the annual meeting. The company can ask the SEC to reject the proposed resolution on several broad grounds if:

◆ The resolution deals with business operations and is like similar resolutions that were defeated in the past by significant majorities

◆ The resolution contains anything illegal

◆ The resolution is an act of vengeance against the company or members of management

◆ The resolution contains false information

The complete list includes 13 reasons a company can ask the SEC for permission to omit the resolution. The SEC has complete guidelines on its website: www.sec.gov. The company's proxy statements contain procedures for submitting proposed shareholder resolutions. If the SEC declines management's request, the shareholder resolution will be included with the proxy material sent to shareholders. The board of directors and/or management submit their objections to the resolution and why shareholders should vote against it. If shareholders sign over their proxy rights, management will have their votes on the issue.

Each year, approximately 1,000 shareholder resolutions are filed, however, most are either withdrawn or omitted before they ever come to a vote by the shareholders. The cards are clearly stacked against shareholder resolutions getting to a vote. It is even less likely that a shareholder resolution will pass, since management and the board of directors oppose almost all. This is not to suggest that the tactic is ineffective. The threat of a shareholder resolution and the media attention it can bring is often enough to get management to work out some type of compromise with the socially responsible investors behind the resolution.

Red Flag

The SEC is considering limiting the already difficult process of filing shareholder resolutions. SRI mutual funds and institutional investors have vowed to fight any changes in the regulations limiting their right to introduce shareholder resolutions.

Forces Management to Address Issues

Shareholder resolutions may force management to deal with some issues such as environmental reporting and executive compensation. When management ignores the expressed concerns of SRI investors, a shareholder resolution is the next step. Because of the limitations placed on the process by the SEC (500-word limit and so on), it is difficult for these maneuvers to succeed. That doesn't stop socially responsible investors from trying. Shareholder resolutions can take on many different causes, but they are often presented in the same format.

Sample Shareholder Resolution

The following is an actual shareholder resolution filed for vote at the spring of 2007 annual meeting of Apple Computer by As You Sow Foundation:

> ELECTRONIC WASTE TAKE-BACK AND RECYCLING
>
> PROPOSAL NO. 10 ON APPLE PROXY STATEMENT
>
> WHEREAS Apple Computer emphasizes a commitment to environmental leadership. Yet the technical innovation responsible for leadership in designing and marketing products has not extended to developing adequate end-of-life programs.

The National Safety Council has reported that only 11% of discarded computers are recycled, compared with 28% of overall municipal solid waste. Electronic waste constitutes 2% to 5% of the US municipal solid waste stream and is growing rapidly.

In April 2006, the company agreed to take back old computers without charge when a new Mac is purchased. This, in addition to free recycling of iPods, is a welcome step, but does not yet make the company a leader on electronic waste policies. Our competitor Dell recently agreed to take back all Dell computers for free regardless of whether a purchase is made.

Other companies have taken more significant actions to provide free recycling to supplement fee-based systems. In 2005, Dell sponsored one-day free recycling events that collected 175 tons of equipment. It partners with Goodwill Industries to offer electronic recovery and reuse programs in several states. Hewlett-Packard partnered with Office Depot to offer free nationwide recycling, resulting in recovery of 10.5 million pounds of equipment. Apple needs to show leadership by developing similar broad-based programs.

Dell and Hewlett Packard have both announced public computer take back goals so stakeholders can measure progress against those goals. Dell recycled 72% more product in fiscal 2006 than 2005. Apple has not announced take back goals.

Recent reports indicate that large amounts of discarded computers are being improperly shipped to developing countries. Shareholders need assurances that the company is taking measures including tracking custody of recycled materials to ensure recycling vendors don't export hazardous wastes.

Electronic waste is usually smelted to recover metals, sometimes with plastics contained in the system and case. When plastic combusts, it can create harmful dioxins. The company should disclose measures it is taking to ensure that smelting of e-waste is not creating new environmental problems.

The company has lobbied against legislation, asking computer producers to take responsibility for most of the cost of recycling. Apple appears to want taxpayers to foot the bill. Dell and Hewlett Packard support producer responsibility legislation.

We believe Apple can avoid financial, legal and reputational risk and gain competitive advantage by taking additional measures to develop a leadership position on collection and safe disposition of old computers.

BE IT RESOLVED that Apple Computer's board of directors prepare a report, at reasonable cost, studying ways to improve its computer recycling programs, to be released within six months of the annual shareholder meeting.

SUPPORTING STATEMENT

The report should include a commitment to set public take back goals for end-of-life equipment; study the feasibility of using Apple stores as take back centers, take back partnerships with resellers, and other measures to stimulate recycling. It should discuss measures taken to prevent improper export of hazardous waste, the environmental impact of its recycling processes, and explain its lobbying position on take back legislation.

Electronic Waste Takeback & Recycling

Lead Filer:

As You Sow Foundation
Conrad MacKerron
San Francisco, CA 94104

Success Stories

Shareholder advocacy is often more successful behind closed doors out of the media's bright lights. There frank talks can proceed and often agreements are reached without forcing the issue to a shareholder resolution.

One week before the annual meeting and vote on this shareholder resolution, Steve Jobs, the CEO of Apple, announced an aggressive take-back and recycling program by the company. That was enough to convince the As You Sow Foundation to withdraw its resolution at the last moment. This isn't always the outcome of talks with companies, but it does show that shareholder advocacy works. In this case, it took several years of talks and shareholder resolutions to get to the desired outcome.

Annual Meeting and Proxy Voting

The annual meeting is required by law and is the time for voting on major issues before the corporation. As a shareholder, you have the right to vote your shares on the issues before the corporation. Generally, shareholders vote on issues that are major concerns, such as election of directors, mergers, and so on. You also have the right to vote on shareholder issues (and have the right to bring shareholder issues, as we noted in the previous section). If you can't attend in person, you can designate a proxy to vote your shares. Companies provide shareholders with a form prior to the annual meeting that they can sign and return designating a board member or someone else as their proxy. The proxy form allows for a vote in favor of or against each resolution on the ballot, or you can abstain. Not voting your shares is an automatic abstention and, essentially, a vote for management.

This is how managements often control corporations they don't own—by accumulating enough proxy votes to control the outcome of all votes. In the past, many mutual funds that owned stocks voted with management or abstained without much consideration, unless the vote would directly affect the company's financial prospects or stock price. One of the reasons some people are drawn to socially responsible investing is that SRI mutual funds take their proxy votes very seriously, as we have seen through their shareholder advocacy. Mutual funds are also required to hold annual meetings.

> **Responsible Tip**
>
> Some corporations limit attendance at the annual meeting or in some way restrict the people who can attend. With thousands of shareholders, it would be impossible to accommodate everyone.

Proxy Voting

Shareholders vote for board members and on other major issues at the annual shareholder meeting. The vast majority of shareholders exercise their voting rights by proxy. A proxy gives another party the legal right to vote the shareholder's shares on matters before the corporation. Proxy statements are sent to shareholders before the annual meeting detailing important matters to be decided. These include:

- ◆ Election of new board members

- ◆ Executive and director compensation

- ◆ Any matters brought up by management, such as proposed mergers, major acquisitions, and so on

Proxy statements generally give management or a designated director the right to vote your shares according to your wishes. Occasionally, a group of shareholders will attempt to gather enough proxies to oust management. This is done by encouraging shareholders to sign their proxies over to the dissenting group. Often called proxy fights or battles, they sometimes occur when a company or group is attempting to take control of a corporation. If they get enough proxies, they can gain control of the board of directors and fire management. Many corporations stack the terms of board members so that only a few are up for re-election in any year. This makes it more difficult for another company or group to take over a corporation, but it also limits the influence of shareholders in disagreement with management. The issue of stacking board member terms is discussed in more detail in Chapter 3.

Responsible Tip

Thanks to the Internet, many companies let you cast your proxy vote electronically using a third-party verification system to prevent voting fraud. It is likely that this will be the preferred means of voting in the near future, especially for environmentally conscious firms.

Your Rights in Proxy Voting

Voting for board members or on other issues before a corporation is not always as straightforward as it may seem. Companies have different classes of stock with different voting rights and different ways of counting votes that may or may not work to your benefit. It is important that you understand the different possibilities so you can make your votes count.

Most companies issue two types of stock: common and preferred. Despite its more important sounding name, preferred shares carry no voting rights at the annual meeting (or any special meetings). Preferred shareholders do get first dibs on dividends and that's why they are attractive to some investors. Common stock usually earns one vote for one share, but not always. Some companies issue two classes of stock, A and B, when it first goes public. Both are shares of common stock, but with different voting rights.

For example, when Google, the Internet search engine company, went public, it issued dual-class shares of common stock. Class A shares were sold to the public and conveyed one vote–one share rights. But the founders retained Class B shares, which were one share–ten votes rights. This is done so companies can sell significant, even a majority, of its stock, and the founders can retain control through voting rights. You should know this before investing in a company with a dual-class structure. It does not necessarily make the company a bad investment, but you should know that the founders would retain the right to do what they want with the company.

The other area you need to understand in proxy voting is that votes are counted in a different way. In most cases, you have statutory or straight voting rights. These are simply one vote per one share of common stock. Some companies, however, allow cumulative voting, which can benefit individual investors. Under cumulative voting, you have votes equal to your number of shares times the number of directors up for election. For example, if you own 100 shares and four directors are up for election, you have 400 votes. You can apply these votes to one, two, three, or spread them out evenly over all four candidates.

The Least You Need to Know

- You have rights and responsibilities as a socially responsible investor.
- Shareholder advocacy is an important part of socially responsible investing and a role the mutual funds play.
- Shareholder resolutions force management to confront issues that are important to socially responsible investors.
- Boards of directors should be constituted to represent the interests of the shareholders, not management.
- Proxy voting is the method most investors use to vote on major issues, including shareholder resolutions, at the annual meeting.

Chapter 12

Mutual Fund Proxy Voting Victory

In This Chapter

- ◆ Understanding the history of mutual fund proxy voting
- ◆ Investors gain transparency in funds' proxy votes
- ◆ Influence of mutual funds
- ◆ Rights of mutual fund shareholders

Mutual funds, along with institutional investors such as pension funds and foundations, own most of the outstanding shares of stock. This puts them in a powerful position to influence change, but they haven't always taken advantage of their position. Socially responsible mutual funds have been upfront about their proxy voting policy and records. Traditional mutual funds, however, up until 2004, generally had no proxy voting policy and almost never disclosed how they voted their shares in the many companies they owned. Studies indicated mutual funds often just went along with management almost without thought. It was a rare case when a traditional mutual fund would challenge a management decision or proposal.

Prior to 2004, mutual fund shareholders had little understanding of the connection between the fund and the companies in which it owned shares, or whether the proxy votes were in line with the shareholder's values. Since 2004, funds are required to disclose their proxy votes, and the track record on voting for socially responsible issues (shareholder resolutions) has slowly improved. Regardless, most traditional mutual funds still choose to side with management on most shareholder resolutions, which is to say the funds either vote against the resolutions or abstain.

> **Responsible Tip**
>
> Even though transparency in fund business always makes for better investor relations, it took action by the Securities and Exchange Commission (SEC) to force mutual funds to disclose proxy voting guidelines and voting history.

Proxy Votes Not Always Known

Mutual funds invest in stocks and bonds with a wide variety of investment strategies and styles. Socially responsible mutual funds are just one segment of a very large industry (8,000 different funds). The SRI funds, in most cases, work hard for transparency when it comes to their investments. As we noted in previous chapters, shareholders of individual stocks have the right to vote on important issues before the corporation. Mutual funds as shareholders of individual stocks have the same rights. For each stock a fund owns, a proxy statement is issued prior to the annual meeting. Prior to 2004, how most traditional mutual funds voted their shares was largely unknown to investors in the fund. In August of 2004, all mutual funds and later all *investment advisers* were required to disclose their proxy votes. Most mutual funds opposed this SEC requirement.

This provided a window into the operations of funds and how they used their proxy votes. In many cases, it was not a pretty picture.

> **def•i•ni•tion**
>
> **Investment advisers** are financial professionals who make buy and sell recommendations for a fee or percentage of the assets they manage.

Recognizing that traditional mutual funds may not have the same imperatives as socially responsible funds, it was still shocking to many investors how little thought was paid to shareholder resolutions and how easily fund votes went to management. As fund shareholders became aware of voting patterns, they began to question proxy-voting patterns. Even if a fund was not an SRI fund, investors saw value in supporting some of the shareholder resolutions offered to annual meetings of companies owned by the mutual fund.

Mutual Funds Own Many Stocks

Mutual funds own many different stocks and have the opportunity to look at a large number of proxy votes on socially responsible issues. It is not uncommon for an actively managed stock-based mutual fund to own from 30 to 100 different stocks. Index funds can own even larger numbers of stocks. This puts mutual funds in the position of seeing many different shareholder resolutions each year. A fund, like an individual shareholder, has three choices when it gets a proxy statement from a company prior to the annual meeting:

1. It can vote with management. This remains the most frequent response to a proxy statement.

2. It can ignore the proxy statement and not send it in or abstain from voting. This has the same effect as voting with management.

3. It can thoughtfully vote its proxy, perhaps supporting some initiatives and opposing others, but doing so with a reason and purpose.

When most major mutual funds choose the first option, they give up the opportunity to play a role in change for the better, SRI advocates insist. Of course, the mutual funds may not see it that way. Some believe social or corporate responsibility issues are not matters for shareholders to decide—in other words, management is in a better position to judge the benefits of a particular course of action. One mutual fund frequently abstains from every SRI vote on the grounds that these are day-to-day business matters best decided by management. In surveying funds about their commitment to socially responsible shareholder

Responsible Tip

If you ever wondered how managers can control a company where they only own a very small percentage of the stock, this is how. When major mutual funds and other institutional investors vote their proxies with management, it empowers management to continue business as usual.

resolutions, researchers noted that the complexity of deciding whether a resolution is really a benefit or a negative makes keeping score difficult. A vote against a shareholder resolution may be the socially responsible thing to do in some cases because not all shareholder resolutions are brought by SRI investors.

SRI Advocates Wanted to Know

The issue of how mutual funds voted (or didn't vote) their proxies grew out of a concern by several SRI advocates who complained to the SEC. Their complaints were that the lack of transparency denied fund shareholders rightful information about what their money was supporting or opposing. Those advocating full disclosure noted it could be done easily and inexpensively by the funds. Their main argument, however, was that the funds had a fiduciary duty to shareholders to formulate proxy voting guidelines and follow through with reports on how they voted.

Traditional mutual funds resisted the change on several grounds, including the argument that shareholders really weren't interested in this information. SRI investors proved that argument was wrong when thousands of letters supporting the reforms flooded the SEC. Some suspected funds were reluctant to disclose voting patterns because it might be discovered that they sided with management in an attempt to win retirement fund management business from the companies.

Industry observers noted that during this period there were numerous corporate scandals, although they were just the latest in a long line of wrongdoings. The mutual fund industry could be criticized for (or suspected of) conflicts of interest if this relationship between funds and companies continued. It is not difficult to imagine a mutual fund representative bargaining its proxy votes for a business relationship from the company.

The results of the reform have opened a window on how mutual funds fulfill their fiduciary responsibility with respect to voting their

> **Success Stories**
>
> Socially responsible investors and others pushed the SEC to rewrite the rules and make the voting records of mutual funds public information. The funds countered, saying there was no interest from investors in this information, but thousands of letters supporting the new rules convinced the SEC otherwise.

proxies. Of particular interest to SRI investors is how the traditional funds voted on socially responsible shareholder issues, ranging from corporate governance to environmental issues. This is important because it gives investors who want to invest in a traditional mutual fund, but are still concerned about SRI issues, a chance to see how the fund has voted on specific shareholder issues in the past.

Votes on Key SRI Issues

There are over 200 socially responsible mutual funds, but that doesn't mean every investor will find all of their investment needs met in this small part of the market. If you need to look to more traditional funds to fill your investment goals, but are still concerned about SRI issues, you can track how mutual funds vote on those issues. Some funds are very forthcoming with their proxy voting guidelines and voting histories, while others are much less so. Several studies found it was difficult to find someone who could speak knowledgeably about the fund's proxy voting policy and voting record, especially in larger fund families. While the voting record of some funds was clear and consistent, other funds were more difficult to track because of seemingly inconsistent votes (this also is confounded by shareholder resolutions that may be titled the same, but have different objectives). Unless investors choose one of the few large mutual fund families that is open and consistent about its proxy voting guidelines and actual votes, it may be difficult to determine how a fund will likely vote on future issues.

Disclosure by Large Mutual Fund Families

Many investors look to large *mutual fund families* for their investment needs. These large investment companies have many different types of funds under one umbrella company. The advantage to the investor is you can often move your money from one fund to another without paying any fees, so as your investing goals change, you can adjust your investment portfolio. These huge firms are one of the first places many investors start when looking for a fund that fits their investment goals.

These huge firms have had a spotty record when it comes to disclosure of proxy voting guidelines and votes. Some are more forthcoming than others are. While finding the information is important, it is also necessary to review it carefully before investing if you are concerned about

def•i•ni•tion

Mutual fund families are groups of funds managed by one investment company. The funds are called a family because they share common management, and investors can often move their money from one fund to another within the fund without penalty.

how the firm may vote its proxies (on your behalf). One of the largest investment companies in the world is Vanguard. The firm has more than $1.1 trillion in assets under management and more than 183 domestic and foreign mutual funds of various types. It counts over 9 million institutional and individual shareholders, according to its website. With financial power like this, Vanguard could be a significant influence in the corporate world for change. But, like most traditional mutual funds, Vanguard doesn't view that as its role or responsibility. Vanguard does a better job than many funds of listing it proxy voting guidelines, which outline what issues it believes are important and how it will normally vote on them should the situation arise in a proxy vote.

In general, Vanguard's proxy voting guidelines suggest it supports efforts that add or protect the company's value. It is generally supportive of many of the same issues that are important to SRI investors because they also make good business sense. These include:

♦ Nonclassified boards of directors

♦ Independence of boards of directors

♦ Reasonable executive severance packages

♦ Policies that enhance shareholder rights

♦ Policies that restrain dilution of stock

When it comes to those issues classified as "corporate and social policy issues," Vanguard takes a different approach. They view these topics as more "day-to-day" business activities and contend that a company's management is in the best position to decide whether these issues are important to the fiscal well-being of the firm. Their policy states:

"Proposals in this category, initiated primarily by shareholders, typically request that the company disclose or amend certain business practices. The Board generally believes that these are "ordinary business matters" that are primarily the responsibility of management and should be evaluated and approved solely by the corporation's board of directors. Often, proposals may address concerns with which the Board philosophically agrees, but absent a compelling economic impact on shareholder value (e.g., proposals to require expensing of stock options), the funds will typically abstain from voting on these proposals. This reflects the belief that regardless of our philosophical perspective on the issue, these decisions should be the province of company management unless they have a significant, tangible impact on the value of a fund's investment and management is not responsive to the matter."

Vanguard's voting record on these issues, according to its website, is almost always to abstain. SRI advocates point out that an abstention is the same as a negative vote against the shareholder resolution (or a positive vote for management). SRI proponents also note that companies can ask the SEC to exclude shareholder resolutions that deal with "ordinary business matters," so presumably if an issue makes it to a proxy vote, the SEC has determined it is not in this category.

None of this should be taken as critical of Vanguard. On the contrary, the company is one of the better mutual fund firms at disclosing its proxy voting policies and its actual votes. One helpful feature on Vanguard's website is a summary of how the fund voted on broad categories of issues for the previous year. This summary gives the investor a quick look at how the fund responded to the various issues. Vanguard also

Responsible Tip

Mutual funds that choose to abstain from voting on shareholder issues automatically vote with management because shareholder resolutions brought by SRI investors are almost always opposed by management. A nonvote works the same as a no vote.

provides a voting record by fund, which then breaks down the voting record for each company owned by the fund during the past year. This format is used by other mutual funds and while it provides a great deal of detail, it would be more helpful if it were summarized.

Traditional Mutual Funds Can Influence Companies

The increased disclosure ordered by the SEC has made a significant difference in the amount of information mutual fund investors have regarding the proxy votes the funds cast. But it is not clear that this transparency has measurably altered the voting outcomes of the funds as a group. It is possible that the potential for increased visibility has made some funds more thoughtful about how they voted, but it is also possible that any slight increase in votes for corporate or social issues have come as a natural evolution in the investing process toward embracing more socially responsible company policies and practices.

Corporate governance is a socially responsible investing issue, but it is also a big concern of traditional investors. Clearly, lapses in these areas have cost everyone money and scandals drained confidence from the market. In many cases, the traditional funds are in agreement with SRI investors on corporate governance issues such as making the board of directors more independent of management, not overdoing the compensation of executives, and other issues.

When it comes to social or corporate responsibility issues, however, it is a different story. In most cases, funds side with management or abstain from voting. In addition to the argument put forth by Vanguard in the previous section, funds have noted that many of the SRI proposals either lack sufficient fiscal analysis or do not demonstrate any material fiscal value to shareholders. SRI investors often argue that most of the socially responsible initiatives will pay a fiscal dividend at some point in the future. But this it is not the compelling evidence that traditional mutual funds want to hear as they are more concerned with how changes may effect a company's ability to generate the level of expected earnings in the short term.

Red Flag

Before the reforms of 2004, there was a concern that mutual funds might try to influence other business with a company by voting for management. Mutual funds are the preferred investment vehicles for 401(k) retirement plans, and this can be lucrative business for mutual fund companies.

Traditional funds also note that one reason they invest in a company is their confidence in its management. When management opposes shareholder resolutions, funds will often defer to the managers as a matter of trust.

Mutual Funds Feeling the Heat

One of the highest-profile socially responsible issues is climate change, which is a broad term for shareholder resolutions that address concerns over global warming, greenhouse gas emissions, and other factors. The number of shareholder resolutions specific to climate change was at an all-time high for 2007. More companies are being pressured by shareholders and others to do something about their contribution to the global warming problem. Inaction at the federal level has not stopped some states from setting targets for lowering greenhouse gas emissions. Every developed country in the world except the United States has acknowledged this is a serious problem that is being made worse by human activity. As noted earlier, some companies will be convinced to take the appropriate steps without being pressured by shareholder resolutions or bad publicity, however, many still see planning for or dealing with the impacts of climate change as potentially added expenses with no obvious or immediate payback.

Many shareholders, including a significant number who would not consider themselves outside the mainstream of the investment community, will push companies to adopt policies on climate change and to back those policies with real operational changes where appropriate. As shareholder resolutions are brought to annual meetings, mutual funds will be asked to vote their proxies on climate change and other important corporate social resolutions. There are other important social, corporate, and environmental issues before corporations, but we'll use climate change to illustrate how mutual funds have responded to a current issue.

Responsible Tip

Socially responsible investors file shareholder resolutions on a number of important issues each year. Many of these issues also have unexamined economic risks associated with them. They deserve as much consideration as climate change.

Is Climate Change a Real Problem?

This question is a significant part of the problem facing those who are concerned about climate change—a number of people led by government officials have simply denied that climate change is happening or that humans can do anything to stop it. The United States is alone among the world's developed countries in not acknowledging the problems of greenhouse gases and the need to reduce their emissions. Of course, we are also the largest source of greenhouse gas emission on a per capita basis, so admitting that the emissions are a problem would put us in a tough position. Detractors suggest that to implement the controls needed to curb emissions might push the economy into a deep recession. Yet Europe and parts of Asia have already begun plans to roll back emissions to 1990 levels—thanks to alternative (to burning fossil fuels) energy sources.

In 2005, the CEOs of several major companies, including Ford, General Electric, Duke Energy, and others stated that climate change was a threat to the economy and some form of mandatory controls were needed to help us compete in a world market where carbon resources were shrinking. These aren't wild-eyed radicals, but business leaders of some of the most respected industrial giants in the country. They are concerned that something needs to be done about climate change and it should begin now.

While climate change concerns can be about saving or protecting natural habitats, to many investors and a growing number of business leaders it is also about addressing real economic risk. If companies aren't addressing these risks without prompting, shareholder resolutions are the next step. Unfortunately, proxy-voting procedures often guarantee that either the fund will vote against any shareholder resolution or it will abstain from voting at all. Mutual fund shareholders face another obstacle if the funds have a policy of supporting management against almost all shareholder resolutions.

 Red Flag

Climate change has become a political issue rather than a question of risk management. In the political arena, facts don't always count as much as emotion and rhetoric. Several states have tired of the national dialogue going nowhere and taken steps to address the problem.

The voting patterns of 100 of the largest mutual funds managed by 31 investment companies during 2005 revealed that none of the funds with holdings that received climate change shareholder resolutions voted for any of the propositions. Overall, the greatest weakness is proxy-voting guidelines that direct funds to either vote against or abstain from voting on environmental issues. The study was conducted by the Investor Responsibility Research Center for Ceres, which is a network of investment funds, environmental groups, and other public interest organizations. Ceres membership represents more than $400 billion in assets. Investor members include state and municipal pension funds, socially responsible investment firms, religious groups, union funds, and foundations, according to information on its website.

The Ceres study and others in the industry believe that climate change is an unacknowledged risk that investors should evaluate along with other traditional risk factors when considering a company for investment. Mutual funds, like all investors, evaluate the risk of an investment and decide if the potential return is worth the possibility that it will not meet its investment objectives. Missing or underestimating a risk can be devastating to an investor because it skews the risk-reward relationship. If an investment actually carries a higher risk than the investor calculates, the potential return he expects will not be sufficient (the higher the risk an investor takes, the more potential reward must be available).

If climate change is an unacknowledged risk as the Ceres study and others believe, mutual funds that dismiss environmental shareholder resolutions as a matter of policy are not fulfilling their fiduciary responsibility. By automatically voting with management (against) such shareholder resolutions or abstaining from voting, mutual funds are exposing their shareholders to unnecessary risk.

> **Responsible Tip**
>
> Investing is about managing risk so that potential reward is appropriate for the amount of risk taken in a portfolio. The more risk an investor is exposed to, the higher the potential reward. If a risk is hidden or not factored into an investment, the investor cannot correctly evaluate whether the investment fits her tolerance for risk.

What Industries Are at Risk?

In many ways, Europe is ahead of the United States in acknowledging the risk of climate change and factoring in those risks to company planning and evaluation. Some industries at risk due to various consequences of climate change include:

♦ **Insurance companies**—Natural disasters beyond what insurance companies have traditionally reserved for pose an economic danger to the industry. Large insurance providers in Europe factor in climate change–driven natural disasters in their risk analysis and planning.

- **Utilities**—Power companies are among the biggest sources for carbon dioxide emissions, accounting for up to 40 percent of the U.S. total, according to the Ceres report. Several of the major electrical providers have issued risk reports. If the government were to take seriously the reduction of greenhouse gases, energy providers could be at risk for major changes.

- **Heavy manufacturing**—Companies engaged in heavy manufacturing (steel, oil and gas refining, chemicals, and so on) are at risk for mandatory retrofitting of processing equipment and energy generation systems to reduce greenhouse gases.

- **Automobiles**—Automobile emissions are major sources of green house gases and other pollutants. Alternative energy sources will help, however, much stricter gasoline mileage requirement could be a serious risk for this industry that has managed to fend off the restraints so far. If gasoline prices continue to rise, a growing consumer base that is concerned about its contribution to the climate change problem may push the industry very hard to find better solutions, including looking for answers from imports.

Representatives of these and other industries and along with many financial professionals have taken the risks of climate change seriously. They are building risk models or adding climate change to existing risk models so that they can better evaluate the threat and discern a course of action. Investment professionals that accept climate change as a legitimate risk are working to help companies and investors figure out what the risks are, how to mange them, and what the potential opportunities are (if any).

Responsible Tip

Mutual funds automatically voting with management are not acceptable for many investors as the risks of climate change become more widely known and more precisely defined for certain industries.

Mutual funds that do not tap into this assessment of risk may be missing a key ingredient in evaluating a business. The blanket policies of voting for management or abstaining on socially responsible issues are irresponsible. Funds need to adopt a more open attitude that leaves room for them to consider shareholder resolutions rather than dismiss them summarily. Funds also need to push companies they invest in to fully disclose their exposure to climate change liabilities and what they stand to gain or lose based of how the company reacts to shareholder resolutions.

What Is the Track Record on Climate Change?

In a summary of a research post on SocialFunds.com, Jackie Cook, a senior research analyst with the Corporate Library, noted that an examination of proxy voting records from 2006 showed support by funds of climate change resolutions at less than 19 percent among traditional funds. Another study looking at a different grouping of traditional funds found support for climate change shareholder resolutions at less than 7 percent.

For SRI proponents, these numbers are perplexing, because they believe compelling financial justification supports steps to curb greenhouse gas emissions and other environmental actions that will help slow climate change. Yet most management teams are still opposing the shareholder resolutions and apparently not having success in negotiating with climate change advocates. Given the rising public tide behind this issue, it makes sense for businesses to address it head on and begin to formulate a response to the problem.

As more shareholder resolutions are brought to companies, more mutual funds will have to face their own insistent shareholders who will want to know how the fund voted and why. Investors are going to insist on a plan and strategy to move the company forward in response to what they perceive is a worldwide crisis. To the extent that companies and mutual funds ignore the warnings, they do so at their own peril. The time is coming soon when mutual fund investors (and not just SRI investors) will demand a much higher degree of accountability from the funds and the companies the funds own.

How to Know What Your Fund Is Doing

Most traditional mutual funds are posting their proxy voting guidelines and how their funds voted on their websites, although you may have to look to find the information. Some of the links to proxy voting information can be found under "investor relations," or the "about (fund name)" link. If the site has a search function, the easiest path may be to enter "proxy" and do a search.

The Least You Need to Know

◆ Investors in the funds did not always know how mutual funds voted their proxies since 2004.

◆ Reform gave mutual fund investors access to how funds voted their proxies.

◆ Voting records of mutual funds on shareholder resolutions brought by SRI investors has not improved with disclosure.

◆ Climate change is an example of an unacknowledged risk that mutual funds ignore by voting for management on shareholder resolutions.

Part 4

SRI Investment Opportunities

Socially responsible investors have many of the same basic
opportunities as traditional investors. Mutual funds are the most
widely used investment product, but investors can also choose
individual stocks and bonds, as well as venture capital funds.
Although investors have choices of funds, the number of SRI
specific funds is much smaller than traditional mutual funds.

Chapter **13**

Overview of Mutual Funds

In This Chapter

- ◆ Why mutual funds work for investors
- ◆ Types of mutual funds
- ◆ Mutual fund styles
- ◆ Diversification and asset allocation

Socially responsible investors use mutual funds more than any other investment product—and with good reason. Mutual funds make it easy to invest by doing all of the hard work (research, monitoring, buying, selling) for you. That professional help is valuable, but it comes with a price and, if you're not careful, expenses can cut deeply into any profits. For many investors, reasonable expenses are a small price to pay for the professional management and ease of investment that mutual funds offer.

Investors can choose from a wide variety of mutual funds with different investment styles and objectives. Many investment companies manage families of funds to attempt to provide a cross section of offerings to keep as many of the investor's dollars as possible. Socially responsible mutual funds offer investors many opportunities, however, their offerings do not compare in scope with traditional mutual funds. Some investors find that they cannot meet all of their investment needs with just SRI mutual funds and must use traditional funds to complete their portfolios (this is another reason it is important to understand proxy voting by traditional mutual funds). Socially responsible investing is still investing, so it is important to understand that part of the process. While mutual funds make the investing process easy, not all funds are the same. An informed socially responsible investor is more likely to reach both goals of affecting change and meeting financial objectives.

Popularity of Mutual Funds

Mutual funds are the single most popular investment product on the market and with good reason. Investors pool their money and a team of professionals manages it for them. The investors share in any profits or losses. Mutual funds come in different investment styles and with different objectives, so investors can find one that matches their needs and aligns with their tolerance for risk. Mutual funds invest in stocks, bonds, cash, or all three, depending on the fund's objectives. Some funds invest for growth, while others focus on income, and others still blend both growth and income. Finding a mutual fund that fits most reasonable investment needs is almost a certainty. SRI mutual funds can be found that fall into most of the standard categories, however, you will have fewer to choose from than out of the universe of traditional funds.

Mutual funds are not risk-free investments, however, you do enjoy the benefits of professional management making the decisions about when to buy and when to sell. Mutual funds also give you easy and quick access to your money should you need to pull out some cash for an emergency or to pay large bill like college tuition. Mutual funds also let you invest incrementally in whole dollars, which is what you do if you contribute to a company-sponsored retirement plan such as a 401(k).

Responsible Tip

Socially responsible investing is another way of expressing your values, but it is also an investment strategy that should consider traditional investing parameters and fundamentals.

Benefits of Mutual Funds

Mutual funds benefit the millions who invest in them either on the open market or through a company-sponsored retirement plan. Socially responsible investors will find many of these benefits especially important to them. Mutual funds take most, but not all of the work of investing off the investor and turn it over to professional money managers. Investors still have a responsibility to monitor their investments periodically and make necessary adjustments as warranted by changes in fund performance and their own life circumstances. The three main benefits to investing through mutual funds are professional management, diversification, and convenience.

> **Red Flag**
>
> Professional management is a great benefit to owning mutual funds, but it doesn't mean all professional investment managers are good at what they do. You shouldn't send in your money and blindly trust that everything will be okay.

Professional Management

Mutual funds are managed by investment professionals who typically have years of experience in the stock market. An investment management company hires researchers, analysts, portfolio managers, and others to run the mutual funds it offers. Most mutual funds belong to a family of funds that is managed by an investment management company, which can spread the expense of the financial professionals over all the funds it offers. Professional management is one of the distinguishing features of mutual funds because it is a value-added service that offers investors access to research and expertise that would be too expensive for most individual investors to afford privately.

Portfolio managers have different styles and approaches to investing. Some are more aggressive and trade frequently, while others tend to be on the conservative side with fewer trades. The portfolio manager's investment style should match the mutual fund's goals. Socially responsible funds typically require more research than most traditional funds, so the investment management team is important to the financial performance, as well as meeting the SRI goals.

Diversification

One benefits of investing in mutual funds is easily achieved diversification. Diversification is the spreading of your investment dollars over a number of stocks or bonds so a poor performance by one investment has little effect on the total holdings. Simply stated: Don't put all your eggs in one basket. A mutual fund may own 40 to 60 different stocks (or more). Few individual investors can own that many different stocks.

def•i•ni•tion

A **sector** of the economy is a grouping of similar businesses. Economic or industry sectors describe sections of our economy that function and are influenced by many of the same factors. Some examples of sectors include technology, retail, health care, or oil and gas. Stocks are also grouped by sectors.

You do need to exercise caution when buying multiple mutual funds, however. If several mutual funds own essentially the same stocks, you haven't diversified as much as you might think. For example, if you owned three different mutual funds, but all invested heavily in technology stocks, you would be vulnerable if that *sector* of the economy was depressed. You should be diversified by industry sector as well as by number.

Convenience

The mutual fund industry has made it easy to become an investor. You can begin investing in many mutual funds with as little as $1,000 to open an account and some offer even lower minimums. Subsequent contributions can be as low as $25. Most mutual funds can set up an automatic debit to your checking account so that each month an amount you specify is withdrawn by the fund and deposited into your account. This is a painless and effective way to have a regular investment plan. You can change the amount invested at any time.

Another convenient feature of mutual funds is their liquidity. You can usually convert your shares to cash within two business days without penalty as long as you are not withdrawing from a retirement account prematurely. This liquidity means you have access to your money if you need it for an unexpected major bill or if you have been saving for a major expense (such as college).

You buy mutual funds in whole dollars unlike stocks, which are bought in number of shares. With mutual funds, it is okay to own fractional shares, so investments and redemptions are in whole dollars (the only exception would be if you completely liquidated your account and owned fractional shares, those would be converted to cents).

Figuring Share Price or NAV

Mutual funds calculate a share price called the Net Asset Value (NAV) at the close of trading each day the market is open. The NAV is the fund's assets minus its liabilities and divided by the number of outstanding shares. This gives you a per-share price or NAV. This is what you pay if you buy shares and what you receive if you sell shares—less any fees or expenses.

Responsible Tip

If you want to buy or sell mutual fund shares, the price you pay or get is determined at the end of the day when the NAV is calculated. If you invest $2,000 and the NAV is determined to be $20 per share, you own 100 shares.

Risk and Reward

Investing ideally obtains the most reward for the least amount of risk. Another way of saying that is investors should expect a reward that is proportional to the amount of risk assumed. A high-risk investment like a futures contract should pay a larger reward than buying a risk-free U.S. Treasury Note. If the potential reward is not appropriate for the amount risked (the chance is that you will not achieve your financial goal or lose money), investors would be wise to look for someplace else to invest their money. Investors can take steps to minimize risk in their portfolio. Even if all your investments are in mutual funds, you still need to examine the composition of the funds, their goals, and investment styles to manage your risk.

Diversification

We have already noted that diversification is one benefit of owning a mutual fund. Most mutual funds own a large number of stocks and/or bonds, so a few clunkers won't dramatically change the performance of the fund. If you own more than one fund, compare the holdings of the two for overlap. You may find that you own two funds, but they own essentially the same stocks. You can avoid this by checking the types and styles of funds before you buy to make sure all your purchases aren't falling in the same categories.

Investment styles are very important ways to diversify. The three that are commonly recognized are growth, value, and blend. We'll discuss them in detail later in this chapter. One way to diversify is to buy funds in several different investment style categories. Market conditions sometimes favor one style over the other for a period, but may swing back and favor a different style. Being invested in all the major styles can protect you from market swings.

Investment styles are often combined with company size to create a way to talk more specifically about investments. The most common way investment professionals measure a company's size is by market capitalization or "market cap." This calculation produces a comparable number that is a way to compare companies in any industry. You calculate market capitalization by taking the current per-share price and multiplying it by the outstanding shares of stock. For example, if a company had 70 million shares of stock outstanding and the current per-share price was $50 per share, the market cap would be $3.5 billion ($70,000,000 \times \$50 = \$3,500,000,000$). The $3.5 billion represents how much money is would take to buy the company for cash on the open market if you could purchase all the shares at once for the same price.

Obviously, a company's market cap changes with its stock price, but this method reduces the value of all companies to a single number.

Responsible Tip

Market cap is a better way to determine the worth of a company. Using sales numbers or other metrics is only meaningful when comparing the company with others in the same industry.

Many mutual funds invest according to market cap as well as investment styles. Companies are assigned to large, mid, or small cap categories and then by investment styles. There is no universal agreement on where the size categories break, but this is one way to consider them:

♦ Large cap—$10 billion and up

♦ Mid cap—$2 billion to $10 billion

♦ Small cap—Less than $2 billion

Just as market condition sometimes favor one style, they may also favor a particular size company. You want some diversification in your holding by size, also.

Large cap stocks are often older, more mature companies that offer more stability—although with the way some high tech companies take off, a number of young companies have made it to the large cap category very quickly. This category is misleading in that a large number of companies have market caps well over $50 billion. For example, the average market cap of the *Dow* in the spring of 2007 was $147 billion. It takes some more investigation to see if a fund that claims to be investing in large cap stocks is buying the largest cap stocks or those near the cutoff point of $10 billion—it makes a difference.

On the other end of the size spectrum, small cap stocks may represent young emerging companies that have potential for tremendous growth, but also come with a much higher degree of risk. Smaller companies must grow or capture a niche so small and specialized that it doesn't attract competition, in which case it likely will never grow. Larger companies have greater resources to overtake smaller competitors and either buy them or drive them out of the market. Smaller companies have a much higher failure rate than mid or large cap stocks. The point is investing in small cap stocks should produce a higher return than an investment in a large cap stock—if not, the investor is taking too much risk for too little reward.

Responsible Tip

Asset allocation is so significant that many investment professionals consider it the single most important decision investors make—more important than the actual investments.

Asset Allocation

Many investment professionals believe maintaining a proper asset allocation is the single most important key to investment success. Asset allocation is the process of deciding how to apportion your investment dollars among the three major classes of assets: stocks, bonds, and cash. Some add real estate as the fourth asset class. These asset classes represent the spectrum of where you can place your investing dollars. How you split up your investments among these assets is the allocation part. Defining the asset classes is straightforward:

- **Stocks**—Common stock in companies. In mutual funds, this could range from aggressive growth stocks to more conservative income stocks. Stock funds can also invest in industry sector such as technology stocks or health care stocks. You can also invest in stock funds that own foreign stocks for diversity from U.S. markets.

- **Bonds**—Bonds issued by companies, municipalities and the U.S. Treasury. Bond funds can also be aggressive or conservative, although most are organized to be more conservative. Bonds as an asset, counter the volatility of stocks and are an important part of every portfolio.

- **Cash**—Money market funds, bank CDs, savings and so on. Cash is the most conservative asset, although you may not earn enough to have a real return after inflation and taxes. But cash is an important part of every portfolio, although not a significant part. There is no substitute for cash when you need it in a hurry, especially if it is in an account you can get to without incurring a penalty.

Asset allocation is important because each of these classes of assets performs differently and what weight you give to each determines how aggressive or conservative your investment strategy is. This is particularly important for people planning for, nearing, or entering retirement. By changing the asset mix, you can be more proactive in building a nest egg early in life and more conservative in protecting it later in life.

A younger investor may want to be more aggressive and allocate more of her assets to stocks and less to bonds and cash. As she nears retirement age, it makes sense to "dial back" the

Red Flag

Some investors who have not saved enough for retirement are tempted to take extraordinary risks in an attempt to score big gains and catch up. This is a dangerous and almost always losing strategy. If you need to catch up, find a way to put more money into savings—don't risk what you have on wild gambles.

aggressive position by decreasing the amount allocated to stocks and increasing the amount designated to bonds and cash. At retirement, she will still want some of her assets in stocks, but the majority of her holdings should be in some form of bonds and cash. Here's how that might look:

Building to retirement:

◆ Stocks—80 percent

◆ Bonds—15 percent

◆ Cash—5 percent

Nearing retirement:

◆ Stocks—60 percent

◆ Bonds—30 percent

◆ Cash—10 percent

At Retirement:

◆ Stocks—30 percent

◆ Bonds—55 percent

◆ Cash—15 percent

These are illustrative guides only. How you divide your assets among the classes depends on your personal situation and your tolerance for risk. In a thorough analysis of asset allocation, consider the degree of risk and composition of the stock and bond classes at each stage. Appendix A has resources for more information on asset allocation and other considerations.

Types of Mutual Funds

Mutual funds come in a variety of types that you can fit into your asset allocation plans. All of these types apply to socially responsible funds, but some obscure traditional fund types aren't be found among SRI funds. The investments the portfolio manager makes determines fund types. There has been controversy about funds taking names that makes them sound like one type of fund, but their investment patterns don't reflect that definition. Funds are supposed to follow their stated investment guidelines, but again this hasn't always been the case. The lesson is: be aware of what the fund is buying and how closely it sticks to its stated purpose. Here are the main types of mutual funds:

- ◆ **Money market funds**—These funds invest in short-term bonds and other money instruments. The rates you'll earn in money market funds fall in between regular bank savings accounts and bank CDs. There is no penalty for early withdrawal, so you can consider money in these funds as good as cash. Almost every family of funds includes a money market fund.

- ◆ **Stock or equity funds**—These funds invest in common stock. This type represents the largest group of mutual funds. Stock funds cover a wide range of styles and sizes, for large cap growth funds to small cap blend funds. One way to look at the range of stock funds is to use a style box, which is a concept pioneered by MorningStar. com. The table below illustrates the nine possible combinations of investment styles and size. An investor can quickly see where their funds fall on the scale and where new funds might be added that would not overlap existing holdings.

Responsible Tip

Money market funds may pay better than bank accounts, but they are not federally insured. Although mutual funds do offer some protection against fraud, you are not protected to the same degree a federally insured bank account offers.

Investment Styles

Size	Value	Blend	Growth
Large	_____	_____	_____
Mid	_____	_____	_____
Small	_____	_____	_____

Most stock funds look to grow their value (price) over time, although the larger, more mature stocks combine this with dividend income. Smaller stocks tend toward growth and seldom pay dividends. Stock funds are also characterized by where they invest. Domestic equity funds buy U.S. stocks. International funds buy stocks in foreign companies, while global equity funds buy stock in foreign and U.S. companies.

♦ **Bond funds**—These funds are also known as income or fixed income funds and they invest in corporate and government debt (bonds) with the goal of providing current income. Bonds are an effective counter to the stock market's ups and downs. As investors near retirement, more of their holding should be directed to bonds, which are safer than stocks. But some bond funds shoot for very high returns by investing in what are known as junk bonds, and can be very risky and should be used cautiously. Bonds are not risk-free. Higher interest rates or soaring inflation can hurt bond funds. People in retirement should keep a minority portion of their assets in the stock market to protect against inflation.

♦ **Balanced funds**—These funds blend stocks and bonds in some proportion to achieve some growth and income. The fund usually states what percentage of the assets are in stocks and what are in bonds—60 percent stocks and 40 percent bonds would be typical. A variation of these funds are called life cycle funds and some have specific dates so investors of a certain age can invest and the fund automatically adjusts the stocks-to-bonds ratio, as the investor grows older.

♦ **Index funds**—An index fund removes any decision making from the portfolio managers by replicating a popular stock market index such as the S&P 500. Index funds are inexpensive to manage and, consequently have very low expenses. The funds mirror the components of a stock or bond index. If the components change—for example, a stock is removed from the S&P 500 and another is added—the fund does the same. Your return will be the same as what the index does, but with less expenses.

Responsible Tip

Index funds are often considered a core holding by investment professionals, which means they believe every investor should have some assets in an index fund as a conservative bet on the market.

♦ **Specialty funds**—Many specialty funds on the market that invest in specific areas. Sector funds invest in only one industry sector, for example, retail businesses. Regional funds invest in specific geographic regions, both domestic and foreign. Specialty funds can be risky because of the concentration in one industry or region. Some investment professionals consider socially responsible funds specialty investments, however, given the broad range of choices available to SRI investors that label is not justified.

Investment Styles

Portfolio managers focus on achieving the best investment results possible for the funds they manage. There is no single road to investment success. Some investment professionals choose a strategy known as value investing that seeks out undervalued stocks and holds them for the appreciation they hope will occur when the stock market recognizes their true value. Other professionals look for growth stocks that have the potential to grow at a faster rate than the market in general. These stocks can experience rapid growth for short or long periods depending on the company and industry. Then, others blend both methods for their funds. At times, market conditions have favored one strategy over the other. Value investors have the edge by many calculations over long periods, while growth investors can score major returns over shorter periods. Of the two, pursuing a growth strategy is the most risky.

Growth Mutual Funds

Growth mutual funds look for stocks with a higher than average growth rate. Ideally, the fund will spot the stock before everyone else does and be able to buy before the price starts moving up. The primary concern for investing in a growth stock is how much more can it grow. Fund managers set their own expectations for growth rates and those expectations will vary depending on the size of the company, the industry, and the risk factor. A small, high-risk technology stock would be expected to grow at a phenomenal rate quarter-to-quarter. An older, but still growing company might not have the same expectation. The danger in investing in growth companies is that at the first sign growth is slowing or stopping, investors will bail out of the stock, and the price will fall sharply. With growth stocks, knowing when to sell is as important as knowing when to buy.

Value Mutual Funds

Value investing does not focus on buying stocks with low per share prices, but invests in companies that the stock market has undervalued. Value investors spend a great deal of time analyzing a company's financials to determine a fair market value. This gives them an idea of what the stock should be selling for on the market. If the stock is under priced, it could be because the company is in an industry that is out of favor

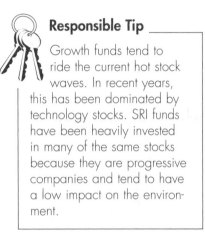

Responsible Tip

Growth funds tend to ride the current hot stock waves. In recent years, this has been dominated by technology stocks. SRI funds have been heavily invested in many of the same stocks because they are progressive companies and tend to have a low impact on the environment.

with investors or some bad news has tainted all stocks in the industry. Value investing buys stocks at a bargain price and waits for the market to correct its pricing, which will give the fund a nice profit. Value funds are typically long-term investments.

Blended Funds

Blended funds combined both strategies of value and growth, choosing investments rather than strategies to guide purchases. With an adept manager, these funds can shift investments to value or growth depending on where the market is paying the biggest rewards.

Management Styles

Mutual funds are managed using one of two styles: active or passive management. A fund manager using active management believes he can pick stocks that will achieve the best returns for his fund. The manager may buy and sell stocks as their return changes. Some managers turnover 100 percent of the stocks in their portfolio each year in search of the highest return for the fund. Actively managed funds incur more expenses due to research and trading costs. Passively managed funds are typically thought of as index funds that buy a group of stocks based on a stock market index and hold that group until the index changes its composition. Passively managed funds usually have lower expenses because little research or trading is involved. Most SRI funds fall into the actively managed funds category to the extent that stocks are researched and screened for social and environmental factors and then analyzed for financial soundness. Although SRI index funds can be considered passively managed, they are not completely on automatic. Companies in the index are still screened for social and environmental policies. A serious lapse in one areas could drop them off.

Investment management companies that run actively managed funds believe it is possible to outperform the market or passively managed index funds by selectively buying and selling stocks. Some actively managed funds do beat the market as measured by indexes such as the S&P 500, however, very few beat it consistently. A fund manager's approach to stock selection may fit a particular set of economic and market conditions producing superior results. When those economic and market conditions change, as they always do, the winning strategy may fall apart. In addition, actively managed funds have the increased trading expenses and taxes dragging down gains that passive index funds don't bear. For SRI funds, actively managed doesn't necessarily mean excessive trading. SRI funds are more actively managed for social and environmental factors than economic or market changes.

Responsible Tip

Mutual fund expenses, whether from loads or operating expenses, are a significant drain on return and have a direct impact on whether the fund will meet its return objectives.

Mutual Fund Expenses, Fees, Taxes

Mutual funds feature professional managers who do the research, screening, and make investment decisions for fund investors. This expertise comes with a price tag as you might expect. It is reasonable to pay for these services, however, you should be cautious because long-term investment success is directly tied to expenses and fees charged by mutual funds. The higher the expenses charged to shareholders, the lower the chances you will achieve the return you need. The funds you must consider include a sales fee, called a load, and the actual expenses of the fund, which is known as the expense ratio. Some funds have no sales fee or load and are cleverly known as no-load funds. This doesn't mean they don't charge you expenses, but they don't charge a sales fee or load. Stock mutual funds also make capital gains distributions, which are tax bills they incur when the sell a stock for a profit. Some gains will be short-term, while others could be long-term. The tax treatment is quite different.

Sales Expenses or Loads

There are several ways to buy mutual funds. Many no-load (no sales charge) funds can be bought directly from the management company, although some discount brokers sell them, also. No-load funds mean just that—you do not pay a sales commission to buy or sell the fund. This lowers you cost of getting into and out of the fund, which increases your profits or reduces your losses. Many financial experts urge investors to stick with no-load funds for this reason.

Loaded funds charge a sales fee that goes to the person who sold you the fund. The person is usually a stockbroker or other investment professional. Many of these mutual funds are sold only through financial professionals. The two types of sales loads are a front-end load and a back-end load.

- ◆ **Front-end load**—A fund with a front-end load charges you a fee when you purchase the fund. The fee is deducted from your investment and paid to the salesperson. For example, if you invested $2,000 in a mutual fund with a 5 percent front-end load, the fund would take out $100 for the salesperson's commission and invest $1,900 in the fund.

- ◆ **Back-end load**—A back-end load is also called deferred sales charge. It charges a sales fee on a sliding scale only if you sell the fund within a certain number of years. The fee might be 6 percent the first year, 5 percent the second year, and so on until the fee

 Red Flag

Despite what salespeople may say the only correlation between fund performance and sales commissions is negative, not positive. The more expenses a fund pays, the lower its return.

disappeared if you held the fund until the seventh year. Although this fee sounds like a better deal if you plan to hold the fund for a long time, it can be very expensive if you decide to sell before the load has expired. The reason is you pay the percentage on the fund balance, not the original amount. If the fund has gone up since you bought it, taking 3 or 4 percent off the profits may be a big hit.

Sales commissions are defended as the price for the salesperson's help in selecting the right fund for you. But you should be aware that no empirical evidence supports that claim and salespeople only recommend funds that pay them commissions, so you aren't getting a look at all the options.

Mutual Funds and Expense Ratios

One expense you can't avoid is the expense ratio. This is the fee you pay the investment management company that runs the mutual fund. The fee covers administrative costs, research expenses, trading fees, the fund manager's fee, and 12B-1 fees. The 12B-1 fee is a neat little charge where the mutual fund can charge shareholder for advertising itself.

Index funds with their passive management have the lowest expense ratios thanks to the low cost of operating these funds. An expense ratio of 0.2 percent of assets for passive index funds is among the lowest, while an actively traded stock fund might run as high as 2 percent. The higher the fees, the less likely the fund is to beat the S&P 500 or any other stock index.

Taxes and Mutual Funds

Mutual funds that buy and sell stocks may generate long or short-term capital gains tax liabilities. These are distributed to shareholders, usually toward the end of the year. Actively managed funds are less tax friendly because of the number of trades they make. Most of the gains they distribute are short-term, which means they are taxed as ordinary income to taxpayers. Long-term capital gains are taxed at a more favorable rate. Passively managed funds seldom distribute capital gains because there is little trading in the fund. Most of the gains these funds distribute will be long-term capital gains.

The Least You Need to Know

◆ Mutual funds are the most popular investment product for traditional and SRI investors.

◆ Mutual funds offer several benefits for investors.

◆ Mutual funds invest in stocks, bonds, or both.

◆ Mutual funds can be actively or passively managed.

◆ Expenses directly impact the possibility a fund will achieve its goals.

Chapter 14

SRI Mutual Funds

In This Chapter

- ◆ The benefits of using SRI mutual funds
- ◆ How socially responsible mutual funds work
- ◆ SRI mutual funds and retirement accounts
- ◆ SRI mutual funds and expenses

Mutual funds are the investment vehicle of choice for most socially responsible investors. As noted in Chapter 13, mutual funds are the most popular investment product, and their design and benefits make them particularly suited for SRI investors. The process of selecting stocks (and/or bonds, in some cases) for a mutual fund lends itself well for reviewing a company for social, corporate, or environmental concerns. This is usually the first cut in the process, depending on the financial objectives of the fund. Once a pool of companies is identified that meets the socially responsible criteria for the fund, the mutual fund team pours over details of the financial statements to evaluate the firm from an investment perspective.

As we noted in Chapters 11 and 12, shareholder activism is important for some SRI investors. These investors will look for ways to engage the company through the mutual fund. With that exception and the screening for social and environmental issues, SRI mutual funds are just like traditional mutual funds. Because they are registered securities, they must follow the same laws and regulations as the other funds. Investing in socially responsible mutual funds feels just like investing in traditional mutual funds except you know your investment dollars are supporting your values.

Most Popular SRI Tool

Mutual funds are a good fit for socially responsible investing. Their structure and benefits make them an ideal investment product for a group of like-minded investors. The mutual fund is the evolved form of the tried and true concept of pooling money for investment purposes. Despite wildly divergent backgrounds, investors in traditional mutual funds are attracted to the investment philosophy and success of a mutual fund. Socially responsible investors have a stronger bond. They share a set of values that they express through investing in a mutual fund that honors those values in its investment practices. In some cases, there is also a religious, political, or other bond. The professional management of mutual funds is an added benefit to the screening process for SRI funds. In addition, many funds engage companies in dialogue to encourage changes in social, economic, or environmental policies.

Responsible Tip

No special financial or investing knowledge is necessary to invest in socially responsible mutual funds. They are just like traditional mutual funds with the exception that certain social and/or environmental values are given the same importance as financial considerations.

Professionals Handle Stock Selection

One main benefit of using mutual funds is the professional management that evaluates and makes investment decisions. Professional managers add value to mutual funds that most investors can't because they have the expertise and time to devote to the investments. Like traditional mutual funds, SRI funds have defined goals that the managers follow so investors know the parameters within which decisions are made. For example, a fund may exclude alcohol products, but allow investment in an otherwise qualified company if alcohol sales are less than five percent of its revenues. This parameter gives the manager a frame to work within and the investor a degree of comfort in knowing where the boundaries are.

Fund managers at socially responsible funds have the extra step of social, economic, or environmental screening that their peers at traditional funds don't have. This extra step is what makes investing in SRI funds acceptable to investors who are concerned about profiting from businesses that violate their values.

> **Responsible Tip**
>
> It is important to understand exactly what a socially responsible mutual fund does and does not find acceptable in a company. No company is perfect, so some accommodations have to be made. The fund's prospectus spells out exactly what the parameters of inclusion and exclusion are and what latitude fund managers have in selecting stocks.

Socially responsible investing fund managers use two methods to identify investment candidates from the many possibilities. The first method is screening which uses certain data points that the company must meet before moving on for further analysis. The other method is often called best-in-class. It involves finding the best companies in a grouping or industry sector. In some cases, a modified version of both methods is used. It is important to note that the analysis doesn't stop at this point. Once a company or group of companies is identified as potential investment candidates, SRI funds continue with rigorous traditional analysis of the company as an investment candidate.

The Screening Process

Many new SRI investors believe that screening just excludes certain types of businesses. While that is true for some funds, exclusion screening is only part of the picture. A more complicated and subjective screening process known as qualitative screening looks, not to exclude, but to include companies. Qualitative screening is more difficult because it identifies those companies that have exceptional social, economic, or environmental qualities.

Exclusion Screening

At its most basic level, socially responsible investing screens out investments in companies that profit from activities and products the investor finds contrary to your values. The most common exclusions include alcohol, tobacco, weapons, gambling, and the nuclear industry. These "exclusion screens" exclude companies that are involved in the offending businesses or industries.

Think of these excluded businesses and products as pebbles and regular companies as grains of sand. The sand passes through a fine wire screen easily, but the pebbles don't. The mutual funds and, by inference, the fund investors will not own or do business with those "pebbles" if possible. An absolute screen would eliminate a company with any connection to the excluded products. A less strict screen called a threshold screen, allows up to five percent of a company's sales to come from an excluded product. This would probably allow many hotels to be included in the SRI fund, even if they feature a lounge in the lobbies of their properties as long as the alcohol sales didn't amount to more than five percent of the total revenue.

Red Flag

The Securities and Exchange Commission is picky about investment companies choosing names for funds that are misleading. But before you assume a fund is SRI by its name, read the prospectus, or go online to one of the resources in Appendix A to verify the fund is truly SRI.

The original SRI funds were organized in many cases by religious groups that didn't want to support activities that were contrary to their beliefs. A number of these funds still exist today and have grown to include other religious and ethical beliefs. Most major religions have funds that support their beliefs and adhere to those beliefs in its investment practices. But not just the "sin" products earn exclusions in the screening process, and not just religious organizations practice exclusionary screens. Environmental and labor issues, human rights, women's and minority rights, all have places in this process with various screens.

While exclusionary screens satisfy many with strong feelings about certain products or services, critics point out that the process does nothing to affect change. Companies the screens exclude rarely suffer with the

possible exception of some occasional bad publicity. Many other investors have no qualms about owning the stocks, so a market always exists
for the equities. For some SRI investors, the first priority is to avoid
profiting from the companies that violate their values. Exclusionary
screens prevent this from happening. Other investors more interested
in trying to change corporate behavior may find these screens counter-
productive since change must come from inside (via shareholders).

Qualitative Screening

Qualitative screening differs from exclusion screening in that it is
looking for companies rather than eliminating companies. Qualitative
screens examine companies in a broad range of industry sectors looking
for those that are outstanding examples in the areas of environmental
stewardship, employee relationships, and other positive social and economic policies. Qualitative screening is used by SRI investors who want
broader representation in industry sectors, rather than being driven to
certain sectors that traditionally produce the most survivors of exclusionary screens (for example, technology).

Some qualitative screens look for top performers in those areas of
concern to socially responsible investors, while others may look for
companies that are likely targets for shareholder activism. These could
be companies that are leaders
or near leaders in their market
segment, but who fail to meet
the standards of SRI investors.
Rather than exclude them, investors might choose to invest and
engage companies in dialogue
to change their behavior—
persuading if possible, and using
shareholder resolutions if necessary to affect change in policy.

Responsible Tip

If you are particularly
interested in shareholder
activism, identify funds
that are strong in this area,
and then decide which one
makes the most sense for you
from an investment perspective.

Not All Screens Are Equal

It is important to note that not all screens are created the same or have
the same goals. As we'll see in further examinations of SRI mutual
funds, the industry is broadly defined at best and investors should not

assume that definitions literally translate from one investment company to another. You can count on the intentions of most funds being pointed in roughly the same direction, but how one fund chooses to reach its goal may be slightly different from another. Screens and investment professionals' stock selections reflect the people behind them along with their preferences and prejudices. When a fund says it uses a qualitative screen to identify investment targets, don't assume you understand what that means without checking into the terms of the screen and knowing what values the fund focuses on. You should know if the fund practices total exclusion, threshold exclusion, qualitative screening, or a combination.

Best-in-Class Modeling

Another strategy employed by SRI investors could be called best-in-class. This strategy seeks companies with the best environmental, social, and economic record in an industry sector. The companies may have other problems, but within their grouping, they standout. These companies may be open to changing their other areas of concern to socially responsible investors or improving upon those areas where they are already doing well. By investing in best-in-class companies, SRI investors can express their support for in-place policies and procedures and encourage the company to expand its socially responsible efforts into other areas of corporate life and governance.

One way to approach best-in-class modeling is to look at companies from a perspective of *sustainability*. By this measure, companies that maintain at a high level of long-term social, ecological, and economic performance are considered best-in-class by the sustainability measure. This gauge of corporate performance is gathering interest, as we'll see in Chapter 16 and in other areas of the book. Efficient practices today that can be maintained for an indefinite period are, by definition, good for the environment, the population, and the business.

Complimenting that approach is a concept, first coined in 1992, called *eco-efficiency*. This idea, which started out as a simple concept, but has grown into a complex business strategy, is to minimize the ecological impact a company and its products have on the world. This means a company thinks about every step in the production, distribution, and disposal of its products. The company will try to reduce the energy required to make the product; reduce the packaging material and/or use recycled packing material; find ways to efficiently distribute the product; and make the product and packaging easily recyclable. That is the practice of eco-efficiency. It is more detailed and complicated when it comes to actually implementing programs, however, the goal is simple.

Socially responsible investors use sustainability and eco-efficiency as two examples of companies that are well managed.

def•i•ni•tion

Sustainability is the concept that companies respect the environment through all stages of product development, manufacturing, and disposal so future generations will have access to the resources they'll need. Many companies file sustainability reports detailing their efforts, such as controlling green house gases.

Eco-efficiency is the practice of examining the life cycle of products and determining where energy can be saved and environmentally friendly steps taken in the process.

Ease of Investing

Investing in socially responsible mutual funds will be familiar to investors with a history in traditional mutual funds. Many funds are sold directly by the investment company and are no-load, that is they charge no sales fee. Other SRI funds offer different classes of shares depending on when you pay the sales fee. Although this was covered in Chapter 13 on general information on mutual funds, it bears noting as it specifically applies to socially responsible funds. The different share classes are:

- ◆ **No-load funds**. This is not really a class of shares, but represents funds that sell directly to the investor and do not charge any sales fee or commission. Some discount brokers may sell no-load funds, but you are usually better off buying directly from the investment company that manages the fund. You have access to people at the fund to clear up statement problems or other questions you might have and it is easier if you are dealing directly with the fund.

- ◆ **Class A shares**. Class A shares charge a sales fee when you buy the mutual fund's share. The fee can range up to five percent of the purchase, which means on a $10,000 purchase $500 goes to the salesperson and $9,500 is invested. For most investors, this is your best choice even if is hurts on the front-end. But be very selective about paying a high fee for a fund. Research has shown a strong negative correlation between fees and investor return.

- ◆ **Class B shares.** Class B shares are also known as a deferred sales charge because you don't pay a fee when you buy the fund. But, unless you hold it for a specific number of years, you'll pay a fee when you sell. The fee is often on a sliding scale that declines as years pass.

- ◆ **Class C shares.** Class C shares are known as level load funds because you pay a small fee when you buy the shares and a small fee each year thereafter for a certain period.

Responsible Tip _____

You can buy many SRI funds directly from the investment management company without a sales charge. One problem facing the SRI mutual fund industry is many of the investment companies are small and do not have the economies of scale that traditional invest-ment management companies enjoy. That makes it difficult to keep expenses low.

Which is the best deal for investors? Hands down, it's the no-load funds. Despite the sales pitches you'll hear, over time the no-load funds win in the performance category. If you find a loaded fund you just have to buy, choose Class A shares if you plan this as a long-term investment. If you are thinking short term, choose Class C shares. Despite their apparent appeal, Class B shares should be avoided. As a group, their returns are the lowest of all share classes.

SRI Funds and Your Retirement

One question new SRI investors ask is if SRI mutual funds are accept-able and appropriate for their retirement accounts. The answer to the first part of the question is, yes, they are acceptable. A growing num-ber of defined contribution plans offer SRI funds as part of the pool of available funds. Defined contribution plans are 401(k) or 403(b) retirement plans offered through your employer. These plans usually feature a set of mutual funds that participants can choose from to allo-cate their retirement contributions to as part of their retirement plan. You can choose the SRI fund as well as traditional funds to round out your retirement plan. The second part of the question—are SRI funds appropriate for retirement accounts—depends on the individual funds, its goals, limitations, and other characteristics. But a traditional mutual fund would have to bear up under the same scrutiny before it could be judged appropriate for your retirement fund.

SRI Mutual Funds Work Like Other Funds

It is worth noting and repeating that socially responsible mutual funds are registered investment products with the Securities and Exchange Commission. As such, SRI mutual funds must abide by the same rules, regulations, and laws as traditional funds. For example, they you must be given a prospectus on a fund before you can buy it, although those two actions frequently happen simultaneously.

More important, SRI funds fill the same needs as traditional mutual funds, because many have the same financial goals. The only difference is the SRI fund layers an additional step of screening in or out certain companies based on their record in environmental, social, and economic issues. Some SRI funds target retirement dollars, specifically funds known as asset allocation or life cycle funds. We'll discuss these fund types in detail in the chapters on mutual funds. They are funds specific for the retirement market, and as noted above, are designed to act like their traditional counterparts.

 Responsible Tip

Whether you put all or only part of your investments into SRI funds is a personal decision. Although the selection is more limited than the universe of traditional mutual funds, SRI funds can fill almost any investment need.

Most Acceptable for Retirement Accounts

Most SRI funds are acceptable for retirement accounts as witnessed by the growing number of defined contribution plans that include them in their offerings. This is good news for consumers, because saving for retirement in a defined contribution plan is an important way to build a retirement portfolio, especially if your company matches part of your contribution.

But defined contribution plans aren't the only way you can use SRI funds in your retirement. If you are eligible to contribute to an IRA,

SRI funds can be used to fund that retirement tool also. IRAs have annual contribution limits, some income caps, and other qualifications. See Appendix A for more information on IRA rules.

SRI Funds Work for College Savings

In addition to retirement accounts, SRI funds can be purchased through some *529 College Savings Plans.* These plans are typically offered through the state but use one or more investment companies to assemble a set of mutual funds for investors to select as allocation choices. The funds grow in a tax-deferred environment, and if used for a qualified educational expense, the distributions are tax-free.

def•i•ni•tion

> **529 College Savings Plans** let you put aside a certain amount of money each year in a special account where it grows tax-deferred. Individual states offer these plans and each has certain income requirements. If the distributions are used to pay for qualified education expenses, they are tax-free.

A Question of Expenses

There is a truth about all mutual funds that investors should know: high expenses (sales loads and operating expenses) mean a lower return. Some funds with high expenses may outshine the averages for a period, but over time, the funds with lower expenses historically are more reliable in producing the best returns. Sales people and fund managers argue that to get the best talent you have to pay more or you are compensating the sales person for selecting the best fund. But history doesn't bear out those claims for the long-term investor.

Of course, a fund with low expenses managed by an incompetent is not going to do well. But all things being equal the lower the fund's expenses the better your chances for investment success. That doesn't mean you should put all your money in an inexpensive index fund and forget it (although you will find people who will recommend just that). Actively managed funds, which will have higher expenses than index funds, do beat the market on a consistent basis. The key to deciding whether an expense is too high or not is to examine the value received for the fee or expense. It is this "value added" that SRI funds bring to the investment table. Because they are by definition, actively managed funds, many SRI funds may have expense ratios that are higher than their traditional peers, however, you can't assume SRI funds' expenses are automatically higher just because of the socially responsible component.

Value Added by Expenses

Some types of funds, both traditional and SRI, have higher operating expenses because of the additional costs in managing and researching the components that go into these funds. For example, global funds that invest in securities from foreign countries often carry higher expense ratios than domestic funds. It cost more to research and manage foreign stocks and bonds. But many investors find this type of diversification is important to the health of their overall portfolio, so paying the extra in operating expenses is not an important issue.

The important question is, does the higher expense ratio "buy" me an important component of my portfolio? Could I add that same component at a lower price from another fund? Many traditional funds invest in large-cap stocks. You should not pay a sales fee (buy a no-load fund) or a high expense ratio (over 1 percent) to invest in such a fund. Specialized funds, such as technology, small-

Responsible Tip

Expenses are important, but SRI investors get double value for the expense ratios in most actively managed SRI mutual funds. In addition to the traditional financial analysis, SRI funds do social screening and shareholder advocacy.

cap, or others that required more and specialized research will often carry higher expense ratios. For example, traditional funds specializing in small-cap stocks often carry expense ratios of 1 to 2 percent.

Screened Funds May Carry Higher Expenses

Socially responsible funds like to think of themselves as moving into the mainstream of investing, but in a discussion of expense ratios, you should consider them with the specialized funds. It would be incorrect to say that all SRI funds have higher expense ratios than comparable traditional funds. The mutual fund market is very much a buyer beware situation—between multiple share classes (A,B,C) and unjustifiably high expense ratios—some mutual funds make it very difficult to earn a decent return.

Since SRI screened funds perform value-added services for investors, it should not be surprising that their expense ratios tend to be higher than reasonably priced traditional funds. Screened SRI funds still must do the same research as traditional funds, in many cases, plus the socially responsible component. For some screened SRI funds, this is an elaborate screening process and shareholder activism. Although the number of actively managed, socially responsible funds is growing, the numbers are still very small compared to the universe of traditional funds. This reduces your choices when shopping for an SRI fund that fits your social and/or environmental values. The good news is the market for SRI funds is growing and new funds are being added. The larger the market for SRI funds becomes, the more resources will be available to all funds for research and other assistance. In addition, more professionals will become skilled in SRI research and managing SRI portfolios. All of these factors will tend to push expense ratios down over time.

Responsible Tip

Socially responsible index funds can act as a gauge of how the universe of socially responsible stocks (or bonds) is doing. Investors can use the index funds to measure the performance of the SRI fund.

SRI Index Funds Generally Less Expensive, But Less Engaged

Traditional index mutual funds are very popular because they are offered at an extremely low cost to investors. The indexes mimic some market index such as the S&P 500, so investors will do no better or no worse (less expenses) than the index does. For the many investors who believe actively managed funds do not add much in terms of value, but lots in terms of costs, index funds are their answer.

Socially responsible index funds follow the same concept as traditional index funds, except they track indexes of socially screened companies. The oldest socially screed index is the Domini 400 Social Index, which was created in 1990 by KLD Research & Analytics. One year later, the Domini Social Equity Fund (ticker: DSEFX) became the first socially responsible index fund. The Domini 400 Index tracked 400, primarily large cap stocks that had passed a social screening. The index roughly paralleled the concept that the S&P 500 was the proxy for the total market. The Domini 40 would be the proxy for the total SRI market. We'll discuss SRI index funds in more detail in Chapter 15.

Although SRI index funds are generally less expensive than actively managed SRI funds, they may not be as inexpensive as their traditional counterparts. Some newer SRI index funds rival traditional index funds in the expense ratio department.

Socially responsible index funds can provide investors with a solid investment in a broad base of socially screened stocks. But that's where the involvement of the funds generally ends. Don't expect much in the way of other socially responsible initiatives from the funds, because their expense ratios don't provide enough money to support that activity. As we'll see in Chapter 15, the pressure is on SRI index funds to keep expense ratios low or lower them further.

The Least You Need to Know

- Socially responsible mutual funds use professional management for social and financial decision-making.

- Different types of screens will produce different results.

- SRI funds make socially responsible investing easy.

- SRI funds are appropriate for retirement investing.

- SRI funds may, but not always, have higher expenses than their traditional counterparts have.

Chapter 15

SRI Index Mutual Funds

In This Chapter

- ◆ How index funds work
- ◆ The role of SRI index funds
- ◆ Index funds provide broad or narrow market coverage
- ◆ Exchange traded funds on the rise

There is an ongoing war in the mutual fund industry between the investment professionals who believe it is possible to selectively pick stocks that will outperform the market and another group that says the market will win in the end. The index mutual fund is the latter group's answer: you don't try to beat the market; you mimic it. That's not the whole story of index funds, but by definition, they are created to match or mimic a market index.

Indexes are usually created to track a specific market or segment of the market. Index mutual funds are organized to mimic the market so investors can participate in the performance of that market or market segment. In the traditional mutual fund world, index funds have very low expense ratios. If they are managed correctly, the fund's performance will parallel the movement of the index. This gives investors the opportunity to passively share in the gains or losses of this market or market segment.

For SRI mutual funds, the same index fund concept is true. The difference is SRI mutual fund indexes must be screened or they will not be any different from traditional indexes. This meant new indexes had to be created or existing ones substantially modified.

How Index Funds Work

In the world of traditional mutual funds, the best-known index is the S&P 500 index. It is a broad-based selection of 500 leading stocks and is considered a proxy for the whole stock market. Many traditional mutual funds compare their results to the performance of the S&P 500 index. If the fund can show a higher percentage growth than the S&P 500 index, the fund manager can boast of "beating the market." Other indexes cover different segments of the market, some larger and some smaller.

Indexes are model markets constructed to track the performance of the whole market or a segment of it.

Responsible Tip

Socially responsible investing index funds can be a relatively inexpensive way to invest in socially responsible companies. Be sure you know what screens were used to filter companies before you invest in an SRI index funds.

To better follow SRI index funds, it is helpful to understand indexes and how they work. Not all indexes are created the same. How the value is calculated can make a big difference in when market movement affects its total.

Creating an Index

An index of stocks (or bonds) is a mathematical exercise in grouping stocks to be tracked and deciding on how the index will be calculated. Several methods of calculating changes in an index exist. In the next section, we'll look at two different methods.

In simple terms, an index begins with a value and then tracks the changes in prices for the stocks making up the index. As each stock changes price, the index is recalculated based on the method chosen and a new index value is posted. During the trading day, this is done in real time. Stock splits, dividends, and other events are accounted for in the index recalculation. Occasionally, companies are dropped from the index and new companies added. The index is adjusted accordingly.

How Two Famous Indexes Are Calculated

The S&P 500 index is the most widely used index by investment professionals as a proxy for the whole market, but it is not the best-known index to the public. That honor belongs to the Dow Jones Industrial Average, better known as the Dow. While the S&P 500 tracks 500 stocks, the Dow covers just 30. The Dow has been around longer and carries much more emotional appeal than the S&P 500. Investment professionals view the Dow with caution, but respect the fact that it represents the mood of institutional investors who hold most of the stocks in the Dow. Their actions (buy or sell) can drive the whole market either up or down.

The Dow is 30 of the largest *blue chip stocks* on the market. These companies are the rock-solid leaders in their industries and represent the safest of equity investments. While no stock investment can be considered completely safe, these companies represent conservative investments, which is one reason most

Responsible Tip

Not all indexes are the same, so be careful when comparing one to another. Depending on the selection criteria, you may be comparing apples to oranges.

of their outstanding shares are owned by institutional investors. The Dow is a price-weighted index, which means a change in price for any component of the Dow affects the index the same. For example, a stock selling for $20 goes up $1 in price and a stock selling for $40 goes up $1 in price. Both price changes would have an equal affect on the index.

def•i•ni•tion

Blue chip stocks are considered the highest quality and safest stocks. They are usually large, older companies that have survived many market cycles in tact. The 30 stocks that comprise the Dow Jones Industrial Average (the Dow) would be considered blue chip stocks. Some believe the term comes from the game of poker where the blue chips are always the most expensive.

The S&P 500 has 500 of the leading companies in its index. Most of them are large-cap stocks, but not all. Because it covers a much broader segment of the total market, it is considered a total market index. The S&P 500 is a market-cap weighted index, which means more importance is given to larger companies than to smaller companies in calculating changes to the index. A $1 change to Microsoft will count much more than a $1 change to a smaller company. This skews the results toward large companies, but the index is still representative of the broad market—it covers about 70 percent of the total market's value.

Tracking Identified Sector

The traditional mutual fund market is extremely competitive and produces new indexes and new funds on a regular basis. In addition to the broad market indexes such as the S&P 500 and the Dow, a number of stock sector indexes track a narrow segment of the market—for example, technology stocks or energy stocks. These sector or segment indexes let investors follow a particular industry or segment of the economy by buying the leading companies through the index fund.

Low-Cost Passively Managed Funds

As we noted in Chapter 14, traditional index funds can be quite inexpensive to operate and are often offered with expense ratios as low as 0.25 percent. Because they are passively managed, the funds have very low expenses and can keep costs down. This is a powerful argument for investing in index funds exclusively.

How SRI Index Funds Work

Socially responsible index mutual funds follow the same principles as traditional index funds with the exception that a screening process of some type creates the index. SRI indexes range from broad market coverage to a more narrow focus. The main concern is what is screened in and what is screened out. These decisions define the index and the index fund.

A criticism of SRI indexes and index funds is that some are contrived and may not represent a true value to the shareholders. Another criticism is that some indexes were created to make SRI investing more appealing to institutional investors who own most of the total assets invested in socially responsible funds.

Most indexes keep the list of members out of public access areas, although you can usually buy a copy. The important thing for SRI investors to remember is that multiple screens create indexes and it is important to know what goes into those screens so you can judge how "socially responsible" the members of the index are.

Responsible Tip

While index funds can provide a lower cost way to do SRI investing, if you are passionate about a cause (for example, the environment) you may find index funds don't have the punch that regular SRI funds with strong advocacy programs offer.

Full SRI Market Coverage

The growth of the SRI mutual fund market has given rise to the need for more indexes to measure different segments of the SRI market. This coincides, somewhat, with the growing interest in traditional index mutual fund investing as a low-cost alternative to actively managed funds.

Some influential names in investment research have joined the industry with SRI indexes of their own, which adds to the creditability of the movement. But there are still indexes on the market that seem to have been created by organizations with little background in indexes or investment management. Because SRI indexes are inherently subjective in how and what screens are applied, investors should be cautious when investing in index funds.

Example of Broad Market of SRI Index

The first SRI index was the Domini 400 Social Index started in May of 1990. It was an answer to the S&P 500, but not a duplicate of that index. The Domini 400 consists of 400 socially screened companies. KLD Research & Analytics created the index to provide a way for SRI investors to measure their performance. It also demonstrates the affect of social, environmental, and governance screens have on the risk/ reward equation.

The Domini 400 is a *float*-adjusted, market cap weighed index. It is similar to the S&P 500 in that changes in larger companies count more than changes to smaller companies' stock prices. It differs in that the index uses a float-adjusted basis rather than *outstanding shares* to judge a stock's market capitalization. Float adjusting means the index only counts shares of stock that are actually available for trade. It does not count shares of stock held by founders, a control group, or others that are not generally available on the open market. KLD Research believes this makes the index a more reliable indicator of market conditions.

def•i•ni•tion

Float is the number of shares of common stock actually being traded in the market.

Outstanding shares are the number of share of common stock that have been issued and are available for trading, but some may not be currently on the market (for example, they could be held in reserves).

KLD Research licenses use of the index to mutual funds and exchange traded funds that want to build a product on it. Up until November 30, 2006, the Domini Social Equity Fund was the largest and oldest socially responsible index fund in the industry. On that date, the fund transitioned to an actively managed fund. (More on the Domini Social Equity Fund in Chapter 16).

Although the Domini 400 serves the same purpose as the S&P 500, it is not a mirror or substitute for that index. Only 250 of the 400 firms in the Domini 400 come from the S&P 500. Of the remaining, 100 are mid-cap stocks and 50 are small cap stocks. According to the KLD Research website, this is the performance of the Domini 400 index relative to the S&P 500 index:

	One Year*	Three Year*	Five Year*	Ten Year*	Since 5/1/90 Inception*
DS400 Index	15.59%	9.51%	10.65%	5.92%	11.82%
S&P 500	16.13%	11.76%	11.81%	5.98%	11.27%

* Annualized Returns

Because the Domini 400 index is more heavily represented in the technology and financial services sectors than the S&P 500, it will show better returns during those periods when those sectors are doing well. But the index excludes many energy companies, industrial concerns, tobacco firms, and others, so it will not do as well when its core sectors turn down as they did following the tech crash in 2000.

Red Flag

The mutual funds and exchange traded funds mentioned in this chapter are for illustration purposes only. Their inclusion is not a recommendation to buy or sell the securities.

Investing in the Domini 400 Index

You cannot invest directly in the Domini 400 Social Index because it is not a security. The index is licensed to investment companies for use in building investment products such as mutual funds and exchange traded funds. The Domini 400 is licensed to Green Capital Management for use in its Green Century Equity Fund. The fund is a stock index fund based on the Domini 400. According to fund information, its objective is:

> The Green Century Equity Fund seeks to achieve long-term total return, which matches the performance of an index comprised of the stocks of 400 companies selected based on social and environmental criteria. The Fund seeks to achieve its objective by investing in the stocks, which make up the Domini 400 Social Index.

According to a prospectus dated November 28, 2006, the Green Century Equity Fund had a total operating expense ratio of 0.95%.

Based on information from the Green Century Funds website (www.greencentury.com), here is how the fund compared to the S&P 500 in returns over several periods.

Responsible Tip

Small mutual fund companies have a difficult time holding expenses down. Larger companies can spread certain overhead costs over more funds and keep individual fund costs lower. Smaller fund companies with only a few funds under management don't have those economies of scale.

Annual Total Returns as of 6/30/07

	Green Century Equity Fund	S&P 500 Index
One Year	18.25%	20.59%
Three Years	7.75%	11.69%
Five Years	8.09%	10.70%
Ten Years	5.57%	7.13%

Green Capital Management is typical of many SRI investment companies that combine investing and shareholder advocacy. In addition to the Green Century Equity Fund, the company offers the Green Century Balanced Fund. Contrast this with traditional mutual fund companies that may offer dozens of funds in the same family. A group of nonprofit organizations dedicated to environmental issues owns the company. According to the Green Century Funds website, all of the profits earned by the management company go to these nonprofit groups to further their goals of supporting a variety of environmental issues.

Sector SRI Indexes

Although not as well-known as the broad market indexes, some smaller indexes cover very specific parts of the SRI spectrum. These indexes focus on certain parts of SRI investing that may appeal to particular investors. One example is The Wilderhill Clean Energy Index (www. wilderhill.com). The index philosophy is:

> A priority of the WilderHill Index (ECO) is to define and track the Clean Energy sector: specifically, businesses that stand to benefit substantially from a societal transition toward use of cleaner energy and conservation. Stocks and sector weightings within the WilderHill Clean Energy Index are based on their significance for clean energy, technological influence, and relevance to preventing pollution in the first place. We emphasize new solutions that make both ecological and economic sense, and aim to be the leaders in this field.

This index is obviously very narrow in its focus, as opposed to the Domini 400, which took a much broader look at the SRI market.

You cannot invest in this index directly, but an exchange-traded fund, The PowerShares WilderHill Clean Energy Portfolio, that mimics the index is available. Exchange traded funds are similar too, but not the same as mutual funds. At the end of this chapter is a discussion of SRI exchange traded funds.

> **Responsible Tip**
>
> The traditional mutual fund industry also has its specialty index funds, which focus on sectors or geographic regions.

Examples of SRI Index Funds

The evolution of socially responsible index funds followed the same logic that propelled the growth of traditional index mutual funds. Investors were looking for an inexpensive way to buy "the market" or a well-defined part of the market. Traditional index funds were developed along with a variety of parameters including market breadth, company size, economic sector, and so on. SRI index funds use some of these same parameters, but they also layer on their social, environmental, and governance screens. Thanks to modern screening tools and proprietary research databases, investment management companies can construct indexes based on a wide variety of financial and SRI parameters. This gives SRI investors a relatively large choice of funds to consider. It is important for investors to exam each SRI fund, including index funds for it sector representation and actual holdings. If you are not careful, you may end up with several funds that essentially own the same stocks.

Examples of Domestic Index Funds

As noted above, the Domini Social Equity Fund was the first and for many years, the largest SRI index fund before converting to an actively managed fund in 2006. Before its conversion, the Domini Social Equity Fund was a huge player in the SRI market (it remains so, after its conversion). Since the 1990s when the Domini Social Equity Fund was started a number of other index funds have sprung up, including some from among the most respect names in the traditional mutual fund world. Their entry into the SRI market and index funds proves that socially responsible investing is not a passing fad but a legitimate part of the financial scene.

One of the most respected names in SRI mutual fund investing is Calvert, which has developed one of the best management teams for its funds. Calvert offers its own SRI index called the Calvert Social index. The index contains 641 companies that have been screened for social, economic, and environmental concerns. The companies are large-cap growth stocks.

Responsible Tip

The traditional index mutual fund market has the resources of world-class research firms to build on—Standard & Poor's, Russell, Dow Jones, and others. The SRI market is still developing its own counterparts.

This index is used to form the Calvert Social Index Fund, which is a large growth fund. The fund begins with the top 1,000 firms and begins a rigorous screening process, according to its website to weed out the unacceptable stocks. The fund mimics the index and adds or deletes stocks as the index does. With an expense ratio of 0.75%, the fund is competitive with traditional index funds as well as SRI index funds.

A mutual fund industry giant, Vanguard has a SRI index fund based on the FTSE4Good US Select Index, which a London-based, U.S. version of a global index of socially responsible companies. Vanguard had been using Calvert's Social Index up until the end of 2005 when it switched to the FTSE4Good US Select Index to pattern its Vanguard FTSE Social Index Fund. Vanguard is a leader in low-cost index funds and this fund at 0.25 percent expense ratio is no exception.

Although the Vanguard fund is categorized as a large-cap growth fund, it does have some mid-cap stocks in its holdings. The fund holds 425 stocks. Compare the economic sector holdings with the Calvert Social Index Fund and the S&P 500 index.

Economic Sectors	Calvert Social	Vanguard FTSE	S&P 500 Index
Energy	2%	2%	11%
Materials	1%	1%	3%
Industrials	7%	4%	11%
Consumer Discretionary	10%	15%	10%
Consumer Staples	7%	5%	9%

Health Care	13%	17%	12%
Financials	27%	39%	21%
Information Technology	27%	15%	15%
Telecomm Service	5%	2%	4%
Utilities	1%	1%	4%

Percentages rounded

Both Calvert and Vanguard are large-cap growth funds, however, because they use a different index to constitute their funds, the holdings by economic sector show some distinct differences. Vanguard is clearly more heavily weighted toward financials, while Calvert is spread more evenly between financials and information technology. This difference doesn't make one fund bad and the other good, but it does mean that under certain market conditions one funds may register a stronger return than the other. Contrast both funds to the sector weighting of the S&P 500 index, which has no socially responsible screening. You can see that while the two SRI funds address a broad market, they do not come close to duplicating the S&P 500 in their representation of the economic sectors. Both Calvert and Vanguard have over two-thirds of their investment in Health Care, Financials, and Information Technology. The S&P 500 has only 48 percent in the same three sectors.

> **Red Flag**
>
> Socially responsible investing is not "just the same" as traditional mutual fund investing. That doesn't mean it is inferior, but it is not the same. Don't be fooled that you are getting the same representation in a broad market SRI fund as you would get in a traditional index fund.

Exchange Traded Funds

Exchange traded funds (ETFs) are relatively new investment products that have caught on with some investors. ETFs are very much like index mutual funds. In fact, ETFs track stock and bond indexes just like index mutual funds do. But ETFs differ in some significant ways from mutual funds. These differences may work to your favor or not, depending on the type of investor your are and what your investment goals are. ETFs allow you to buy a basket of stocks just like an index mutual fund does. The major difference between ETFs and mutual funds is how they are bought and sold.

Trading ETFs Just Like Stocks

Exchange traded funds are bought and sold just like shares of common stock on the stock exchanges. Their prices change continuously during the day as the underlying stocks change in value and the supply and demand for the ETF shares pushes the price up or down. You buy ETFs on the open stock market just like you buy shares of common stock, which means you pay a commission to a stockbroker when you buy and when you sell. But an investor has no ongoing expenses to pay like an expense ratio in mutual funds. If you want to trade ETFs like stocks, you can. All the various stock market trading orders and strategies are available for ETF trading. You can buy 200 shares of an ETF in the morning and sell 100 shares back that afternoon if you wish.

Responsible Tip

Usually ETFs experience some hot action during volatile markets as traders move in and out of positions. Typically, these folks are trading SRI ETFs, but funds tied to faster moving stock indexes such as the Nasdaq.

Exchange traded funds track a variety of SRI indexes, from the Domini 400 Social Index to some very small and specific indexes. A rule of thumb, which is true for index funds as well as ETFs, is the more narrow and specific the index, the more volatile it may be. Without any other industry sectors to offset negative news, a narrowly focused index fund, or ETF can suffer a significant reversal.

A Broad Market ETF Example

Barclays Global Investors has an ETF that follows a KLD index fund with broad market coverage. The KLD Select Social Index is an SRI index designed for investors who appreciated the values of SRI investors, but wanted more diversification in their holdings, which generally means they were less risk tolerant. KLD created the Select Social Index by choosing several hundred large companies from all economic sectors, except tobacco. Rather than screen out companies for poor showings in one of the usual screens, KLD under-weights poor performers and over-weights companies that score well in its SRI screens. This gives investors the diversification they need. Barclays uses this index as the basis for their ETF they call the iShares KLD Select Social Index Fund. The term "iShares" is your tip that this is an ETF and not a regular mutual fund.

On the other end of the size and focus scale, PowerShares Capital Management is using The Wilderhill Clean Energy Index to produce its own ETF called PowerShares WilderHill Clean Energy Portfolio. This ETF covers 37 companies that support and produce cleaner energy production.

 Red Flag

Some SRI investors are very passionate about their causes are drawn to these very narrow ETFs. Be warned, however, that such focus may mean the market for these shares is thin and it may be difficult to sell your shares if you need to in a hurry.

Who Should Use ETFs?

What are the advantages of ETFs over index funds? You can use a variety of stock trading tools and strategies that are not available to index mutual fund investors, and if you are investing in a highly volatile sector ETF, you may want that flexibility. In addition, there are no ongoing expenses that even no-load mutual funds charge. That may not mean much if you are comparing an index fund with a 0.25 percent expense ratio with an ETF bought from a discount broker, but if the index fund has a ratio approaching 1 percent it will make a difference for the long-term investor.

If you are not planning on trading, but holding for a long-term investment and can get a no-load index fund with a reasonable expense ratio, you will probably not help yourself by switching to an exchange traded fund.

The Least You Need to Know

◆ Index funds provide a way to invest in broad or narrow market coverage.

◆ SRI index funds track groups of stocks that have been screened for various socially responsible values.

◆ Index funds can define a broad or narrow piece of the SRI market.

◆ Exchange traded funds are an alternative to index funds that trade like stocks.

Chapter  16

More About SRI Mutual Funds

In This Chapter

- ◆ The different types of SRI mutual funds
- ◆ Examples of different types of SRI mutual funds
- ◆ The financial focus of SRI mutual funds
- ◆ Foreign SRI mutual funds examined

Socially responsible mutual funds come in many of the same major types as traditional mutual funds. This makes it easy to use them in your investment planning because they have the same general attributes as their traditional mutual fund counterparts. Although you won't find all different types of funds available to traditional mutual fund investors, a good assortment of SRI fund types are available.

The biggest concern for SRI investors is the possibility of a limited selection of some mutual fund types that meet their value goals. Investors looking for different styles of SRI mutual funds have a more limited selection. Most equity funds fall into the large growth or blend categories. Very few value SRI mutual funds are available. This will likely change as the industry expands and redefines its boundaries, but for the immediate future, value investors may have a difficult time finding many SRI equity funds to consider.

Bond funds offer even fewer choices for investors. What does this all mean? Some SRI investors will look to traditional funds to fill holes in their portfolios where SRI funds are absent. Other investors will make do with what the SRI industry has to offer and add new products as they become available.

Types of Funds

MorningStar.com, which is the premiere source for mutual fund information on the Internet, makes no distinction between SRI funds and traditional funds other than to note the difference in their commentary. Socially responsible mutual funds perform a dual role for many investors. As an expression of the investor's values, the funds employ investment policies that seek to honor those values through purchases they make and don't make. As an investment, the funds seek the maximum return on the investor's capital for the appropriate amount of risk. While those roles may not be in direct conflict (some would argue they are), the dual responsibilities of mutual funds often involves some compromises on both roles.

Most SRI investors know they are not going to find a fund that contains a set of perfect companies in its portfolio. All companies are flawed in SRI areas to some degree. But some SRI funds may choose to run very tight screens while others make different decisions. As we noted in Chapters 9 and 10, screens can not only to exclude, but also include. To fulfill their other responsibility of maximizing return, SRI funds may use indexes, screens, and other tools to achieve a more balanced portfolio. Each fund has a type designation that gives investors an idea of what the manager's investment goal is. These fund types are self-assigned and can vary from fund to fund in the exact definition.

Responsible Tip

It is not uncommon to find articles in the traditional financial media questioning the practicality of constructing a truly diversified portfolio of purely SRI mutual funds. You have to judge how comfortable you are with the selections available.

What's the Fund's Focus—What's Its Type?

A fund type refers to the overall investment strategy of the fund. For example, a growth mutual fund would invest in growth stocks—those stocks expected to grow faster than the rest of the market by a considerable amount (20 percent or more). An income fund would invest in securities (bonds and stocks) that paid current income in the form of interest payments and dividends. The Securities and Exchange Commission, which regulates mutual funds, is strict about funds that say they are one type of fund, but invest as if they are another type of fund. But the rules governing what funds can invest in are very loose and dependent on what the fund outlines in its prospectus. A growth fund could say in its prospectus that it invests in growth-oriented stocks, but may from time to time invest in other types of stocks if conditions warrant.

Red Flag

Any fund can call itself socially responsible and claim to do screening. The level of screening is not regulated and there is no governing body that sets any standards for what truly is an SRI fund and what is not. Buyer beware. Some funds are so loosely constructed that their screens don't mean much and almost any company can pass through.

MorningStar.com has its own proprietary way of classifying funds. They make the determination by what the fund actually owns, not what the funds says it will own in the prospectus. MorningStar analyzes the fund's holdings, and based on those findings, puts the fund in a grid that identifies its style and type. MorningStar's findings may not agree with how the fund characterizes itself, but it is hard to argue with labeling a fund based on what it is, rather than on what it says it is.

It is important to know what a fund's true style is so you can find the right fit for your portfolio. Some funds' names tell you what type of fund they are—Aquinas Growth Fund, for example, lets you know its intentions. On the other hand, the Appleseed Fund doesn't tell you much all by its name (it's an all-cap value fund).

Mutual Fund Type Definitions

As noted above, not all types of mutual funds are found in the SRI universe, but new funds are being added each year and some may fill in where gaps in types exist now. Here are definitions of the more common equity mutual fund types you will find in the socially responsible universe:

◆ **Growth funds**—Growth funds invest in stocks that have higher than average growth in earnings and revenue potential. The goal is an ever-rising stock price. These companies seldom pay dividends, but reinvest profits to finance more growth. Growth funds are for investors with an above average tolerance for risk. The distinction for SRI investors is that some industries may be precluded even though they are high-growth candidates. For example, some SRI funds that have strict environment screens would eliminate many energy and exploration companies. But these can be high-growth companies if market conditions are right. An example of an SRI growth fund is the Citizens Core Growth Fund (WAIDX).

Responsible Tip

Socially responsible investing growth funds tend to be heavy in technology, financial, and services sectors of the economy. These can be environmentally friendly, but may not always be in favor of the market. If you own one or more of these funds, have a good idea of what its holdings are so you can cushion any blows if these sectors fall out of favor.

◆ **Aggressive growth funds**—Think growth funds on steroids. These funds invest in younger companies, often technology or other sectors that have the potential to score very high returns. Aggressive growth funds may invest in initial public offerings and may use more sophisticated trading strategies such as options to achieve higher returns. When these funds hit the market right, they can score tremendous returns, but like any high-risk investment, they can also suffer severe losses. This is not an investment for the faint of heart. Many companies that might fall into this category might also score well or SRI screens, however, they can

be very risky investments, especially young, technology companies. Not every investor will be comfortable with this level of risk.
Few if any, SRI funds will categorize themselves as aggressive
growth, but depending on their holdings, may fall into this category.

♦ **Value funds**—Value funds look for value stocks, which have been
under-priced by the stock market. Value stocks are often companies that are out of favor for some reason or have had bad news
that dropped the stock price below its intrinsic value. When the
market corrects the pricing, value investors will see a substantial
profit if they have bought correctly. Value funds attract investors
who are interested in a long-term investment. SRI investors can
be value investors, too. But many value stocks are old line companies the may be stuck in their ways and not interested in the
environment any more than is legally required. Fewer value funds
are available to SRI investors than growth funds. An example of
an SRI value fund is the Aquinas Value Fund (AQEIX).

♦ **Income funds**—Income funds come in several variations, but
the general focus is to produce immediate income, either monthly
or quarterly. Most income funds invest in a variety of bonds,
dividend-paying stocks, and other interest-paying securities.
Equity income funds invest strictly in preferred stock (dividend
paying). Other income
funds invest in risky junk
bonds and other high-risk
debt instruments. SRI investors need to know where
the income fund is investing
and what its risk profile is
to make an informed judg-
ment about the fund. An
example of an SRI income
fund is the Parnassus Equity
Income (PRBLX).

> **Responsible Tip**
>
> Investors at or in retire-
> ment favor income funds
> for the immediate cash
> they generate. These funds
> invest for immediate income
> so retired people can use the
> money for living expenses.

♦ **Balanced funds**—Balanced funds combine stocks, bonds, and
cash in a pre-determined mix. The funds seek some capital appreciation along with income. Balanced funds generally have a set
proportion of stocks to bonds to cash ratio (with some wiggle

room). This gives investors a fixed balance that reacts to changes in the market and economy with the balance of the three asset classes. Investors benefit by the complementary interaction of the three asset classes (stocks, bonds, cash), which is a classic positioning for portfolios. Balanced funds can be appropriate for SRI investors at or nearing retirement if they can find one with the right mix of stocks, bonds, and cash. An example of an SRI balanced fund is the Calvert Social Balanced A (CSIFX).

♦ **Index funds**—Index funds mimic a SRI index that captures a certain segment of SRI stocks or bonds. Index funds are designed to let investors "buy" the market represented by the index, which means they can participate in any profits or losses that market experiences. Most index funds are pure, however, some managers do try to enhance the returns with some decisions outside the index. SRI index funds are a conservative buy that tracks a market index such as the Domini Social Index. An example of an SRI index fund is the Calvert Social Index A (CSXAX).

♦ **Foreign or international funds**—Foreign or international SRI funds invest in companies outside of the United States. An example of an international SRI fund is the Domini European Social Equity Fund (DEUFX).

♦ **Global funds**—Global funds invest in any country including the United States. An example of a global SRI fund is the Citizens Global Equity Fund (WAGEX).

Responsible Tip

The investing world has numerous names for a variety of mutual funds. The same fund may be called two different names. The important aspect for investors is what the fund does, rather than how it is named.

Bond funds have their own types and we'll cover these in Chapter 17.

What's the Fund's Financial Focus?

Not to belabor a point, but socially responsible investing is still investing. Unless you have no interest in the potential return from your socially responsible investment, it is important that you consider the financial aspect of where your money is going as well as your values.

Fortunately, the number of SRI funds is growing providing investors with more selections to fit both their values and financial needs. Investors can access many resources to help them understand the financial aspects of a fund they are considering. With the exception of the very small funds, you can find comment and commentary on most of the larger SRI funds. Appendix A has a list of online resources that you can use to check out a fund. These resources will help you determine the fund's financial focus or goals, which aren't always discernable by the fund's title.

Using exclusively SRI funds to build a portfolio may be satisfactory to some investors, but others may find the selection too limited or missing some elements that are available in the traditional mutual fund universe. Because SRI mutual funds are not exactly like traditional mutual funds, investors may want to consult a financial professional familiar with the socially responsible investing. We'll cover this in more detail in Chapter 19.

Responsible Tip

Constructing a portfolio with a limited universe of SRI mutual funds may have been a daunting task at one time. It is much less so now, however, some investors still find working with a financial professional beneficial toward getting the most from their SRI investments.

A Question of Risk and Reward

Investors have to ask about any prospective investment whether the risk of losing money is worth the potential reward. This is true no matter what the investment—the risk must be appropriate with the potential reward. If the risk is high, but the potential reward is low, then the investor should look for something else.

Socially responsible investing is no different. Aligning risk and reward is an important part of investing success. One way investors can learn about the relative risk of investing in a particular SRI fund is to evaluate the investing style of the fund. Does the fund stick with larger, more mature companies or is it after smaller, younger companies? Some general rules can give you an idea about the amount of risk a fund is willing to take in order to meet their goals.

- Larger is less risky than smaller

- Growth is more risky than income

- Growth is more risky in the short-term than value

These aren't absolutes because it still depends on the fund manager's expertise in buying and selling decisions to make the fund work or not. Whether you are investing in a mutual fund or individual stocks, however, these guidelines are more often right than wrong. They are defeated by mismanagement, fraud, and other factors of human making, but in a fair test, they will hold true.

Your concern with risk is an important part of how you choose which funds make up your portfolio. If you have a low tolerance for risk, you'll want to stay away from funds that focus on small-cap, young companies. The potential rewards may be high, but if you can't sleep at night, this is clearly not the right level of risk. You might consider a fund that blends mid-size and larger companies for some extra growth potential with some of the risk tempered.

Conflicting Values and Financial Goals

An important factor to consider when investing in an SRI fund is what industries or sectors their negative screens exclude. This is where your values and your financial goals may come in conflict. How much will it hurt the fund's potential performance (if any) to have certain sectors excluded? For example, large growth funds will move money into sectors that are expected to outperform the rest of the market by a substantial amount in the near future. In recent years, energy companies have been standouts in this capacity. Exxon-Mobil, thanks to rising oil prices and rising demand, posted record profits and its stock soared. It was not the only energy company that benefited from this economic situation.

Red Flag

Chasing hot sectors is a way for any mutual fund or investor to lose money. Successful investing is usually the result of a thoughtful long-term strategy. Adjustments are always a part of any strategy, but sector hopping is seldom a winning plan.

What about the SRI funds that exclude energy companies from their holdings on environmental or other reasons? Were there equally attractive alternatives that did make it through the SRI exclusion screens? Tobacco, alcohol, gambling, weapons manufacturers, and other industry categories that are frequently screened out have all, at various times, been very profitable. When SRI fund managers can't invest in these sectors at those times, their funds may suffer in comparison to traditional peers. As we noted in Chapter 2, the penalty for investing in SRI funds as opposed to traditional funds is hard to measure, but doesn't appear to be large and in some cases, there is no penalty at all. Still, what may be true for the entire SRI industry, may not be true for every individual fund.

You may be attracted to an SRI fund by its social and/or environmental policies, but it is important to be fully aware of the fund's financial focus, too. The key is to understand how the fund is performing in the present market and how it might perform under different market and economic conditions. You may not be able to predict with accuracy what the fund will return, but you can see where there could be problems. In markets that reward funds that are broadly invested in energy and defense stocks, how will this fund do? What if the favored sector is technology or services? Are there large gaps in coverage because of excluding screens that will make the fund vulnerable to lower returns?

Investors must decide if they value their financial returns higher than their social responsibility values. Some investors augment the SRI investing with traditional funds to protect themselves financially against potential loss. With the large and growing number of SRI funds and the increasing sophistication of fund managers, however, pure SRI investors are finding enough opportunities without significant penalties to satisfy both goals.

Foreign SRI Funds

Your portfolio of investments should contain a portion of assets invested in the economies of countries other than the United States. This is a prudent strategy whether you are an SRI investor or not. We live in a global economy and having a small portion of your assets invested in other economies is good hedge against the U.S. economy. Investing in foreign companies that have been screened for socially responsible values is a real benefit of using a mutual fund. It can be complicated to do social screening on U.S. companies, but uncovering the relevant information from foreign firms can be a real challenge, especially since many countries don't require the level of detailed reported that we demand in the United States. On the other hand, a number of foreign companies have been out in front on many socially responsible issues. They have taken leading roles in shaping energy policies and worked hard on workers' rights.

Responsible Tip

Foreign mutual funds can have a high degree of risk if they invest in emerging markets. Few SRI funds are involved in this area because those companies that can afford to practice SRI typically are more mature and operate in more mature markets.

As noted in a previous section, two forms of foreign mutual funds exist: the global fund and the international fund. Both will help you diversify you holdings, although the international or foreign fund is the most pure in that it does not invest within the United States.

What You Need to Know

By paying careful attention to what the fund does and where it invests, investors can diversify their portfolios with some assets invested in SRI companies from Europe to Asia. It is important to know whether the fund is a global or an international fund. Global funds are perfectly acceptable. Be sure, however, you understand how much of the fund is invested in the United States and in which stocks. You'll want to avoid holding a fund that invests in stocks that you already own through other funds.

The risks of investing in a fund that owns stocks in foreign companies include all the standard risks of investing plus some that are unique to owning overseas companies. One challenge is the currency exchange rate between the company's domestic currency and U.S. dollars. The fund converts the U.S. dollars of its investors into the currency of the country and buys the stock. The value of the stock may rise or fall depending on some of the usual factors such as earnings, competition, demand, and so on. But there also can be gains or losses in the difference in the exchange rate between the country's currency and U.S. dollars. For example, if a fund bought a company's stock when the exchange rate was $1 for 1.5 of the country's comparable units, a $10,000 investment would buy 15,000 units worth of stock. When the fund wanted to sell, the exchange rate had fallen to $1 to 1.25 units. Assuming the price remained unchanged, the fund would only receive $8,333. (This simple example ignores trading costs, fees, taxes, and so on to focus on the impact of exchange rates.) Fortunately, the funds have tools to mitigate currency fluctuations, such as currency trading positions and other options.

In addition, investing in major economies of Europe is made easier by the adoption of the euro as a regional currency of 13 of the member states of the *European Common Market*. This facilitates trading securities in these European countries by eliminating multiple currencies. It has also led to tremendous growth in European stock markets, which also make it much easier and safer for funds to buy and sell securities in these countries.

Investors should also note that investing in foreign countries includes political and economic risks that are different and potentially more volatile than those in the United States are. Some countries also have difficult taxation rules that make it harder to profit from trading activity. While the United States has stringent registration of securities, other countries may not have the same standards so the potential for fraud and other misdeeds exists.

def•i•ni•tion

The **European Common Market** is made up of 27 member states in Europe who share a common trade and agricultural policy. A number of common political and financial policies facilitate interaction among the member states. A common currency, the euro, has been adopted by 13 of the members.

They haven't adopted a single currency (although the U.S. dollar is close), but the Pacific and Asian economies and markets are prime areas of U.S. investment. Several SRI funds target these regions, which have experience tremendous economic growth in the last two decades. No SRI funds will be found investing in Chinese companies in any significant way, but the China market began booming in 2006–07. Capitalism has come to China in a big way, although it is unclear how unfettered the totalitarian government will let it become. Major concerns include human rights abuses of workers, massive environmental problems (China is a huge consumer of coal-fire electricity), and over-population.

It is not on everyone's investing radar screen, but several international SRI investing funds include Australia in their portfolios. Australia and New Zealand represent a pocket of western-type government and culture in the South Pacific at a time when populations, cultures, and religions of Southeast Asian countries are gaining prominence in the national political and economic arena.

Some Examples of International and Global Funds

For most investors, global or international funds shouldn't make up more than 15 percent of your portfolio. You have several choices for SRI funds in these two categories. These are recommendations, just examples of the types of funds available. Because funds that invest in foreign companies are somewhat more complicated, these examples may help with your understanding.

The Citizens Global Equity Fund (WAGEX) is a global fund that invests in United States and foreign stocks. The fund holds approximately 42 percent U.S. and the rest in foreign stocks.

Although this fund does not use the S&P 500 index as a benchmark, its holdings bear a remarkably close distribution to the index.

Economic sectors	Citizens Global Equity Fund	S&P 500 Index
Energy	11%	11%
Materials	8%	3%
Industrials	12%	11%
Consumer	12%	10%
Discretionary Consumer Staples	5%	9%
Health Care	10%	12%
Financials	21%	21%
Information Technology	12%	15%
Telecomm Service	6%	4%
Utilities	5%	4%

Percentages rounded

The fund may also hold some of its assets in cash equivalents. These percentages are subject to change and presented for illustration purposes only.

The social criteria for this fund are spelled out on its website www. citizensfunds.com.

Global funds straddle the foreign and domestic markets, which can be a plus under certain economic and market conditions. But they can also work against themselves with gains in one geographic area canceled out by loses in the other.

The Domini European Social Equity Fund is a relatively new international fund that invests strictly in European companies. The fund targets mid- to large-cap companies. Some 25 percent of the fund's holdings are in British companies followed by

Responsible Tip

Global and international funds are gaining popularity in the SRI community as the concept of worldwide social responsibility spreads.

France and Germany. A look at the holding by economic sector compared to the S&P 500 index shows how the fund differs from a U.S. composite. This, in part, is reflective of the different composition of the European and U.S. economies.

Economic Sectors	Domini European Social Equity Fund	S&P 500 Index
Energy	6.5%	11%
Materials	5%	3%
Industrials	9%	11%
Consumer Discretionary	14%	10%
Consumer Staples	4%	9%
Health Care	13%	12%
Financials	35%	21%
Information Technology	2%	15%
Telecomm Service	7%	4%
Utilities	4%	4%

*Percentages rounded

The fund may also hold some of its assets in cash equivalents. These percentages are subject to change and are presented for illustration purposes only.

The social criteria for this fund are found on its website at www.domini.com.

An international fund that invests strictly outside the United States can act as a counter to the U.S. market. But as markets become more interrelated, there is some suggestion that this counter is disappearing. If we are truly headed for a global stock market, investing in a purely international fund may lose some of its counter to the U.S. markets. We aren't there yet, so it's still a good idea to have a small percentage of your assets overseas.

Are They Right for You?

Are global or international SRI funds right for your portfolio? That's a question best answered by you when considering how far you want your values to spread in influence and what financial role they may play in your portfolio. Socially responsible investing is very much active in other markets besides the United States. Canada and Britain have had socially responsible investing movements for a number of years. Other countries in Europe have also carried the banner of SRI investing in areas such as worker rights and the environment. The environment in particular is a powerful movement outside the United States and will be influential in shaping investments for many years to come.

For SRI investors in the United States, this overseas focus on the environment and human rights will present opportunities to join like-minded investors in a number of foreign countries. Because the United States is lagging behind other developed countries in implementing significant environmental standards on greenhouse gases, we will not be the leader in this movement unless policy is changed significantly. The countries and companies that lead in these issues will likely come from overseas and global and international funds will be a way to participate.

The Least You Need to Know

- SRI funds span the most common types of mutual funds.
- SRI funds' style considers the question of risk versus reward.
- Global and international SRI mutual funds present opportunities and risks.
- Investing in foreign-based SRI mutual funds presents risks and opportunities.

Chapter 17

Investing in SRI Stocks and Bonds

In This Chapter

◆ The benefits of investing in individual SRI stocks

◆ How to evaluate individual SRI stocks

◆ Investing in SRI bonds

◆ Evaluating SRI bonds and bond funds

In previous chapters, we discussed the many benefits of using mutual funds for socially responsible investing. The professional management, diversification, and ease of investing make a compelling case for these funds. A mutual fund's knowledgeable staff that checks the social and environmental screens and engages in shareholder advocacy benefits investors looking to invest in situations compatible with their values. But some investors want more control over their investments. They may object to what they consider inordinately high expenses or they may just prefer to get their hands dirty when investing their money—do the research and so on themselves.

Whatever their motivation, these investors want more control over their money and more interaction with the companies they own. Thanks to a number of resources, it is possible for individuals to discover many SRI aspects of individual companies. Many companies are issuing environmental or sustainability reports. Other sources of information exist that compare companies standing on SRI issues. Individual investors can file shareholder resolutions and many do. Bonds, which are loans to governments and corporations, also play an important role in investing and a growing role in SRI investing.

Why Own Individual SRI Stocks

Owning individual stocks (as opposed to shares of a mutual fund) offers investors several benefits and poses several challenges. From a pure investment perspective, many investors only own individual stocks, while a great many more only own mutual funds. A smaller number own both, which is probably a smart strategy. Not every investment professional will agree with that statement. Some say stick with mutual funds and let a professional make those hard decisions for you. Others say there is no reason to pay ongoing expenses that eat away your profit, when holding a stock doesn't cost a thing. From the SRI perspective, mutual funds can provide a much better job of screening funds—if they do their homework, but individual investors can do a good job if they follow some simple steps.

The Benefits and Drawbacks of Owning Individual Stocks

From an investment perspective, owning individual stocks (as opposed to shares of a mutual fund) offers some distinct advantages. One big advantages is no ongoing expenses to eat away at any profits—or to add on to a loss. You will pay a stockbroker a fee when you buy the stock and when you sell. More important, investors gain a more intimate knowledge of the company behind the stock when looking after eight to ten individual stocks in a normal portfolio. Mutual funds that own dozens of stocks (index funds may own hundreds) don't provide much opportunity for investors to fully understand the company.

If you own individual shares in a company, you are a direct owner of that company, unlike mutual funds where you own shares in a fund that owns shares in the company. This direct ownership means the company deals with you in matters of proxy votes, dividends, and so on. In addition, you don't have to pay for the privilege of being an owner. Thanks to discount stockbrokers, commissions are quite low and that's the only cost (other than taxes on dividends) of owning shares of stock. You pay another commission when you sell the stock and possibly a capital gains tax on profits.

Remember, going it alone in the investment world is just that. Unless you pay for investment advice, you must do your own research and decide which stocks work best for your portfolio. You'll want to monitor the companies behind these stocks to make sure your original reason for buying the stock continues to make sense. If a stock begins a dramatic decline, do you sell or ride it out hoping the price will rebound? You'll have to decide if the drop is due to something wrong with the company or its market. When all of these decisions are yours, some investors see the benefit of paying professionals at mutual funds.

Responsible Tip

Taxes on dividends are lower than most personal income tax rates, however, Congress frequently looks at the rate for an additional source of income and adjusts the rate upward.

But even these challenges don't deter the true believers, because they enjoy this type of investing and they know that all things being equal, your chances of making a higher return on your investment are with individual stocks and not mutual funds.

The Case for Investing in SRI Stocks

There is an existing system of information sources and support to help investors buy and sell individual shares of stock. What about doing socially responsible screening though—how hard is it for individuals to do that type of research? It is not as easy as researching the financials of a company because the government requires an open-book reporting policy for companies that trade on public stock exchanges. For the most part, that requirement doesn't extend to socially responsible areas—those areas aren't defined that way for easy researching.

Companies must report major legal and regulatory actions to shareholders and those filings are a matter of public record. You can find them at the Securities and Exchange Commission website and through several free and paid sources. See Appendix A for more information on where to locate these resources. These reports are not the easiest to decipher, but major labor relation actions such as discrimination settlements, union arbitrations, and so on are reported here. In addition, if the company has major findings against it by the Environmental Protection Agency or any other federal or state regulatory agency, you should be able to locate those. Another good source of information is to Google the company and check out the news archives for stories on any legal problems the company has had.

The searches won't uncover the problem that hasn't been reported yet or isn't severe enough for civil or criminal action yet. A good SRI screening by a mutual fund or a screening services may pick up this type of problem that an individual investor might have a difficult time uncovering.

Red Flag

Using mutual funds to pre-screen your potential investment list carries a bit of risk. A good SRI mutual fund constantly re-screens its holdings and if a company doesn't make the grade, it is dropped from the holdings. You may not know the company is dropped or why.

One answer to the research problem is to let mutual funds do it for you. Either through funds that you own or by researching funds, you can often discover what companies SRI funds own. This gives you a pre-screened list to start your personal research. The key is understanding what screens the fund applies and how those screens fit with your values.

Do Your Own Stock Screening

For many SRI investors, the point of owning individual stocks is so they can do the screening and selecting themselves. They feel more comfortable about investing when they have done the legwork to their standards. The same is true of the SRI standards. As we have previously noted, socially responsible screens come in a variety of levels of thoroughness.

A do-it-yourself investor likely has specific ideas about what the company should look like from an investment perspective and what SRI standards it should meet. These investors are not usually eager to turn over either type of research to another party. Fortunately, many tools available to individual investors make sophisticated research possible for little or no money. SRI research lacks the depth of tools that traditional investing offers, but resources are available for individuals to help them with that aspect of socially responsible investing.

You Can Set Your Own Financial Criteria

The Internet has opened a huge amount of information to investors willing to do their own research. The tools to process the volumes of information are surprisingly robust considering many are free or available at modest costs. Stock screens, profiles, commentaries, and more are all available online and, for the most part, free.

Many major information sites provide a variety of stock selection and qualification tools. Some sites provide a basic level of service and offer a higher level of offerings for viewers who choose to subscribe to a premium service. For example, MorningStar.com, one premiere websites on the market for mutual funds and stocks offers pages of free information and commentaries. The information includes investing lessons as well as market news and educational articles on a variety of investing and personal finance topics. Investors are becoming more sophisticated in their knowledge of investing and the available tools.

The better online brokers usually offer tools for portfolio management and stock/fund selection. Most tools are straight up returning unbiased recommendations. However, investors should be alert to the possibility that some online calculators may be stacked in favor of encouraging customers to buy more stock, mutual funds, or other securities.

> ### Success Stories
>
> Morningstar.com is an excellent place to start for mutual funds, but it also has great tools for stock investors, too.

Stock and Mutual Fund Screens Do Heavy Lifting

Financial screens help investors sort through the thousands of stocks or mutual funds to narrow down the field for consideration. These screens consider financial data and ratios only, so are only suitable for the investing side of the decision. But they do a good job at cutting through mountains of financial data to help investors in the initial selection process. The screens limit the field to a smaller number for the investor to pursue further.

Investors can use the pre-set screens offered by some sites or construct their own using easy to understand menus. These screens examine fundamental financial information and ratios. Investors can sort though thousands of stocks or funds in seconds to find the targets that fit the parameters they enter into the screen. Some screens offer a basic service at no charge and a premium version for a small subscription fee. The premium screens can be quite sophisticated in the parameters you can look for in a company. Some very high-end tools perform complicated analysis on stocks or groups of stocks, but most investors don't need this level of sophistication.

Building with SRI Values

The financial side of investor's investigations is just part of the process for socially responsible investors. Investors must also screen the companies based on their values and the issues that are important. When an individual acts alone, it may be helpful to find a sympathetic listener who lets you talk out your SRI positions. The act of explaining your values to another person is a good way to be focused on which social, ecological, and governance issues are important. Articulating your goals, writing them down are good ways to set them firmly in your mind and prepare for doing your due diligence on the values portion of the investment.

Responsible Tip

You can set up Google to alert you anytime a company you are following makes the news. This is a handy device for keeping an eye on your investments. Make sure you set the alert to the period you want the search (daily is probably too often).

As noted above, reading a company's annual report, 10-Q form, and other required filings will alert you to major civil or criminal infractions. Likewise, a review of news media articles using an online search engine such as Google will help investors spot any red flags such as boycotts, labor disruptions, or other incidents that land the company in the news.

A growing number of companies are providing SRI type reports along with the usual and required financial disclosures. Most reports are not required by any regulatory body, however they are reviewed for misleading or fraudulent statements that might lead a person to buy the stock under false pretenses. These reports, despite the regulatory review, are not likely to put the company in a bad light, even if that's where they deserve to be. They can be a starting place for further investigation. Caution should be used is accepting reports of ecological or socially responsible activities as absolute truths. Some companies spend more money promoting their good deeds than they spend of the actual deeds themselves. This tells you where their motives are.

An example of research available to individual investors is the website www.cookingyournestegg.org. The website focuses on global warming and looks at the top 24 mutual funds, but individual stock investors can use its results to find information about companies they may be considering. Many of the funds are large cap, growth funds, so it is skewed that direction, but the information is helpful if those are the companies you are considering.

Although the website was designed to help people see the global warming exposure they may have through the mutual funds they own, individual stock investors can use the tool also. The calculator asked you to select the funds you want to review and when you submit your list, it shows you the companies in each fund with financial risks to global warming issues. You can click on the company name and get specific information about why the website believes this is the case. The reports also list companies that have taken or are taking steps to improve energy efficiency, reduce greenhouse gases, and other measures to reduce financial liabilities for global warming issues. You get a look at both negative and positive reports on global warming issues.

Unless you are looking at small cap stocks, there's a good chance the companies you are considering are in one of the mutual funds—especially since several are broad-based stock index funds.

> **Success Stories**
>
> You can see the affect of global warming in your own life by using one of the carbon calculators available on the Internet. These calculate your carbon footprint based on a series of questions. A good one can be found at: www.climatecrisis.net/takeaction/carboncalculator.

Where Do You Draw the Line?

A problem facing the whole SRI investing community is the lack of a universal definition for the many terms that make up the process. The current term that is on everyone's lips is sustainability. How sustainability is defined depends on who you are talking to and about what. We'll get into a more detailed discussion of sustainability in Chapter 21, but for now, the debate raises an issue for individual investors. How do you decide which companies are in and which are out based on the social and environmental screens you assign from your values? We all accept that no companies are perfect, so at what point do individual stock investors say, "This is as far as I will go. Anything beyond this point is grounds for excluding the company."

Even if it is not articulated in that manner, mutual fund managers and other professional investors reach the same decision. Given that social, environmental, and governance information may not be as hard and clear as financial ratios, these decisions are always subjective to some degree. If you are able to articulate the most important three values and make them your absolutes, it is easier to address the lesser concerns on a case-by-case basis. For example, you could say my most important three values are:

- No sin investments (alcohol, tobacco, gambling, pornography, and so on)

- No war-related profiting

- No major polluting processes

If a company scored perfect on all three of these, could you overlook a settled discrimination suit if it appeared the company had ended the illegal practices? Investors must be prepared to make these types of decisions and compromises. Nothing is magic about holding fast to three primary values, however, you should consider some small number as primary values and others as secondary. This allows you to stand fast on your primary values and consider the secondary values as somewhat negotiable.

Responsible Tip

Perfect is the enemy of good—this saying is an example of how wanting an investment with no flaws will stand in the way of moving forward with a SRI investment plan.

Shareholder Advocacy as an Individual

Individual investors have the same rights as mutual funds and institutional investors to bring shareholder resolutions and other advocacy actions to a corporation. It will be more difficult because the process can be cumbersome and time consuming, but a determined individual can prevail.

Corporations have the right to request shareholder resolutions be denied, but they must meet certain conditions before the Securities and Exchange Commission will rule in the company's favor. If shareholders understand the rules and craft their resolutions so the SEC can find no fault under its regulations, there is a good chance it will go to a proxy vote. Shareholders who bring resolutions to corporations also have the option of entering a dialogue with the company to resolve the issue before it comes for a vote.

Corporations pay more attention to blocks of votes, but individual shareholders still must be reckoned with when it comes to shareholder resolutions. It takes a determined individual to follow a shareholder resolution issue through the process, but if you follow the regulations, it can be done.

If you have a legitimate issue and one that might be opposed by management, be prepared for a campaign of letters and phone calls suggesting you are not acting in the best interests of the company, all designed to make you back off your action. The company can't go very far with this campaign without running into securities laws, but some will push the limits. The other popular tactic is the "we can't do that because…, but we're already doing this and it's just as good or better."

If the company want to settle and avoid a shareholder resolution, make sure what they proposed actually accomplishes what you want or substantially most of it. Also, make sure there is a public statement that the company is going to do X or no longer going to do Y. Any agreement should be in writing and made public. This is insurance that the company will follow through with anything it commits to do behind closed doors.

Responsible Tip

Don't believe that one person is powerless to make changes. A passionate investor with a just cause has a good chance to make a difference.

Investing in SRI Bonds

Investors should keep some assets in bonds to counter the volatility of stocks—that is an important rule of investing. Stocks, bonds, and cash are considered the three primary asset classes that make up portfolios. Stocks, which can be individual stocks or stock mutual funds, offer the best chance for rapid growth and usually come with the highest risk. Bonds and bond mutual funds counter the volatility of stocks by moving in the opposite direction of the stock market—when stocks are down, bonds usually rise, and so on. But the potential return from bonds, which is current income, is lower than stocks, but also less risky. Cash is usually the safest investment and offers the lowest return.

Most information you can find about socially responsible investing discusses stocks and stock mutual funds. So far, that has been true in this book, also. There is a good reason for that. The selection of SRI bond funds is limited compared to stock funds. Buying individual SRI bonds (meaning bonds from companies judged socially responsible) is not easy or inexpensive, although many investors own individual corporate bonds. Corporate bonds do not offer any tax advantages like municipal or U.S. Treasury bonds offer.

Buying Individual SRI Bonds

Individuals can buy corporate bonds through stockbrokers that carry bonds (not all do). The process is not the same a buying stock and you may have a difficult time because SRI investors want to buy bonds from specific companies. The typical bond investor will ask a stockbroker to find a bond with certain characteristics, such as maturity, rating, coupon rate, and so on. The stockbroker will try to find such a bond in the inventory the company owns and fill the order. If the stockbroker's firm does not have a bond to fill the order, it will buy one from another broker and fill the order that way. An SRI investor will ask for a bond from a specific company because of its SRI rating. The stockbroker will

Responsible Tip

Unless you have a good stockbroker who is familiar with SRI investing, finding individual SRI bonds may be challenging. See Chapter 17 on working with a financial professional for tips on finding an adviser to help you secure individual bonds.

have to find another broker that holds that bond and buy it for resale to the investor. All of these transactions begin to build substantial sales charges and fees to the investor.

The Case For and Against Individual Bonds

Investing in individual corporate bonds has some advantages from the investment side of the process. Corporate bonds tend to pay the highest coupons or interest rates of all bonds. They can provide a steady stream on income for years, which can be especially useful to people in retirement. At maturity, you get your original investment back. For example, a 10-year, 7 percent corporate bond with a face value of $1,000 will pay an investor $70 per year for 10 years and then return the $1,000 face value.

Investors can hold bonds until maturity or they can trade them before maturity. Corporate bonds can be bought at issue or in the secondary market through a stockbroker. The steady income and return of principal are factors that help retired people manage their assets. Rating companies help investors judge the creditworthiness of various corporate bond issues. The higher the rating, the lower the interest rate.

Owning individual bonds for any period can be risky. If interest rates rise substantially, you are locked into a lower paying security. The only way to get out of the lower paying bond is to sell it at a discount (for less than face value). Corporate bonds are subject to being called, which means if interest rates fall, the company could issue new bonds at a lower rate and buy the existing bonds off the market. You would get the principal back, but lose a source of higher interest rate.

Buying and selling individual corporate bonds can be expensive in fees and charges. Most financial advisers suggest you not consider individual bonds unless you are able to commit at least $25,000 and up to $100,000.

Using SRI Bond Funds

The importance of bonds in individual portfolios, but maybe more important in the holdings of institutional investors has created the need for SRI bond funds. Most traditional bonds are held in bond funds and by institutional investors. For most SRI investors, bond funds make the same sense as stock funds do. They combine all the positive elements of stock mutual funds, which are even more important for bonds. The downside is there are not that many to consider.

Convenient and Easy to Set Up

Bond mutual funds, like their stock counterparts, are easy to get started. Most will set up an account for $1,000 to$2,500 initial deposit (although some require up to $5,000 minimum) and will do automatic withdrawals from your checking account. The funds allow you to make withdrawals, which is much more convenient than selling individual bonds on the open market. The funds vary from no-load to loaded share classes. See Chapter 13 for an explanation of sales expenses and share classes.

Professional Management

A key factor for most SRI investors is the professional management of SRI bond funds. The bond market is a sophisticated and complicated network to navigate. It takes a specialized knowledge that professional managers can bring to funds. Few individual investors have the time or expertise to track the market. Socially responsible investing bond funds often are not pure stock funds. They may include U.S. Treasury issues, mortgage pass throughs, municipals, and other debt instruments. You'll want to check the prospectus thoroughly to see how much of the fund is actually invested in SRI corporate debt and how much is invested in the same debt instruments as traditional bond funds. If you want to be as pure of SRI investor as possible, you want to check out the composition of the bond funds carefully before investing.

Responsible Tip

Socially responsible investing bond funds are filling a need of investors to have that asset class available to round out portfolios built with SRI stocks and stock mutual funds. As socially responsible investing grows, more and different funds will become available.

May Be Safer Foreign Investment

Several SRI bond funds focus on foreign bonds. These funds represent the safest way to invest in foreign debt. Foreign SRI bond funds are on the rise and more will be available in the U.S. market as interest in socially responsible investing continues to grow.

Specific risks to investing in foreign debt make using bond funds a good idea. Foreign currency exchange rates, political and economic unrest, different social values, and so on make investing in foreign bonds more challenging than U.S. debt instruments. A good fund manager and research team will earn their expenses in a foreign bond fund by doing the difficult research and making wise buy and sell decisions.

The Least You Need to Know

- Individual SRI stocks offer the potential for significant returns.
- Investors can do their own research on individual SRI stocks.
- SRI bonds provide balance to your portfolio.
- Investing in SRI bond funds is the choice of most investors.

Part

How to Do SRI

How does one get started in socially responsible investing? What are the resources? You can find these answers as well as information on working with a financial professional versed in SRI. Fortunately, there are many resources to help you get started as well as financial professionals versed in SRI. You should also note what critics have to say about SRI.

Chapter 18

Investor Tools

In This Chapter

- ◆ Where to find information on SRI mutual funds
- ◆ Where to find information on individual stocks
- ◆ Where to find shareholder advocacy information
- ◆ Where to find community development information

Information on socially responsible mutual funds is readily available thanks to securities laws that require full disclosure of all pertinent information and the Internet as a means to distribute the information. The problem most investors have is not that they lack information, but that it is hard to make any sense of it.

Investors can get a lot of information from a mutual fund's website, but if it is not put in some context, it is difficult to understand the importance of what you read. Independent websites that track financial products such as stocks and mutual funds can provide a great deal of additional information that is not found on the company website. Many sites also include an analysis of the fund and what is good and/or bad about it.

The same information and analysis is available for individual stocks. SRI investors are obviously interested in more than just a financial return, so you can also find resources on the Web to help you track shareholder resolutions and other advocacy efforts.

Information Sources—Mutual Funds

Mutual funds are the most popular investment product in use today. Thanks in large part to employer-sponsored retirement programs such as 401(k) plans, mutual funds are owned by more households than any other single investment. We explored many of the reasons why investors choose mutual funds in Chapter 13: low initial investment, ease of making additional deposits, professional management, and liquidity. All of these attributes work for SRI mutual funds too as we have seen.

The independent websites that cover investment products include most of the SRI mutual funds in their reports. All but the smallest and newest funds generally turn up in any search on the major financial sites. While large traditional mutual funds are measured in the billions of dollars in assets under management, only a few SRI funds have earned a large label.

Responsible Tip

If you do not have access to the Internet at home, most public libraries offer free access and people to help you get started.

As you examine SRI mutual funds, you will notice that their relative small size is a negative when it comes to expenses. You will also notice that many of them have a relative short history when compared to many traditional mutual funds. This also can be a negative when evaluating a fund for investment.

SRI Fund Websites

Socially responsible investing mutual fund websites are usually good sources of information on the fund. The SEC mandates certain information and disclosures must accompany any sales or marketing information. Most funds will let you download a prospectus or trigger a mailing of one to you. Technically, you can't buy a mutual fund without a *prospectus*, however, that rule is self-enforced. Some of the fund sites provide historic price information, but many don't.

You will find an uneven quality about the websites and the help you'll receive over the phone, depending on the fund and how it is sold. Funds sold directly by the investment company have customer service people to answer your questions, while funds sold by stockbrokers rely on independent agents to sell their fund. In addition to information on the

def•i•ni•tion

A **prospectus** is a legal document that must accompany any application or sales material for a mutual fund. It spells out the terms and conditions of the fund, the risks, the fees, and identifies the principal money managers.

funds offered by the investment company (or fund, for smaller operations), you'll find news on the fund's activity in shareholder advocacy.

The fund should detail its shareholder proxy voting guidelines, which describe the framework within which it makes its decisions on shareholder resolutions. Although not all do it, an informative touch is to list actual votes on shareholder resolutions. If the fund doesn't list its votes on the website, there are places you can go on the Internet to find that information. If you own a SRI mutual fund and it is voting on shareholder resolutions, you should know what it is voting for or against at the stockholders meetings it attends on your behalf.

Many funds are also involved in community development and that activity is shared on the website. If the investment company offers a bond fund and/or money market fund, there's a good chance that some small percentage of those assets are directed into community development projects. Frequently, the fund will use those assets to invest in community development banks or other such organizations that make capital available in low-income areas. Success stories of how community investing in a difficult area improved the lives of residents are a standard feature for sites with community investing. Don't expect this on all sites. Some religious sites have their own projects that are the beneficiaries of their funding.

The investment companies that have several funds often include an educational section on investing. This information is to help investors new to the concept grasp the basics in a hurry. But don't expect a complete, unbiased presentation. For example, articles on saving for college may omit 529 college savings plans because they generally don't include SRI funds in the investment choices, although these plans are often the best choice for parents.

Responsible Tip

Many smaller SRI funds use a professional fund management company to run the fund and do the buying and selling of stock for them within the guidelines established by the fund's founders. This makes sense, especially where a nonprofit group wants to have a mutual fund, but lacks the financial expertise to start and maintain one.

Mostly Free Research on Mutual Funds

Fortunately, investors are not limited to what investment companies want us to know about their mutual funds. Thanks to the Internet and a large number of independent websites, we have access to volumes of information on traditional and SRI mutual funds. You can also access sites that are specific to SRI mutual funds. Some of the best general sites on mutual funds are:

- **Morningstar.com** —Morningstar is the premiere source of information on mutual funds on the Internet. They have owned the top position for many years and no other site comes close to their depth and breadth of coverage of the mutual fund industry. You can learn a tremendous amount about almost any mutual fund using their free service. Morningstar has a proprietary system of categorizing mutual funds based on the stocks they actually own rather than on what the fund says it is. In some cases, Morningstar's category is different from how the fund sees itself. You also get a short commentary on the fund's performance and a ranking by stars of the fund's performance relative to its risk (if Morningstar believes investors are not seeing an adequate return for the amount of risk in the fund, it will be ranked lower). The site also includes information on the past five year's performance and compares it to the fund's category and an appropriate market index. For the serious investor, you can upgrade to their premium membership, which costs $15.95 per month. The premium membership buys you more robust analytical tools and analyst's reports that examine the fund in depth. These tools are unbiased and can be very critical when warranted.

- **Reuters.com** —Reuters is a well-respected in international news gathering for many years. Their site also has an outstanding research section on investments. Lipper Research, a leader in financial information and research services, provides the research. Although the site does not provide the depth of information that Morningstar does, it is easy to access and comprehensive enough to give you an idea of the fund's strengths and weaknesses. You can also buy more in-depth reports on individual funds from Lipper for very modest amounts.

♦ **Investopedia.com** —This is an education site as opposed to a site detailing individual mutual funds. It offers a number to tutorials, including one on mutual funds. If you are new to investing in mutual funds, this is a good place to start. The site walks you through the basics in short, easy to understand lessons. You won't be an expert, however the tutorial will answer many basic questions about mutual funds, and how they work.

Red Flag

Not all information you find on the Internet is trustworthy. Stick with well-known companies for unbiased information. Companies you never heard of may be fronts for some financial organization that wants to sell you some product. Their research and information will usually steer you toward whatever they are selling.

Mutual Fund Key Data

It would be easy if there were only one or two items to compare that would tell you this SRI mutual fund is better than that fund. Unfortunately, it is more complicated than that, but not much. You can use a few pieces of data as a way to eliminate some funds from consideration in the initial pass. As we have noted earlier, one problem facing SRI investors is the lack of SRI funds to consider. This means you don't need a lot of research, but it also means your choices are limited and that adds risk to your investments.

In some cases, only a few funds in a particular segment are available to investors. But segments exist, such as large-cap SRI funds, that provide quite a few choices for investors. In these cases, what should SRI investors consider the key data points?

Expenses Trump Everything

The expenses you pay to own a mutual fund are a drag on any return the fund generates. The larger the expenses, the harder it is for a fund to earn a decent return. In the traditional mutual fund world, a body of evidence suggests that expenses are one of the most important determinants of a fund's success. Mutual funds that charge a sales fee or load and have a high expense ratio are likely to be laggards when you look a performance over a long period. We discussed the nature of loads and expense ratios in Chapter 13.

Responsible Tip

Expenses can be deadly to your mutual fund returns. If you don't look at any other numbers when comparing funds, look at the sales loads and expense ratios. The fund with the lowest fees and expenses will be the one to choose almost every time.

You may hear many arguments to the contrary, but the truth is no research has shown high fees have ever been a factor in a fund's success. Funds with high loads and expense ratios often argue that the fees are necessary to pay the talented fund managers. Unfortunately, even talented fund managers can't overcome the power and truth of simple mathematics. High expense ratios come out of your assets in a mutual fund whether the fund is doing well or doing poorly. If the fund is not doing well, high fees just make it worse. If the fund is doing well, high fees take the top off the profits.

The problem for most SRI funds is that, by their nature, they are actively managed, which means the fund manager must keep a close watch on all the holdings to make sure they are performing well financially and that they stay within the social framework the fund has established as acceptable. This extra research and monitoring is costly and the fund must pay for those expenses in higher than average expense ratios. The problem is compounded by the fact that many SRI funds are relatively small in asset size.

This provides fewer assets to absorb the funds fixed and variable expenses. This also contributes to driving up the expense ratios of SRI funds. Comparing expense ratios to traditional mutual funds yields disappointing results. In most cases, SRI funds have higher expense ratios than many other funds in its category. If you are committed to investing in SRI funds, you have to overlook this discrepancy and compare the SRI to other SRI funds. Some SRI indexes you can use, however, you may learn as much or more by comparing a target fund with other funds in its category.

Responsible Tip

Compare SRI funds to other SRI funds for the best results if you are committed to this type of investing. Most SRI funds do not compare well to the best of traditional mutual funds in the expense area, although they beat some of the traditional funds that are way overpriced.

Five and Ten-Year Performance Data

If you look at financial data on the Web or in marketing pieces, you'll soon notice a disclaimer that warns you: "Past performance is no guarantee of future results." This is a standard issue, regulatory warning that providers of financial products are required to include on all of their material. Most people probably skim right over it because the warning is everywhere. Despite its being ubiquitous, the phrase is an absolute truth. So why pay any attention to past performance? It is helpful to see how a fund has performed in different market and economic conditions. Some fund managers have a hot hand in certain markets, but their investing style is lost in a different market. If an SRI fund has been around for five or more years, the resources listed above will show you how it has done against its category and a market index. You want a fund that can adapt to changes in the forces that move the market.

Fund Manager

Some people go to the racetrack and bet on the jockeys. They know certain jockeys manage to ride winning horses more often than losing horses. They need a fast horse to win, but the race is also won on the skill of the jockey. The same can be said for mutual funds. Fund managers who have done well develop a reputation with investors. If that manager moves to a new fund, it is not unusual to see money follow her. With the exception of index funds, which need no stock picking, SRI mutual funds depend on the skill of a fund manager to buy and sell stocks and bonds at the appropriate time for the best return to the fund.

> ### Success Stories
>
> Fund mangers or portfolio managers as they are sometimes called, do the stock picking and make the buy and sell decisions for most mutual funds. If successful, they earn the fund and themselves a lot of money.

Industry critics argue the fund manager's role is overstated, and with a very few exceptions, they do more harm than good. Investors, these critics say, would be better off investing in extremely low-cost index funds and avoiding stock-picking fund managers who are hot one day and cold the next with their selections.

Information Sources—Individual Stocks

If you want to do some or all of your socially responsible investing the hard way by picking individual stocks yourself, the Internet has a number of excellent resources to help you. The difference between using mutual funds and individual stocks is that stocks are not in the same regulatory category as mutual funds. They typically don't report past price information and don't sell directly to the public in the same manner as many mutual funds. You will want to use the same independent sources noted in the previous section for information on individual stocks.

In choosing a stock, you are really choosing a company, of course and that can entail a fundamental analysis of its financial reports. Learning to analyze companies and identify good investment candidates takes some education and experience. SRI investors must also do the research to discover if the company fits their social screens. Experienced stock investors have sources of information they turn to when considering a stock. Most of the information they need is available free or at a reasonable cost.

If you are an inexperienced investor or don't feel like you have the time to devote to researching individual stocks, you should consider working with a financial professional who is familiar with socially responsible investing. These financial professionals have access to even more research than is available on the Internet and can craft an investment program that will meet your SRI and investment needs. We discuss the benefits of working with a financial professional in Chapter 19.

Responsible Tip

Doing analysis of companies by looking at their financial ratios is called fundamental analysis. Most investors favor this method because they get to know the company and what it does. This tells the investors about the company's strengths and weaknesses. This information helps spot dangers or opportunities before they happen.

Information on individual stocks is easy to find on the Internet. Traditional stock information sites can help gather information of companies and monitor stock performance. Some of the better ones are:

- **CNN Money.com** (www.money.cnn.com) is the financial/ business portion of the CNN website. It is a great source for market news and readable explanations on what is happening in the stock market and why. You can also get financial profiles of individual stocks by entering the ticker symbol or company name.

- **MSN Money** (www.moneycentral.msn.com) offers detailed information on company performance and stock ratios. One of the interesting pieces is a breakdown of ownership. Many investors don't realize how much influence institutional investors and mutual funds have on stocks prices and the stock market. Institutional investors and mutual funds own the majority of stock of almost all large cap companies with solid records. A look at IBM as this book was being written showed that institutional investors owned 65.40 percent of the shares and mutual funds owned 26.86 percent of the shares. That leaves less than 8 percent of the stock of IBM in the hands of individuals and other investors.

- **MarketWatch.com** (www.marketwatch.com) is another content-rich site for people interested in individual stocks. It features more columnists than many other sites, so you get more opinion and commentary. You'll find real recommendations on stocks, although none specifically for SRI stocks. A premium membership buys you even more analysis and insight. The site also features quotes and financial information on stocks.

Finding Information on Shareholder Advocacy

For many SRI investors, the whole point of socially responsible investing is to move companies to change and improve policies on the environment, corporate governance, and other SRI issues. The primary vehicle for this is shareholder advocacy and that is often an important function of SRI mutual funds.

But individual investors sometimes participate in the action also. Either way, several subscription websites help interested SRI investors stay current on the status of various shareholder initiatives. These sites report on the status of the resolutions and if a vote was taken, the results. You can find a copy of the resolution and who was the sponsor. This information is helpful in formulating new resolutions and in monitoring the trends in new issues. SRI investors can see which resolutions were withdrawn and why (usually because the company has agreed to some changes that satisfied the resolution sponsors). Since it is the mutual funds, pension funds, and other institutional investors that file most of the shareholder resolutions, much of the material is geared toward that audience.

> **Success Stories**
>
> Information on recent shareholder resolutions indicates that initiatives on global warming and other climate problems are becoming a major target of shareholder activism.

The most detailed information is contained in subscription-only database websites. If you own shares of stock in a company, you will get a packet of any proposed shareholder resolutions before the annual meeting. This packet will contain any proxy resolutions and instructions on how to vote your proxy. Some individuals interested in shareholder resolutions buy several shares of stock just to gain access to the proxy information. Rules set the minimum you must own to file a proxy resolution. We discussed those rules and more about shareholder resolutions in Chapter 11.

♦ **The Interfaith Center on Corporate Responsibility** (www.iccr. org) maintains a database on shareholder resolutions by year. The most current information is only available to subscribers to the Ethvest Database, but their website has complete information on resolutions from two years back in addition to listings for more current resolutions.

♦ **Co-op America** (www.coopamerica.org) also tracks certain shareholder resolutions, although their main focus is environmental issues.

♦ **SocialFunds.com** (www.socialfunds.com) is a news site that reports on a broad range of socially responsible investing news. One areas they cover is shareholder resolutions. News stories cover filings, resolutions, and votes.

Community Investing

Community investing is an important expression of socially responsible investing for many investors because it is much more personal than buying shares of a mutual fund or a company. As we have discussed in Chapter 8, banks and credit unions in areas under-served by traditional financial institutions help provide needed financial services. These community development financial institutions (CDFI) provide the access to capital that encourages redevelopment of urban neighborhoods though affordable housing and assistance for community centers. Investors can participate in community development financing by investing in banks or credit unions (by opening deposit accounts) or a loan fund. Several sites on the Internet can help you find a community development program near you or one that will fit your needs.

 Responsible Tip

Becoming involved in community development investing is as easy as opening a banking account or making a small loan to a loan fund. Almost every major community has some form of community development effort, either through a community financial institution or with a loan fund.

♦ **The Community Investing Center's** database (www.communityinvestingcenterdb.org) is a comprehensive collection of community development organizations with a simple and advance search function. The simple search function lets you look by organization name or by location or by social sector impact, which means housing, loans, microfinance, and so on. The advanced search function allows investors to get very specific beyond location and focus on investment vehicle (bank deposit, bonds, and so on), length of commitment, the social impact, special interest area (such as daycare facilities, clinics, elder-care, and so on), and the size and liquidity of the financial institution. This may be much more detailed than most investors will need, but the database gives you access to the type of information that will lead you to a community development investment opportunity that fits your needs.

◆ **SocialFunds.com** (www.socialfunds.com) has a search function under its community investing center that allows investors to choose the type of community investing they are interested in and the location. The search engine returns all the community development programs serving the selections. The search function includes international opportunities as well as domestic ones. The site also offers a community investment directory and a free guide to community investment you can download.

◆ **The National Federation of Community Development Credit Unions** (www.natfed.org) is a trade group of credit unions that served low-income urban and rural areas. They provide financial services where traditional financial institutions have abandoned. The website offers a description of what credit unions do and a listing of its national membership.

◆ **The Community Development Bankers Association** (www. communitydevelopmentbanks.org) is a trade group of banks operating in low-income areas. The site offers a list of its member banks.

The Least You Need to Know

◆ Information on SRI mutual funds is available from several free websites.

◆ Expenses, the fund manager, and historic performance numbers will help you choose a fund.

◆ Choosing individual stocks is complicated, but you can find information on the Internet to help.

◆ Resources on the Web will help direct you to community investment opportunities.

Chapter

Using an SRI Financial Advisor

In This Chapter:

- ◆ The role of financial advisors
- ◆ Identifying your requirements for a financial advisor
- ◆ Questions to ask a financial advisor
- ◆ Financial advisors and SRI research

Making sense of investment opportunities can seem like a full time job to many people. What is the best place for your retirement funds? What about a college fund? Saving for a new house? Stocks, bonds, mutual funds, pork bellies? It can all get pretty confusing. When you say, 'I want a comprehensive investment plan and I want it to be socially responsible,' things can really get complicated. Not everyone wants to manage their investments by themselves. You may not feel like you have the time, energy, or expertise to make consistent investing decisions. Perhaps you have accumulated a large sum in your retirement account and are now concerned about making a mistake that might jeopardize your nest-egg. The answer to your anxiety may be a qualified financial advisor.

Several varieties of financial advisors provide different levels of service under different compensation scenarios. Some are quite good at what they do and your money spent for their help will be a good investment in your financial security and peace of mind. Also some financial professionals are less than professional and their advice usually leads to your purchasing high-commission products you don't need. Finding a financial professional that you can trust is not difficult if you stick with those certified by legitimate authorizing bodies. Finding a financial professional with experience in socially responsible investing may be just a bit more difficult.

What Financial Advisors Do

The definition of financial advisors is somewhat blurry because some designations require licensing and certification, while others require nothing. Anyone can call themselves a financial planner as long as they are not trading or recommending trading registered securities (stocks, bonds, mutual funds, and so on). On the other hand, a person cannot buy or sell registered securities without being a licensed stockbroker working for a broker/dealer.

Responsible Tip

Finding the right financial advisor is also about establishing a relationship of trust. They can't do their best work if you are not forthcoming about your financial situation. You need to feel your personal information is safe and that the financial advisor is acting in your best interest.

All kinds of levels of licensing and certifications sit in between these two extremes. As the industry has sought to blur the lines between different practitioners, consumers have become confused. This is unfortunate because financial products have become more numerous and abundant. Financial professionals can help investors sort through the marketing noise and make wise decisions about their money. The field of financial advice has grown along with expanded products and now a host of professionals offers their services. Investors must first decide on which type of financial professional they want to work with and then find one that is familiar with socially responsible investing—not always an easy combination.

Types of Financial Advisors/Professionals

Thanks to changes in the financial services industry, once familiar professional titles are morphing into a variety of different descriptions. A stockbroker may now be called a registered investment advisor, a financial planner, investment consultant, or others. Regardless of what is on the business card, if the person buys and sells stock, they must be a stockbroker licensed by the SEC. We'll summarize and then evaluate three major financial professional functions, each of which have some advantages and disadvantages.

> **Responsible Tip**
>
> What one investor wants (needs) from a financial advisor will be different from what another investor may find helpful. Matching your needs with the skills of a financial advisor is important in achieving your investment and SRI goals.

- **Stockbroker**—A stockbroker is licensed by the SEC after passing a series of exams and works for a broker/dealer. Stockbrokers buy and sell registered securities such as stocks, bonds, and mutual funds. They are usually paid a commission—either a flat fee or a fee per share traded. Stockbrokers are the only financial professionals that can trade securities. Other financial professionals can also be stockbrokers and collect commissions and fees on the sale of securities.

- **Financial planner**—You do not need a license to be a financial planner, although several professional designations require extensive course work. Certified Financial Planner is the most respected of the designations. Some financial planners are compensated strictly by fee for their work, while others may charge a fee and commission on products sold. These financial planners must also be licensed stockbrokers.

- **Money manager**—A money manager is a financial professional you turn your money over to along with the authority to invest it as they see fit. Money managers have discretionary authority over your money, meaning they can buy or sell when they feel the need to do so. Money managers can also be stockbrokers, although they typically charge a percentage of assets under management as their fee.

Red Flag

> The investment business is plagued by scams, as you might expect. Any promises of super high returns with little or no risk should be viewed with a very skeptical eye. Phone calls or e-mails from people you don't know with special deals just for you are not special and they are not for you. Some may even be illegal. Stick with legitimate and realistic investment plans.

What Do Stockbrokers Do?

Before the securities industry began a deregulation program in the late 1970s and '80s, a stockbroker was a person who discussed investment options with clients, recommended stocks, executed trades, and collected fat commissions. All brokerage firms were "full service," meaning they offered their clients advice and buy or sell recommendations. Commissions were fixed and, by today's standards, were very high. Thanks to deregulation, commissions were no longer fixed and the discount brokerage business exploded. Concurrent with these changes in the stockbrokerage industry, other financial providers began to enter new markets. Banks and life insurance companies, in particular, expanded their reach into investment products to complement their existing product base. Life insurance agents began selling mutual funds, while bank employees offered financial advice and products.

In this new deregulated environment, some brokerage houses reduced their commissions and trimmed the services offered in response to the discount brokers. Other firms began offering additional services as a way to generate more commissions and fee income. Financial planning was a natural way for some firms to move in offering additional value to clients. As stockbrokers became investment representatives or some other title that signified responsibilities beyond entering buy and sell orders the compensation structure changed.

A popular way for stockbrokers to distinguish themselves from other commission-charging brokers was to offer wrap accounts to their clients who had substantial assets (usually $50,000 or more) invested through the firm. A wrap account combined commissions and a management fee into one fee, which was a percentage of the assets under management. Firms often have a sliding scale for investors with larger amounts invested paying a smaller percentage. As with any investment product, customers should carefully consider whether wrap accounts make sense for them. You pay a fee, usually quarterly that can be a drain on profits from your investments. If you seldom buy or sell stocks, you are probably better off with a regular account that does not charge an ongoing fee, but does charge a commission when you do buy or sell stocks.

Responsible Tip

Stockbrokers have come a long way since deregulation. They can't survive on taking orders over the phone anymore, so the good ones have grown professionally to add new products and services that improve their value to customers. One common value-added enhancement is a good knowledge of socially responsible investing.

What Do Financial Planners Do?

In another corner of the financial services industry, the financial planning industry was growing at a very rapid rate. It was not too hard to see why. The role of a financial planner is to step back and look at your total financial picture, not just your investments. A good financial planner will examine every financial aspect of your life, including insurance, taxes, whether you have an up-to-date will, retirement planning and more. The planner will listen to where you want to go with your finances (early retirement, elderly parents in need of assistance, child with disabilities, and so on) and help you design a savings and investment plan to get there. The plan will also point out areas of your financial life that need tidying up. The plan will have actionable steps in sequence of importance and in a logical order (take care of the real important stuff first—for example, make sure you have adequate insurance coverage).

As the financial planning industry was developing, it split into two camps. The two groups were split on the issue of compensation. One group charged a small fee to do a plan and then earned commissions on the products recommended in plan. They were licensed stockbrokers and life insurance agents, thus able to earn commissions on any products the client bought through them. The other group became fee-only financial planners. They did not sell any products recommended in their plans, but their fees were considerably higher.

Which is the best choice? Both have good arguments. The fee, plus commission planners say that if they do not follow through by offering the products the client needs to complete the plan, many clients never execute the plan. They see no conflict because selling the client products for their own good. A good financial plan is not very useful if it isn't executed. But a financial plan that is really a glossy justification for selling you high-commission financial products is a rip-off. Whether you get a good financial plan or a marketing rip-off depends, in large part, on who does the work for you. If you know and trust the planner or get a good recommendation from someone you trust, you are probably on safe ground—besides you don't have to follow the buy recommendations if you don't want to.

Success Stories
Both types of financial planners can professionally offer you the services you need. The key is finding the right professional with the qualifications to develop a comprehensive financial and SRI plan that fits your needs.

The fee-only financial planners suggest that since there is no incentive to sell any products to earn a fee, their advice is untainted by personal gain. Fee-only planners can put the client in touch with other trusted financial professionals to execute those parts of the plan that require the purchase of registered securities or insurance products. All fee-only financial planners will use some type of computer-aided program to prepare your financial plan. But you should expect a professional and personalized plan that addresses your specific needs. This only happens if the planner gathers an extensive amount of information on you, your family, and your finances. Be prepared to fill out an extensive questionnaire and answer even more questions from the planner or someone on the planner's staff. Be very suspicious of a planner that spends a minimum amount of time gathering information and produces a plan with lots of color charts and graphics, but little in the way of specific information about your particular needs. How does it help you to know your household income is in the bottom half of the top 20 percent of all households in the United States?

A criticism of fee-only planners is their high expense. This can be the case, so you'll want to know upfront what the planner charges for the initial plan and updates. The cost of a plan varies depending on how complicated your financial life is and what you want. But a competent financial planner should tell you upfront what to expect and what the fee covers—the plan, a meeting with the planner to discuss the action points, follow-up telephone support, and so on.

Red Flag

Be very concerned if any financial professional, especially stockbrokers, pressure you to buy a proprietary mutual fund or other branded financial product. Many major brokerage houses sell their own versions of mutual funds, however these products often carry very high expenses and seldom perform as well as independent mutual funds. These house mutual funds may also be backend loaded with stiff penalties if you want to withdraw your funds before a number of years have passed.

Your safest bet is to go with a financial planner that carries the designation of Certified Financial Planner. These professionals have completed a rigorous set of college-level courses, passed a series of examinations, and exhibited professionalism in the field.

What Do Money Managers Do?

Money managers are investment professionals who are hired to handle client's money. Unlike most other financial professionals money managers usually have discretionary power over their client's money. This means they can buy and sell securities without the client's consent on each transaction. A discretionary account means the client has given the money manager written authority to do whatever she thinks is appropriate and necessary to manage the assets. Most money managers charge a fee that is a percentage of assets under management. The fee can range up to 1.25 percent annually. Most money manager's clients must have a minimum of $250,000 in assets, although some may take clients with less.

Discretionary accounts are for the truly disinterested in their money or those so incredibly busy that they can't possibly take the time to monitor or make investments. For most of us, they are not a good idea, especially if you are interested in SRI investing, which implies a more hands-on approach.

Red Flag

Discretionary accounts give great authority to a financial professional. Be sure this is what you want to do and that you completely trust the person before agreeing to such an account. Elderly investors should have a third party review the financial professional's work to make sure it is in the owner's best interest.

Five Things You Should Do Before Hiring a Financial Advisor

It is strange that some people wouldn't think of using an unlicensed plumber, but will let someone with no credentials other than a business card make changes that will alter that personal finances in a significant way for years to come. Thank goodness we require plumbers to master a level of proficiency before we let them loose on the public (you don't want me touching your plumbing).

Unfortunately, some financial advisors have very little in the way of qualifications for what they advertise. Even obtaining a license to sell stocks, bonds, and mutual funds or a license to sell life insurance doesn't qualify you to be a financial advisor. These licenses primarily ensure that you know the rules and regulations governing the sale of the products—that's not the same as being qualified to give good financial advice.

Before you hire or establish a relationship with a financial advisor, consider these five important steps:

◆ **Registration**—Any financial advisor, regardless of what title they are working under, that will be buying and selling securities must be registered with the SEC and the *National Association of Securities Dealers* (NASD). They also need some form of registration in the state where you live. Financial advisors that provide insurance products (life insurance, annuities, and so on) must also be registered in the state where you live. Insurance is regulated at the state level with the exception of those products such as variable annuities that include a mutual funds aspect. A life insurance agent must have a securities license (stockbroker) to sell variable annuities.

def•i•ni•tion

The **National Association of Securities Dealers** is a self-regulatory organization of securities dealers that licenses stockbrokers and others involved in the registered securities business. It administers tests that professionals must past to be licensed and disciplines members for infractions of securities regulations. The Securities and Exchange Commission oversees its work.

♦ **Qualifications**—Qualifications and licensing are not the same. As noted above, licensing means the financial advisor has passed a test or series of tests on the rules and regulations of the industry and has exhibited a basic understanding of the business. This does not mean a person is qualified to do a comprehensive financial plan. You will also want to probe about the advisor familiarity with socially responsible investing. The advisor should be able to speak knowledgably about SRI and current trends and events. Failure to do so may indicate lip service to SRI as a way to lure in new clients (see Number 4 for more questions). For financial planners, look for the Certified Financial Planner designation. Other meaningful professional designations are in the financial services industry. You can find a list of the more common ones in Appendix A. You will also want to know what additional areas of specialized study the advisor has completed and were any of those in SRI investing.

♦ **Compensation**—You want to be very clear from the beginning on compensation. Is the financial advisor compensated by fee only or commission only or a combination? Does the firm offer a wrap account and is that a possibility for your account? It is also important, and this should be in writing if you are getting a financial plan done, to understand what will be delivered and when. Are there updates included in the initial price or are those a separate cost? If commissions are involved, what is that structure? If you want the plan updated, what is that charge? Does the financial advisor use proprietary investment or life insurance products?

♦ **SRI Experience**—How many years has the financial advisor been working with clients interested in SRI investing? What research tools do you use in preparing investment recommendations? The financial advisor should cite one or more SRI reference databases or commercial products that interface with the databases. A lack of knowledge about these resources or a dismissive attitude may indicate the advisor is not a serious student of SRI investing and may not provide the best recommendations.

Responsible Tip

While it is good to get a referral from a friend or family member, unless you know for sure, don't assume they did any background checking on the professional they are recommending.

◆ **Disciplinary Actions**—You can check whether the financial advisor is facing or has been subject to any disciplinary actions by regulatory authorities. You can contact the SEC, NASD, and state regulatory agencies to see if the person has a record of problems working with clients. The contact information for the regulatory authorities is in Appendix A.

For resources on finding financial advisors and advisors experienced in socially responsible investing, go to Appendix A.

Why and When to Use a Financial Advisor

There are many good reasons to use a financial advisor, if not on a regular basis, at least periodically. While financial advice can be expensive, it can also be the best money you spend. Financial advisors/planners can bring clarity to a confusing array of products and services. Their business is knowing what is current and the importance of how certain personal financial decisions fit in changing economic conditions. When you connect with a financial professional who is also knowledgeable in socially responsible investing, they can add that dimension to your financial planning process. Because SRI investments do not have the depth that other products cover, you may need a knowledgeable professional to help you understand where they best fit in your financial plan.

If you have substantial assets to manage, an ongoing relationship with a financial professional that you trust will pay for itself many times over. The financial advisor/planner will help you stay current with the changing market conditions and adjust your financial plan as your life circumstances change (children are born, go to college, retirement, and so on). Even those with means that are more modest will benefit from periodic consultations with a financial professional to help you stay on track for your goals. Your retirement planning in particular is worth spending some money for a good plan. As SRI investments can be used appropriately in that plan, you should have your advisor help you incorporate them.

Access to SRI Research

A financial professional (one of the above) can help you plan a financial strategy and populate it with socially responsible investment products, whether they are mutual funds or individual stocks. Mutual funds would seem to be the easiest. But with new funds added on a regular basis and older funds changing management and focus, it is important to have a professional who is on top of the changes looking after your portfolio.

Financial professionals can tap into many resources that make sorting through hundreds of mutual funds and thousands of individual stocks more manageable. Most of these tools are not available to individual investors, either because they are too expensive or because you must be a licensed financial professional to access the data. This is where the financial professional will match your values with those products and investments that align most closely. It would take you a very long time to do this and you could not cover the number of possible opportunities your financial professional can scan with the tools at his disposal.

 Responsible Tip

Meeting your socially responsible investing goals is a partnership between you and your financial advisor. The more information you can provide regarding your goals and values, the better your advisor can match those to specific investments.

Your First Steps

You should consider focusing on several of the most important of your values to drive your SRI investing. You should share those values and your SRI concerns with the financial professional as part of the planning and evaluating process. The financial professional has access to some powerful tools that will help her zero in on mutual funds and/or individual stocks that meet the values you expressed.

It is important to have clarity in your values and here's one place it will pay off. With a set of clear values and your financial needs and wants, the financial planner can build a plan that makes everyone comfortable. Software tools available to financial planners let them scan mutual funds or individual stocks to pick out the stocks and/or mutual funds that best meet your individual needs. Some software tools can analyze your existing holdings to determine how close they are to your goal.

The Selection Process

How your financial professional develops a recommended selection of investments will vary somewhat among individual practitioners. But many use a process that begins with constructing a model portfolio based on your financial and investment needs. This model considers your income, age, family circumstances (children, spouse, other dependents, and so on), current assets, financial goals, and so on. All of this information comes from the in-depth fact gathering process.

The model also considers your socially responsible values (environmental concerns, war profits, and so on). With this model portfolio, the financial professional can begin the process of screening potential investments to fit your financial needs. For example, if you need more exposure in large cap growth stocks, the professional may recommend a SRI fund that matches your values in this area or a small selection of individual stocks that also fit your requirements.

Responsible Tip

The question of mutual funds or individual stocks or both should be addressed upfront in the process. That decision will be driven, in part, by the size of assets you have to commit. But you will save your advisor a lot of time if that is clarified early in the process.

Unless you turn your money over to a money manager and give him full discretion to manage your money, you will always have the final say in how your money is invested. You may be more comfortable with mutual funds than individual stocks or want the more direct contact owning individual stocks.

Management for Larger Accounts

If you have $50,000 or more in assets to manage, you may want to consider some of the options available for accounts of this size and larger. As noted above, many firms will handle your account on a fee basis—that is as percentage of assets under management. The array of services for larger accounts grows as account sizes grow.

For very large accounts, firms offer highly personalized plans and services. Surprisingly, a large amount of money is invested in socially responsible products through these services. A study of SRI investments in 2005 found that while mutual funds accounted for $179 billion of invested assets, *separate accounts* managed for individuals totaled $17 billion or almost 10 percent as much as all mutual fund investments. This means a group of individuals had invested a total that equaled almost 10 percent of all mutual fund investments. Of course, like traditional investments, the big institutional investors had the most invested at $1.5 trillion.

def•i•ni•tion

A **separate account** is a general term that refers to a high net worth individual or an institutional client. The financial professional manages the account much as a fund manager at a mutual fund works those assets. Typically, a money manager oversees the allocation and investment of assets. For large institutional accounts, this will involve a team of managers.

The Smaller Large Account

Investors with assets of $50,000 to $150,000 (there is nothing magic about these numbers, I am using them for illustration) can find financial advisors willing to help them using a number of different arrangements. Any of the three basic financial professionals listed earlier in the chapter—stockbroker, financial planner, money manager—can work with accounts this size to help design an investment strategy that fits financial and SRI goals.

Depending on how often you plan to trade, assuming you don't use a money manager, you may want to consider a wrap account that charges an annual fee and may, or may not, charge commissions for trades.

Expect to pay 1.25 percent annually, billed quarterly in advance. There may be other fees to cover trading expenses. These fees are examples only and will vary depending on the company.

Large Account Services

Investors with very large account balances can look for highly personalized treatment in the services they receive and in what they pay. When assets under management pass seven figures, investors can expect and should receive a high degree of individual attention and personalized service. A common charge, although not universal, is 1.25 percent annually. It is often billed quarterly and in advance. Much larger accounts—$250,000 and more—may be charged a lower fee by some firms.

What Separate Accounts Can Offer

Separate accounts for larger SRI investors may give you more flexibility if you can locate a good financial advisor who is knowledgeable about socially responsible investing. Most firms that offer separate accounts require a minimum balance that can be as high as $100,000, but no rules cover the amount. In many cases, separate accounts are for investors with significant assets to invest. One popular service offered through separate accounts is building a private mutual fund.

One criticism of mutual funds is the ongoing expense investors must pay to cover the administration costs. These expenses drain profits (if any) and worsen loses. A financial firm can offer significant investors the option of building a portfolio of stocks that the financial advisor manages like a mutual fund. Of course, you still pay the annual wrap fee, but it is usually lower than most expense ratios and you directly own the stocks. You avoid the under performance that often comes with an actively managed mutual fund, unless you choose to actively trade your stocks (not a good idea). For buy and hold investors, this personal mutual fund offers all the benefits of investing in a traditional mutual fund with lower fees and a greater chance for superior performance. Using a financial advisor plugged into the SRI network will assure you that your investments are as socially responsible—and perhaps more so —than those found in many SRI mutual funds.

The Least You Need to Know

◆ Different types of financial advisors can help you, but some are more qualified than others are.

◆ Which type of financial advisor is right for you is a personal decision based on your current needs.

◆ Question a financial advisor thoroughly before engaging her services.

◆ Be certain your financial advisor has access to SRI research to find the right investments for you.

Chapter 20

Critics of Socially Responsible Investing

In This Chapter

- ◆ Self-defining nature weakens socially responsible investing market
- ◆ Buyer beware in SRI funds
- ◆ SRI portfolio creep for performance
- ◆ Not all SRI investing is tainted

Socially responsible investing has its critics and some of them raise valid concerns to any investor considering SRI investing. There is no industry standard that defines what an SRI investment is and is not. No effective trade group writes or enforces industry regulations governing what investments can be labeled socially responsible.

The result is investment companies and others can set their own standards and their own metrics for measuring performance. This may have been okay when the SRI industry was small and it was easier to understand most of the funds calling themselves SRI funds. Times have changed and with new funds being added regularly, it has become more challenging to stay on top of the SRI industry. Critics point to companies that make up many SRI funds, yet have dismal records on environmental issues and other important concerns to socially responsible investors. How do these companies rate inclusion in SRI funds? Critics suggest the answer is found in the pursuit of fund performance. Enhancing fund performance by lowering standards for inclusion in a SRI certainly seems to be happening; however, that's not the whole story.

SRI Self-Defined

Most movements have an organizing body or central authority that sets a framework for members, including standards of operation, membership requirements, and so on. Socially responsible investing has no such central coordination. One could argue that SRI is not a "group," but an investing style like value investing or growth investing, neither of which is a formal organization. Yet, if you asked 10 people knowledgeable about investing to define value and growth investing in general terms, they would all likely be similar in their definitions. You might not have the same experience if you asked about SRI. Is it negative screening or positive screening or shareholder advocacy or community investing or some combination of all of these? What qualifies a company for inclusion or exclusion? If definition is in the eye of the beholder, how are investors to understand and compare investment opportunities among various SRI funds?

Responsible Tip

Just because socially responsible investing has lofty goals, don't assume that every mutual fund calling itself SRI shares the same lofty goals or sticks to those goals.

What Is Socially Responsible Investing?

A big problem for critics of socially responsible investing is that there is no common definition of what it means. The fact is it can mean different things depending on whether you are an investor, a fund manager, a company seeking SRI status, or a community development official. In other words, it doesn't mean anything and it means whatever you want it to mean.

Socially responsible investing began in America as protests against alcohol, gambling, and slavery. Over the years, things have become more complicated in identifying companies that go beyond the sin industries. Environmental concerns, labor and human rights, defense contracting, and so on, make it hard to find the pure socially responsible company among today's large multinational, multidivisional companies. The problem is one mutual fund that calls itself a SRI fund can hold a company (or several companies) that another fund, also calling itself SRI, has rejected. The investor is left to wonder which fund is correct or are they both wrong?

Responsible Tip

The self-defining nature of socially responsible investing was not a problem in the early days when there were only a few funds. But now there are many funds, including some that have requirements very different from the original SRI funds. It is easy for investors to become confused if two funds are labeled SRI, yet they are very different.

Investors who are serious about socially responsible investing cannot leave it to mutual funds to pick their investments without tracking the fund's holdings. This will make your selection process of a mutual fund longer, but by examining the holdings of a fund, you can tell if the fund is honoring your values with its investment policy. If a fund is going to invest in just about every stock in the S&P 500 and still call itself an SRI fund, you may want to consider if this matches your values.

A Vision Becomes Blurred

Why is it important to have a clear definition of socially responsible investing? For some people, it may make no difference at all. The problem is becoming more acute however, as the number of mutual funds calling themselves socially responsible continues expanding. Are the funds really SRI funds? Are they investing in companies that are not really socially responsible, but have made token efforts at SRI? As you will recall from the chapters on mutual funds, one of the big advantages of investing in mutual funds is the professional staff that does the research and makes the tough decisions for you. Can you be sure those decisions are really honoring your values?

In Chapter 11, we discussed shareholder advocacy where a mutual fund may invest in a company that did not have a great SRI record, but was making improvements. The fund may also invest in companies that were leaders in their industry sectors even though the firm may have a poor SRI record. The fund would engage the company and attempt to convince the management to change and use shareholder resolutions to force votes on important SRI issues. Under these circumstances, some funds would have holdings in companies with poor SRI records. But shareholder advocacy holdings don't explain many of the companies owned by funds claiming to be socially responsible. As cautioned earlier in this book, the rise in popularity of SRI funds means you should make sure investments aren't socially responsible in name only.

> **Red Flag**
>
> If you are interested in shareholder advocacy and invest in an SRI fund because you believe it does advocacy, check before sending in your money. Some funds talk about their role in advocacy, but a deeper look shows that they seldom initiate actions, but tag along when others do. Is that what you want?

Letting Others Define SRI

Almost as bad as not having a central way to organize and define socially responsible investing was letting others define the movement in its early days. As America's economy was switching to a consumer-spending, information-driven economy, new industries that were more environmentally friendly took control of the economy. The mutual fund industry began to take off as Americans had investment income for the first time in several generations. As SRI funds began sprouting on the investment scene, many investment professionals greeted them with ridicule and distain. The idea of values entering the investment decision equation was not only contrary to modern investment theory, but also, for many, seemed un-American. For a variety of reasons, socially responsible investing was hung with a fringe tag and investors were told to expect less than optimum returns by financial professionals.

The early pioneers of modern socially responsible investing worked hard to dissuade the impression that investors were doomed to poor performance if they chose to include their values in the investment equation. As we discussed in Chapter 2, studies were done that argued companies with good SRI records were also good investments because the management was strong and forward-thinking. The industry has been fighting the poor performance label for a long time, despite the fact that some SRI funds have done well during certain periods of market activity.

> ### Success Stories
>
> Many SRI funds did very well in the tech boom because they were heavy in "clean" industries like information technology, Internet, and so on. When that sector was hot in the market, these fund managers looked like geniuses, however when the tech boom ended, the funds' high returns did, too. Performance fluctuations like these set funds up for problems when the market is against its investment strategy.

The mutual fund industry, both traditional and SRI, is consumed with performance measures. Funds that have done well for a couple of years in a row are hailed as the new leaders, only to fall off the charts the next year. Very few funds consistently stay at the top of their categories year-after-year. The problem is the economy and the stock market are both very dynamic, although it seems like they are hardly moving at times. The forces at work are very powerful and when they turn, a nimble mutual fund had better be prepared to turn with them. Unfortunately, the way we measure the economy is almost always as history, so it is difficult to know when these shifts are happening until they have happened. By then, it is too late for some funds. The tech/Internet market effectively crashed in March of 2000. Very few investors knew it at the time, but in hindsight, it's quite clear. Funds that were heavy into tech began to unload their holding when they saw what was happening (this included SRI funds), but as all the other funds unloaded their tech stocks, the bottom fell out of that market and everyone suffered huge losses.

The lesson is mutual funds can have a hot streak when the fund manager's strategy matches the way the stock market is running. As long as she can match the market, her fund will do well. When the market begins rewarding a different investment style, however, she will have to change strategies abruptly or fall behind in performance. This is true of traditional and SRI funds alike.

SRI Integrity Challenged

It is not uncommon in the mutual fund business for the investment company to "subsidize" some of the expenses of a new fund to get it going. Most traditional mutual funds belong to a family of funds where many overhead costs can be shared over all the funds. Starting a new fund doesn't mean everything must be done from scratch. There is nothing wrong with this practice as long as it is disclosed to investors and it must be by regulation. This is one of the benefits of being part of a large investment company—there is efficiency in spreading expenses over multiple funds. This helps the fund's performance in the early years by keeping startup expenses from wiping out any profits. There is another way mutual funds enhance performance and that is by a not so ethical practice called portfolio creep. *Portfolio creep* is one of the charges that critics hang on SRI funds to explain how they are able to post market equivalent returns. It is a serious charge because if it is true, the fund is under-cutting the purpose of socially responsible investing.

def•i•ni•tion

> **Portfolio creep** is when a mutual fund manager begins investing outside the fund's objectives in order to boost performance. Typically, the stated fund strategy is out of favor or there is another sector or style that is currently hot in the stock market and the fund manager pulls in the hot stocks of the day to help him hit his performance marks.

The Problem with Expenses When You're Small

Many SRI mutual funds are not part of a large family of funds, but exist in a very small family or as an expression of an organization's commitment to socially responsible investing. In many cases, the actual operation of the fund is contracted out to an investment company that has the staff and resources in place to operate and service a mutual fund. While this is a convenient way to get a fund started, it can be expensive. Smaller funds struggle to keep expense ratios low. Operating a large family of funds is definitely an advantage because many of the overhead expenses can be shared across all the funds. When a new fund is started, it doesn't have to pay complete startup costs for every

expense. Some resources are already in place with the parent investment company. The investment company wants to keep the expense
ratio low or in line with the rest of the funds. It absorbs certain costs
for the new fund so it can start on the same expense footing as the
other funds. Even though not all expenses must be duplicated, some
new costs are incurred and the investment company may pay those also
for a period until the new fund has enough assets to pay its own way.

The problem with expenses is they drag down the fund's performance.
As noted earlier, the expense ratio is one of the most (and some industry experts say, the most) important determinant of a mutual fund's
return to investors. Because most SRI funds are actively managed (in
addition to financial analysis, there is social and environmental screening), expense ratios tend to be higher than many of their peers. Critics
suggest this puts pressure on fund managers to loosen standards so better performing stocks can be added to the fund to boost its return.

Responsible Tip

Fund managers are often paid a percentage of the assets under
management, so it is in their interest to grow the fund. To grow the
fund, it is important (traditionally) to post good returns on a consistent
basis. Fund managers want to show consistent grow in returns and that
they always beat the index they are measured against. Some will go to
extraordinary lengths to meet these performance goals.

The Problem of Portfolio Creep

Portfolio creep is not what the receptionist calls the fund manager. It
refers to a practice of expanding the investment goals of a fund beyond
what is stated in the prospectus to enhance performance. Mutual funds
must state what the investment objective and strategy is in the prospectus. This information is also used in marketing material. Here is the
statement from Fidelity's Blue Chip Growth Fund:

Objective
Seeks growth of capital over the long term.

Strategy
Normally invests primarily in common stocks of well-known and
established companies. Normally invests at least 80% of assets in

blue chip companies whose stock is included in the Standard & Poor's 500 Index (S&P 500) or the Dow Jones Industrial Average (DJIA), and companies with market capitalizations of at least $1 billion if not included in either index). Invests in companies that Fidelity Management & Research Company(FMR) believes have above-average growth potential. Invests in securities of domestic and foreign issuers. Uses fundamental analysis of each issuer's financial condition and industry position and market and economic conditions to select investments.

There is nothing wrong with the fund that I know of and I am not aware it is guilty of portfolio creep. But notice the objective and strategy of the fund leave a lot of wiggle room for the fund manager to maneuver. The objective simply states the fund wants to grow over the long term—hard to argue with that. It also allows for just about any maneuver the fund manager can justify to meet that objective. The strategy's first two sentences start with "Normally ...", which should tell you that in abnormal situations (whatever that means), something different could happen. The fund's name includes the phrase "blue chip," which commonly means the highest value and best quality, yet it allows the fund manager to invest in companies with a market cap at just over $1 billion, a small company by many standards and not a blue chip by any standard. The fund manager can invest in foreign stocks, which many would argue do not fit any definition of blue chip stocks. Again, this is not an unusual definition of a strategy and many other mutual funds could have even looser guidelines. (Note: Fidelity Blue Chip Growth Fund is not an SRI fund. I did not choose an SRI fund on purpose so as to not single out one fund over all the others. This language is common and similar wording can be found in most mutual funds.)

Responsible Tip

It makes some sense to give fund managers room to maneuver during the stock market's different cycles, however, SRI investors are in those funds for a specific reason related to their personal values. When the fund strays from those values, it has betrayed the investors in a way that is worse than straying from the financial objectives.

This is the most damning charge of SRI funds—that to boost performance standards were lowered or abandoned in favor of investments that helped the fund stay competitive. Some SRI funds have felt the need to remain competitive so they could continue to attract new money and retain assets. Since expense ratios are a percentage of assets, the fund must have a certain level of assets to cover fixed costs. The reality is for the mutual fund business that unless you show good performance, institutional investors who own the bulk of mutual fund shares will dump you for a better performing fund. Since mutual funds issue and buy back their own shares, the loss of major investors can be a severe financial blow forcing them to sell assets, possibly at a loss, to redeem the investors' shares. As the shares are redeemed, share prices continue to fall and more investors want out. This is a cycle no fund manager wants. Portfolio creep is one of the ways mutual funds counteract that drain by stepping outside the stated strategy for investments in stocks that are hot at the moment to give performance a boost. It works sometimes, but not always. If SRI funds are guilty of this, investors are being betrayed who invested because their values were as important as the return.

A number of people in the socially responsible community believe the concern over performance on the part of SRI funds is wrong and doing a disservice to the industry. They suggest that people should invest in SRI because it is the right thing to do and whatever return you get is what you get. They object to the marketing that equates investing with your values to getting a good financial return on your investment. Critics argue that pursuit of the highest possible return on investment is what drives bad corporate behavior including short cuts that pollute, manufacturing practices that exploit, and all the other social ills SRI investing is suppose to avoid.

Responsible Tip

Is it realistic to expect SRI investing to be competitive with traditional investing? Some would say that is the wrong question and the industry has hurt itself by trying to answer it. They suggest that SRI investing should be done because it is the right thing to do—not the financially smart thing to do.

SRI Mutual Funds for Real Change

Like many debates, you have the points of view on both ends of the spectrum and most of the rest of us in the middle. Most vocal critics charge that socially responsible investing has become not much better than the soulless pursuit of profit at all cost it is purports to replace. Of course, if SRI funds do not survive, what will be gained? SRI investing should be approached like all investing, with both eyes open. As noted earlier, investors should examine the holdings of funds they are considering. If you find companies on the holdings list that don't make sense to you, either look for another fund or call a fund representative and ask for an explanation. Investors who blindly buy any mutual fund, SRI or traditional, without knowing what it holds, have no one but themselves to blame if they are surprised or embarrassed by its ownership some day. But you must expect that no fund is going to be perfect and no company is going to be perfect by strict socially responsible terms. If you want to be sure your SRI investment does make a difference and is reflective of your values, you should plan to spend time doing some research or have a financial professional you trust help you.

The Marketing of Social Responsibility

Ten years ago, you seldom heard a company talk about its commitment to the environment or lowering greenhouse gases. Twenty years ago, environmentalists were considered weirdoes and called tree-huggers. As the world has become more concerned about the degradation of our environment, it has become good business to tout a company's real or spun concern for the earth in appropriate marketing material. As the corporate spin machines increase the number and volume of their eco-messages, some of this passes for legitimate progress and gains the companies inclusion in SRI funds. SRI critics are concerned that investors are being led to believe companies are environmental champions when they have simply made a few cursory steps toward environmental responsibility and turned on the marketing machine. Unfortunately, too many funds calling themselves socially responsible buy into this "progress" and reward the companies by including them as having passed an SRI screen.

When most of the Fortune 500 (the largest 500 hundred publicly traded companies) show up in one SRI fund or more likely, most SRI funds, you have to wonder how stringent the screens can be. The most vocal SRI critics argue that the industry has lost its vision by sticking to screens that are so porous companies like Enron (the corporate scandal of several years ago) can stay on SRI roles up until it went into forced bankruptcy. Enron destroyed tens of thousands of workers' retirement plans and robbed millions of billions of dollars in market value as the company went from bankruptcy to liquidation.

Red Flag

The marketing of socially responsible companies will continue and accelerate. All the research points to the importance of conveying a company's concern for the environment and other SRI values, so expect to see more marketing. Whether there will be any changes remains to be seen.

This is not to say that all SRI funds are ineffective, because that is not the case. But, with new funds entering the market competing with existing funds for investment dollars, fund managers will be under even more pressure to produce performance. As with traditional mutual funds, some boutique or smaller niche SRI funds will continue to do well because they don't try to compete with the rest of the market. The larger and broader-based funds, however, are at a disadvantage, especially if they stick to looking like traditional funds. Marketing these funds as "just as good as" or "just like …" is a signal that the funds may have abandoned strict SRI standards for a brand of socially responsible investing that is easier to market.

Genuine SRI Funds

How hard is it to find a genuine socially responsible fund? That, of course, depends on your definition of what SRI is. Most SRI funds can be specific about a few things they are against. The problem comes in filling out their portfolio in a way that reflects those values. Critics charge that too many funds are very liberal in their interpretation of how a company qualifies as socially responsible. Investors may want to invest in companies that have no military connection, however a firm could interpret that as excluding companies that made weapons. There is much more that goes into making war besides weapons and many investors who are strongly opposed to war would be just opposed to investing in a company that made night vision goggles as they would be opposed to investing in a company that made rifles. Genuine SRI funds would screen out all war related companies.

Genuine SRI funds would require companies that professed to be "green" to prove it beyond issuing press releases. For example, companies rewarded for making progress would have to show real and significant progress—converting a fleet of cars to energy efficient vehicles with 15 percent hybrids.

How do you find SRI funds like this? You do your research and examine the holdings of funds that appear likely candidates, realizing that no fund will likely be 100 percent of everything you want. Supporters of SRI investing suggest that it is better to support a fund that is 75 percent SRI or even 50 percent SRI than it is to invest in traditional funds. Important SRI funds are making a difference and it would be unfortunate if the industry suffered because too many funds are getting into the business with a little screening and a lot of marketing. Individual investors will have to decide their own comfort levels.

Responsible Tip

Your best protection in any investment situation is information. You can probably find an SRI solution to your investing needs if you are willing to gather enough information.

The Best Solution

If you have the means, the best solution for those who want as pure of SRI investment as possible is to build your own fund with individual stocks. Doing your own research or using a financial professional, you can take a close look at individual companies and build your SRI portfolio. You don't have to build it all at once, it can be done over a period of years as time and fortune allow. This is one way to feel more certain that your money and your values are in tune. Research individual companies is time-consuming (best to do most of the work yourself, rather than using a screening service), but you will know the company very well and it will be easier to spot changes in the company, for good or bad, that might affect your financial or SRI assessment. You don't have to own too many stocks to have a solid portfolio, eight to 12 will serve most people. If you are into shareholder advocacy, directly owning shares of stock can qualify you for filing shareholder resolutions.

What's an Interested Investor to Do?

It might seem like socially responsible investing is full of potholes for the uninformed. That is partially correct, but you could also say that about traditional investing also. Like SRI investors, traditional mutual fund investors must deal with deceptive sounding fund names (although the SEC is cracking down on this); fund descriptions and strategies that are intentionally broad and vague; portfolio creep that puts investments in your funds that are unexpected; and other forms of surprise and disappointment.

All investors should understand exactly what they are investing in when they buy shares in a mutual fund, whether it's an SRI fund or not. With all of the disclosure laws to protect the investor, there is no reason you should own anything you don't understand. As noted earlier, if the fund owns a company that doesn't seem to fit the SRI fund's screening and objectives, either keep looking or contact the fund and ask why the company was included. In fact, asking questions of companies or mutual funds you are considering is one of the best investment analysis tools you have can use. As a financial journalist for many years, I can tell you that how a question is answered is sometimes as revealing as the answer itself.

Don't expect companies to hand out proprietary information over the phone or violate securities laws with their answers. But as a stockholder you should expect an honest and timely answer to your question. The same is true for mutual funds. Why was that company added when it had a poor environmental record?

If you are totally confused by socially responsible investing funds, don't want to be involved in community development and can't handle investing in individual stocks, you may want to consider making a contribution to support your favorite cause.

But most investors will find enough SRI investment choices for them to invest to reflect their values. It is not as hard as some of the critics make it sound.

The Least You Need to Know

- Self-defining has let socially responsible investing lose any common meaning.

- Mutual funds calling themselves SRI may be more marketing than socially responsible in their investing.

- Portfolio creep happens when SRI funds add non-SRI investments to boost performance.

- Not all SRI funds have sold out for performance.

Chapter 21

The Financial/Personal Commitment

In This Chapter

- ◆ Deciding on socially responsible investing
- ◆ Placing financial values on personal values
- ◆ Setting investment and SRI goals
- ◆ Measuring your progress

If you have gotten this far in the book, there's a good chance you are giving serious consideration to socially responsible investing in some fashion. As noted in the introduction, this book is neither pro- nor anti-SRI. It has presented the basics of what SRI is and how it works, some benefits and some drawbacks. You should be in a better position to decide if this form of investing works for them or not. It's not for everyone and if that's you, at least you are making an informed decision when you move on to another investment strategy or philosophy. Others may have found something that resonates in the socially responsible investing world with the way they believe things should work. If so, you may be ready to make a commitment to SRI.

No rules detail how you invest in a socially responsible way. No regulation says all or even a certain percentage of your investable assets should go to SRI. The decision is entirely up to you. Some investors may want to jump in with both feet and convert all of their investments to SRI. Others may be more comfortable with just a part of their money in SRI investments, at least at first. Social and shareholder activism appeals to some investors—others should be content with investments that are more passive.

Community development investments are gaining popularity and you may find that helping fund projects in your community is immensely more satisfying than owning faceless corporations. The handy thing about SRI is that all different types of opportunities allow investors to a wide choice while still remaining under the same SRI umbrella. You should go into SRI investing with your eyes wide open about potential investment returns that can vary dramatically depending on the form of SRI investment and a number of other factors. You need to think about potential return and your financial goals when you make commitments and changes in your lifestyle that could be upset by a negative market situation.

Deciding on SRI

Using socially responsible investing products for your investments is a major decision and one you and your partner should consider with care. You should feel strongly about some core issues—strongly enough to accept lower than market rates, at times, and willing to stick with your investment plan even when other sectors of the market are rising faster. It is unlikely any investment strategy, traditional or SRI, will be successful all of the time and in all types of market conditions.

Responsible Tip

To borrow a political phrase, the world of SRI investing is a big tent that accommodates a wide variety of investors with different interests and agendas, all calling themselves socially responsible investors.

A major portion of your SRI decision will involve identifying those values you feel strongly enough about to make priorities in your SRI investment plan. Some values clearly lend themselves to SRI investing, while others may be harder to identify as investing goals. Here's where some reading and research can help you see what investment options are available and what other investors have done. You may also want to decide how much of your investment plan should go into SRI. Some SRI investors view it as a way of life, so it is never a question of what percentage of their assets they will invest—it will always be 100 percent. But it is not necessary to make that complete of a commitment if you are not comfortable, at least in the beginning. Decide what feels right for you and either start at that level or have a plan to be at that level by a certain date.

Red Flag

Your level of commitment to SRI investing is not a reflection of you core values. Money is a deeply emotional issue that most people don't fully understand. Don't feel pressured into doing or not doing anything with your money that doesn't feel right to you. If SRI investing feels like the right thing for you, then proceed at your own speed and comfort level.

Consider How Much You Want to Commit to SRI

Some investors are reluctant to start a new program with all of their assets at once. This is understandable and perhaps even prudent. With the SRI mutual fund market growing in numbers each year, selecting investments is not easy. Even with the rapid growth of funds, there are still not near the number or variety of traditional mutual funds. This means your options in some fund areas may not be large. Investors can get nervous when they have only a few funds to select from in a particular class.

How you decide to begin your SRI investment program is a personal decision that must make emotional and financial sense to you. Just because your brother-in-law does it one way and brags about it, doesn't make it right for you. To give SRI investing a legitimate chance, however, you should have enough invested to give you a good reading on how you are going to react to its returns (which may be above, at or below normal, depending on the fund and the market).

You should also be aware of what type of SRI investor you are going to be. Some new SRI investors find that following shareholder resolutions is exciting and they can become involved in social activism through a variety of organizations associated with the same values they share. Other SRI investors are content to periodically read news from the fund, but otherwise take a more passive role in their investments. Neither is right nor wrong, but discovering (if you don't know already) how you will interact with your SRI investments will be instructive in determining how much you may want to commit.

Responsible Tip

Socially responsible investing offers the opportunity, if you want it, to be more involved than other types of investing. SRI investing will raise issues that lend themselves to your personal action as well as what your money is doing through your investments. For example, boycotting products or companies involved with oppression or other human rights violations.

Set Up Investment Plan to Accomplish Goals

If you decide to become a socially responsible investor, you shouldn't abandon basic investing principals—they'll work just as well with SRI products as they do with traditional mutual funds. You don't need to own dozens of mutual funds to have a well-diversified portfolio—four to six funds should cover most investors. Here's a basic outline of a diversified portfolio:

- **Large cap growth stocks** —You'll want most of your money here because, over time, this is where the most consistent returns will come from.

- **Small and mid-cap stocks** —These stocks, especially the small-cap stocks, can be vehicles for rapid growth, but they are more risky than large-cap stocks.

- **Foreign stocks** —A small percentage (less than 20 percent) of your portfolio in foreign stocks provides for growth in the global market.

- **Bond funds** —Every portfolio needs bond funds—intermediate and short-term are usually the best. The closer you are to retirement, the larger the percentage of your portfolio should be in bonds.

◆ **Money market funds** —You can't have too much cash. Three to six months for emergencies is a minimum, while the closer you are to retirement, the more you may want on hand. Your cash can be in bank CDs (consider a community development bank—see Chapter 8) or U.S. Treasury T-Bills.

Socially responsible investing funds have offerings in all these areas although not extensive choices in small cap, foreign stocks, or bond funds. As the industry continues to expand, count on more funds being added, some of which will begin to fill out those thin coverage areas. See Appendix A for more information on different funds that are available.

Virtually all the SRI funds offer an automatic debit service that withdraws a preauthorized amount from your checking account each month (or other period) and buy additional shares of the fund. This is an excellent investment strategy and one that lets investors build wealth in an intelligent manner that runs itself. The strategy is called *dollar cost averaging* and it is one of the best tools available to the average investor.

> **Responsible Tip**
>
> Not only are new funds being added, but some existing funds may focus on areas that are important to SRI investors, such as alternative fuels and so on.

> **def•i•ni•tion**
>
> **Dollar cost averaging** is investing a fixed amount on a regular basis in a mutual fund, usually monthly and through an automatic debit to your bank account. This investment method means you buy fewer shares when prices are high and more share when prices are lower resulting in an overall lower average cost.

Meeting Your Financial Goals

Like any investment program, SRI investing will yield different results depending on market conditions. To achieve your long-term financial goals, you should be prepared to make adjustments along the way. This is true of traditional investing, also. Your long-term results are a factor of the amount invested, the return earned, and the years of compounding. To achieve a financial goal in 20 years (retirement with a certain sum in your nest-egg), you begin with a program that projects out 20 years of an estimated return. Most estimates are never right for very long—the future is too unpredictable. If the return you are earning is less than projected, you will need to increase your investment to still meet your long-term goal. As you go into your investment program, the number of years remaining decreases, so does the compounding. Again, adjustments may need to be made. You may need to take on more risk to earn a higher return to compensate for a shorter compounding period (although this is not usually a good idea as you approach retirement).

Responsible Tip

You can't escape the math of investments. SRI investors have fewer alternatives to switch to than traditional investors do when adjustments need to be made. This is why they should be extra diligent in monitoring their financial progress and make adjustments as needed.

Socially responsible investing faces the same math. If you are falling short of your long-term goal, something is going to have to adjust. Here is where a shortage of product can hurt an SRI investor. If no funds in the area you need are performing, well, you face the dilemma of sacrificing financial goals or your values. This may become less of a problem as new funds and other products are added. Of course, your SRI investment could take off (some have in the past) and leave you to face an embarrassment of riches.

Active SRI Investors

While you can remain a passive socially responsible investor, you may find it more meaningful (and potentially profitable) if you spend some time with your investments. One big criticism of mutual fund investors (traditional and SRI) is that they don't know what they own. This doesn't mean you have to memorize the holdings of every fund you own, but it does mean you should spend enough time studying the list to have an idea of what type of company the fund owns. If you stick with this for a while, you'll soon spot when the fund manager switches strategy and begins bringing in stocks that don't seem to fit the previous pattern.

You'll also want to know what stocks the fund holds to see if it is sticking close to the strategy it advertises in its prospectus. A sharp deviation from the stated strategy, which was why you bought the fund in the first place, may indicate trouble with earnings. Being an active investor, however, doesn't mean jumping from fund to fund or stock to stock chasing high returns. Investing research over the years has shown that frequent trading is not a recipe for success. In fact, frequent traders are more likely to lose than win. Investors in individuals stocks will pay commissions and possibly high taxes on short-term gains that cut deeply into trading profits. Many mutual fund families discourage and may penalize accounts that attempt to frequently trade in and out of a fund—the process disrupts the funds redemption and cash flow cycles.

Responsible Tip

While active investing may pay off for the attentive investor, there can be too much of a good thing. Most research indicates frequent traders—investors who jump from stock to stock or fund to fund—don't do as well as investors who make much fewer adjustments. Trading costs, taxes, and fees can eat into any profits traders generate.

Know What You Own in a Mutual Fund

It is very important to have a sense of what stocks you own in a mutual fund. This information is important for two reasons:

- ◆ **Screening**—Despite screening, you may find the fund holds companies on a regular basis that you believe do not belong in the SRI fund. This may be portfolio creep, which we discussed in Chapter 20, or it may be the company was not eliminated by a screen and you think it should be. Screening occurs (either positive or negative) in just about every SRI mutual fund. The outside consultants that are usually responsible for this information may not see the company the same way you do. At any rate, screening, especially positive screening is very subjective. If you are a regular observer of a fund's holdings (since they may change frequently), you will be tipped if a new fund is SRI in it marketing, but much less so in its investing. If you know what types of companies belong in the fund, you will know if the fund matches your values. Critics of SRI, as we saw in Chapter 20, complain the screens are too loose and let companies through that should be excluded. This is a subjective conclusion that each SRI investor must reach. If you are very passionate about your values, you may find the some screens are too loose for your tastes. This may help you decide on one fund over others or you may decide that it will be easier to be true to your values if you invest in individual stocks. Doing your own screening or employing a financial services professional to help you will take more time and expense, however the purpose of SRI investing is to be true to your values. If you feel strongly enough about your values, the extra work and time will not seem burdensome.

◆ **Investment overlap**—If you own several mutual funds (SRI or traditional), you may believe you have diversified your holdings. Unless you dig deeper, however, you won't know for sure. It is possible that the mutual funds hold many of the same stocks. This means you have bought the same group of companies under different mutual fund names. Your portfolio is not diversified. A major market direction shift might hurt these companies, thus all the funds that own them. This can be a real problem, especially for SRI funds because their investment universe is limited by screening and many funds use one of a small number of outside screening services. If you owned three large cap growth SRI funds, there would be a good chance a substantial percentage of the stocks held by all three funds would be the same.

Responsible Tip

When you hold several funds that own many of the same stocks, you have voided the market protection of diversification. Owning more than one large cap growth fund is probably unnecessary and a waste of money. Spread your investments over different size companies and industries for the best protection against market changes.

Avoid Frequent Trading

Frequent trading is not a successful strategy for most people. Most investors have better results doing their homework before making an investment and sticking with their decision. Investors in individual stocks are more successful with a careful analysis upfront and a buy and hold strategy. If the economy changes or something happens to the company, they can re-evaluate their position. Investors who chase the latest hot tip are often disappointed because they usually buy the hot tip when it has already been bid up past its true value. At some point, the market will reprice the stock according to its true value and the stock will plunge. This usually catches amateur investors in the classic buy high-sell low position, which is not a way to make money. Trading aggressively is best left to professionals and even they have a difficult being right most of the time.

The same is true of mutual funds, although many will not let you hop in and out of the fund chasing high returns at another fund within the same family. Chasing returns is a bad idea even if the fund would allow it for the reasons list above.

Monitor Progress

As an SRI investor, you should be monitoring you progress on two levels, the first is how your SRI investments are tracking to your values. Secondly, you must also watch how they are working toward you financial goals. This sounds more complicated than it needs to be, however, it is important that you remain engaged with your investments. Part of the socially responsible investing experience for many investors is staying current or knowledgeable on important issues. Frequently, SRI investors become involved in social activism around a value that is important to them. Investing with the value in mind is only one part of how they show their commitment to what is important.

> **Responsible Tip**
>
> A management maxim says: If you can't measure it, you can't manage it. The wisdom of this is that you can't track progress or digression without some way to measure. The same is true of your financial and SRI goals.

Measure Financial and SRI Progress

Tracking your financial progress is important, not so you can brag at the office, but to make sure you can meet long-term goals. For most people, the biggest long-term goal is retirement and building your nest-egg is a job that can't be put off until tomorrow. If your investment strategy isn't working as you think it should, making adjustments is appropriate. Some investors find this a challenging task and using a financial professional, especially for this important decision, may be well worth the money. You can go crazy in a very short period if you try to follow the market on a day-to-day basis. In the short-term, the stock market can be a very rocky place with lots of movement in both directions. You should be looking at trends over quarters rather than days or weeks. Even quarters are short by many investment standards. Some argue that an annual re-evaluation is enough. Find a period that is comfortable for you and make adjustments only when you are certain there is a better use of your money in another investment.

Tracking your SRI investments follows some earlier comments in this chapter and others about watching for a change in the character of the stocks added to a fund. Screening is the primary, but not the only way, a stock is included or excluded from some funds. Funds will drop stocks because the company has not followed through on commitments to correct an SRI issue or for some other violation. The investments you should be most cautious of are those added later in the fund's fiscal year, especially if the fund is struggling. These later additions could be "ringers" designed to boost performance, but have nothing to do with SRI. You will have to decide how you feel about this practice.

Stay Involved and Consider New SRI Opportunities

The SRI market is growing in size and product opportunities. If you remain engaged in the SRI industry and follow the news, you will be aware of new products and opportunities that may be a good fit for your investment style and needs. You can find resources in Appendix A to help you stay informed about socially responsible investing and what is new in the industry. These resources are reliable barometers of what is happening in the SRI market, but they are not regulatory groups. They don't have any authority to restrict the use of the term "socially responsible investing" as associated with

Responsible Tip

The SRI industry is growing and major investment houses are taking up the banner. This means there will be more options and opportunities in the future for SRI investors. Staying plugged into the SRI community will alert you to new offerings.

specific funds. The bottom line as with all investing is, do your homework before committing any money to a new product.

No Perfect Investments

Finding the right socially responsible investment is the result of defining your goals and doing your homework. That sounds simple, but it
can be more complicated than it sounds. As we've discussed in several
areas already, setting SRI goals is as important as setting your financial
goals. Both are required to be successful in SRI investing. The sticky
part comes in matching your goals to the proper investment, whether it
is a mutual fund, individual stock or a community development project
through a local organization.

Some people, who practice SRI investing, have very strong feelings
about what and how SRI should be done. Their idealism may make
investment decisions difficult by insisting on very strict standards for
their choices. While nothing is wrong with idealism or insisting on
investments that meet exacting standards, both will limit your ability to
look at a large number of options. If your standards are too rigid, you
may not find any deals to support. At some point, you need to ask yourself if you are accomplishing anything by holding out for investments
that probably don't exist. (You can legitimately ask the same question
if your standards are so loose that almost every company meets your
requirements.)

Responsible Tip

French philosopher Voltaire said, "The perfect is the enemy of the
good." He meant that a search for perfection could prevent us from
experiencing the good that is present now. The same can be said of
socially responsible investing opportunities. Waiting for the perfect one
may blind you to the good ones available today.

Identifying the perfect SRI investment could be compared to finding just the right political candidate to support. You may have to hold
your nose and vote for the best candidate, even though there is much
you wish you could change. Critics of the socially responsible investing industry complain that it has been too quick to settle for companies
that make token steps toward improvements in social, environmental,

or other SRI goals. As we discussed earlier, when some SRI mutual funds are concerned about performance, they change their standards for companies meet their SRI standards. Accepting less than perfect investments is not the same as lowering your standards to meet some performance goal—it is the recognition that companies are expressions of the humans that manage them and as such will always be flawed to some degree.

The Least You Need to Know

- Socially responsible investing involves a personal and financial commitment.

- Set up a plan for your SRI investments and decide how much you are going to commit.

- Monitor your financial and SRI progress making adjustments to your holdings no more than quarterly.

- Acknowledge that there are no perfect SRI investments and find a comfort level with imperfection.

Appendix A

Resources

Resources in this appendix address specific references in chapters where the reader was encouraged to look for more information. The resources are listed by topic.

Environmental Issues

Here are some resources for information on environmental issues and corporate responses:

- ◆ **Interfaith Center on Corporate Responsibility** (www.iccr.org) This organization of institutional investors tracks detailed information on SRI issues. They have some free information, reasonably priced publications, and other services. Their databases track shareholder resolutions and are available by subscription.

- ◆ **The Social Investment Forum** (www.socialinvest.org) This is an organization for financial professionals and institutions, but it has a tremendous amount of good information and links to other sources for individual SRI investors.

- ◆ **SocialFunds.com** (www.socialfunds.com) This mega site bills itself as the largest personal financial site devoted to socially responsible investing. It has hundreds of articles and links to keep you current on the industry.

♦ **Natural Capital Institute** (www.responsibleinvesting.org)
This organization maintains databases on a number of domestic
and foreign SRI stocks and mutual funds.

This is not a comprehensive list, but each of these sites will lead you to
other sites for any additional information you need.

Regulatory Agencies

Several regulatory agencies and commissions at the federal level have
authority over socially responsible investing products or they regulate
and investigate complaints against companies.

♦ The Securities and Exchange Commission is the regulatory body
for all publicly traded companies. Each company must file numerous reports each year. All of this information is available to the
public through the SEC's EDGAR website (www.sec.gov/edgar.
shtml).

You can reach the SEC at:

♦ SEC Investor Complaint Center (www.sec.gov/complaint.shtml)

♦ SEC Complaint Center, 100 F Street NE, Washington, D. C.
20549-0213

♦ The National Association of Securities Dealers is now known as
The Financial Industry Regulatory Authority (FINRA). FINRA
was created in June of 2007 through a consolidation of NASD
and other self-regulatory agencies. You can contact them at:
The Online Complaint Center (https://apps.finra.org/
Investor_Information/Complaints/complaintCenter.asp)

Other agencies that investigate business practices are:

♦ **The National Labor Relations Board (NLRB)** is an independent agency that regulates and monitors union elections and
investigates complaints of unfair labor practices against employers.
The organization also monitors and supervises union elections.

- **The Occupational Health and Safety Administration** (www. osha.gov)   OSHA as it is better known, has already made a name for itself with its safety warnings and the shutting down of dangerous operations. The organization is charged with enforcing health safety standards in the workplace.

- **State labor relations agencies.**   Each state has with its organization a labor relations or labor department. These departments have a variety of duties depending on the state, but they can provide oversight of workplace safety and general worker conditions. You can usually find the agencies listed on the state's website.

Community Investing

Community investing is a very popular part of socially responsible investing, although many do not necessarily connect the two. To find out more about community investing organizations, this government website offers a wide variety of resources: www.cdfifund.gov/what_we_do/.

Stock, Mutual Fund Screens

Stock and mutual fund screening tools can help you narrow down you search for possible investment candidates. These screens search on investing fundamentals.

- **MorningStar.com** (www.morningstar.com)   MorningStar.com is one of the premiere information sites on the Internet. They have free stock and mutual fund screening tools, but if you want their most powerful services, you'll need to subscribe for a modest monthly fee.

- **Yahoo Finance** (http://screen.yahoo.com/stocks.html)   This site has active stock and mutual fund screens with multiple categories to refine your selections.

- **Reuters** (http://today.reuters.com/investing/MarketsHome.aspx) This international website features preset screens and screens you can build yourself.

Almost all of the major business and investing websites carry screens. If one of these does not work for you, look around as some of the other sites for another option.

The North American Industry Classification System (NAICS) is a way of classifying businesses using a numeric code. It replaced the old standard industrial classification system (SIC codes). The NAICS will help everyone involved in industry be more precise in talking about and comparing businesses. For more information visit: www.census.gov/epcd/www/drnaics.htm.

Asset Allocation

Asset allocation is the process of logically distributing your investment dollars among stocks, bonds, and cash to reduce your overall risk. By investing in an appropriate assortment of large and small cap stocks; domestic and foreign stocks; growth and value stocks; along with short and intermediate bonds or bond funds, plus a cash reserve you can reduce your risk that all of your investments will do poorly at the same time. This is the simple explanation of asset allocation, but the concept is the same even when performed with greater precision by a financial professional using the latest software tools and market data.

The SEC offers a Beginners Guide to Asset Allocation on its website: www.sec.gov/investor/pubs/assetallocation.htm.

IRA Contribution Rules

The traditional IRA has been a laggard when it comes to allowing people to invest more annually. The original amount of $2,000 per year was hardly enough for anyone to build a retirement on. The guidelines were revised to acknowledge that participants needed the opportunity to invest more, especially those approaching retirement. If you are married and filing jointly, you can contribute $4,000 ($5,000 if you are age 50 are older). There are income limitations, and Congress has been known to change the rules in the past. Your safest bet is to check with a financial professional to make sure you know what rules are in play for the tax year you want to make a contribution. The same advice applies for deductions, always check with a professional before making withdrawals that could cost you tax penalties and interest.

The SmartMoney.com website has a primer on IRA contribution rules: www.smartmoney.com/retirement/ira/index.cfm?story=supertable.

Mutual Fund Information

The Internet has a number of resources you can use to find information on mutual funds. For SRI funds, you might want to consider these sites:

◆ **Cooking your Nest Egg** (www.cookingyournestegg.org)   This site lets you look at some of the largest mutual fund families and examine their holdings for environmental friendliness.

◆ **Interfaith Center on Corporate Responsibility** (www.iccr.org) This organization of institutional investors tracks detailed information on SRI issues. They have some free information, reasonably priced publications, and other services. Their databases track shareholder resolutions and are available by subscription.

◆ **The Social Investment Forum** (www.socialinvest.org)   This is an organization for financial professionals and institutions, but it has a tremendous amount of good information and links to other sources for individual SRI investors.

◆ **SocialFunds.com** (www.socialfunds.com)   This mega site bills itself as the largest personal financial site devoted to socially responsible investing. It has hundreds of articles and links to keep you current on the industry.

◆ **Natural Capital Institute** (www.responsibleinvesting.org)   This organization maintains databases on a number of domestic and foreign SRI stocks and mutual funds.

Venture Capital Funds

If you would like more information on joining a Community Development Venture Capital or possibly starting a venture capital fund in your community, check out the Community Development Venture Capital Alliance. This network of community development venture capital funds is a good place to start whether you are looking for funding or looking to become involved as an investor (www.cdvca.org/about/index.php).

Active SRI Investors

Not everyone is cut out to be this active type of SRI investor, but for those who are, there are many opportunities to plug into advocacy groups that fight for special issues. One such group is Co-Op America (www.coopamerica.org). This advocacy group is much more action oriented than most and encourages members to become involved in a variety of ways.

Financial Professional Designations

Here is a list of meaningful financial professional designations:

- **Certified Financial Planner (CFP)**   This is the top professional designation for financial planners. The Certified Planning Board of Standards sets the standards for this designation. CFPs have knowledge of investments, estate and retirement planning, insurance and taxes. Candidates must complete extensive course work and pass qualifying exams.

- **Chartered Financial Consultant (ChFC)**   These candidates must complete course work and pass exams on financial planning, investing, insurance, taxes and estate planning. They must also have completed three years of work experience in financial planning.

- **Certified Public Accountant and Personal Financial Specialist (CPA and PFS)**   These professional are CPAs who have taken additional course work that is specialized in financial planning.

- **Charter Life Underwriter (CLU)**   These professionals work for life insurance companies and take the same financial planning topics as the ChFC designation.

These are the most common professional designations for financial planners you will find in the market. But there are several other designations that you may find in dealing with investment companies.

- **Chartered Financial Analysts (CFA)**   These professionals take a three-year independent study to earn their designation. They must have three years of work experience and pass several exams on accounting, ethical standards and portfolio management. Most CFAs work for investment companies such as mutual funds and pensions.

◆ **Chartered Investment Counselor (CIC)**   This is another designation that CFAs can earn after more study, in particular on portfolio management.

◆ **Certified Fund Specialist (CFS)**   A CFS studies mutual funds and advises clients on which funds to buy. If the CFS holds the correct licenses, they may buy and sell funds for clients. Most CFSs work for mutual fund companies.

◆ **Certified Investment Management Analyst (CIMA)**   This designation is for investment consultants with at least three years of experience and focuses on risk management, performance measurement and asset allocation. They are required to take extensive continuing education courses.

Finding an SRI Financial Professional

For resources on finding financial advisers and advisers experienced in socially responsible investing, go to SocialFunds.com (www.socialfunds. com) and download a free brochure on working with an SRI financial professional. The site also has directories of SRI financial professionals by state.

Information on New SRI Funds

For more information on different funds that are available and new funds as they are introduced, some sites that will help you stay informed about the industry are:

◆ **The Social Investment Forum** (www.socialinvest.org)   This is an organization for financial professionals and institutions, but it has a tremendous amount of good information and links to other sources for individual SRI investors.

♦ **SocialFunds.com** (www.socialfunds.com)   This mega site bills itself as the largest personal financial site devoted to socially responsible investing. It has hundreds of articles and links to keep you current on the industry.

Glossary

529 College Savings Plans These plans let you put aside a certain amount of money each year in a special account where it grows tax-deferred. The plans are offered by individual states and have certain income requirements. If the distributions are used to pay for qualified education expenses that are tax-free.

10-K A 10-K reports are detailed annual reports filed with the SEC. They are like annual reports, but contain much more detailed financial and narrative information. The 10-K is due at the end of the fiscal year.

10-Q These reports are detailed quarterly financial statements that must be filed with the SEC within 35 days of the close of the first three quarters of the company's fiscal year. The reports must include any relevant information about the state of the company's financial affairs.

actively managed mutual fund An actively managed mutual fund is one that the manager may use aggressive stock picking strategies attempting earn the highest return possible. This may mean a significant number of trades during the year.

annual report Annual reports are submitted to shareholders at the close of each fiscal year. The year's financial performance is reported along with significant details about the year's activities.

The first part of the report is usually given to dramatic photographs, stunning graphics, and inspiring messages from the president. The back-end of the report contains the important information on finances, operations, and the auditors report.

best of class   Best of class is a way of building a screened portfolio that compares companies to others in their industry rather than against some absolute standard. This means some companies come out as best of class even if the company would be excluded from most other screens. This result is the target of a major criticism of SRI investing.

blue chip stocks   Blue chip stocks are considered the highest quality and safest stocks. They are usually large, older companies that have survived many market cycles in tact. The 30 stocks that comprise the Dow Jones Industrial Average (the Dow) would be considered blue chip stocks. Some believe the term comes from the game of poker where the blue chips are always the most expensive.

carbon dioxide   Carbon dioxide is a colorless, odorless gas produce from the combustion of fossil fuels. It occurs naturally in our atmosphere and acts as a blanket, among other things, to regulate the Earth's temperature. Global warming says we are producing so much carbon dioxide (CO_2) that the percentage is changing and more heat than normal is being retained.

corporate social responsibility   Corporate social responsibility (CSR) is the idea that companies have a responsibility that extends beyond earning a profit for the owners. Some companies take this very seriously and implement a set of policies that have positive impacts on communities, the environment, its workers and other stakeholders. Not all corporate managers agree with this idea.

defined contribution plan   A defined contribution plan is a retirement plan where the contributions to the plan are known, but the ultimate benefits paid at retirement are not. Benefits paid at retirement will depend on the performance of investments made in the defined contribution plan, such as 401(k) retirement plans.

dollar cost averaging   Dollar cost averaging is investing a fixed amount on a regular basis in a mutual fund, usually monthly and through an automatic debit to your bank account. This investment method means you buy fewer shares when prices are high and more shares when prices are lower resulting in an overall lower average cost.

eco-efficiency Eco-efficiency is the practice of examining the life cycle of products and determining where energy can be saved and environmentally friendly steps taken in the process.

European Common Market The European Common Market is made up of 27 member states in Europe who share a common trade and agricultural policy. A number of common political and financial policies facilitate interaction among the member states. A common currency, the euro, has been adopted by 13 of the members.

exchange traded funds Exchange traded funds (ETFs) are very much like index mutual funds in that they are a basket of stocks that mimics an index of a market or market sector. ETFs, unlike mutual funds, are bought and sold on stock exchanges, so you'll need to go through a stockbroker. They trade any time the market is open, just like stocks.

exclusionary screen An exclusionary screen sets a social or environmental threshold that a company must meet. If the company fails to meet the test, it is excluded as a possible investment candidate.

financial planner A financial planner will review your current financial status, discuss your goals and devise a plan to help you reach those goals. The planner may also suggest corrective steps such as additional life insurance or the necessity of a will to solve immediate needs. You do not need a license to be a financial planner, although several professional designations require extensive course work. Certified Financial Planner is the most respected of the designations.

float Float is the number of shares of common stock actually being traded in the market.

greenhouse gases Greenhouse gases are released when fossil fuels (oil, natural gas, coals, gasoline, diesel, and so on) are burned. These gases are thought to be changing the composition of our atmosphere making it denser so it retains more heat. This heating, known a global warming, is a major ecological challenge for the future and companies should have a plan in place to deal with it.

growth investor Growth investing is a strategy that attempts to identify companies with significant growth potential. A growth investor is looking for 20 plus percent growth annually as a minimum. Growth investors make money by knowing when to sell a growth stock before it reaches the limits of its growth. Growth stocks that fail to keep grow-ing often fall sharply in price.

institutional investors   Pension funds, insurance companies, trust funds and other large pools of money are called institutional investors. These investors tend to be very conservative. As a group, they own the majority of outstanding shares of stock and can move the price of an individual stock or the whole market up or down depending on whether they are buying or selling.

investment advisor   Investment advisors are financial professionals who make, buy, and sell recommendations for a fee or percentage of assets they manage.

large cap stock   A large cap stock is a company with a market capi-talization in excess of $10 billion. A large cap mutual fund would only invest in stocks this size or larger.

living wage   Living wage is defined several ways, but it is often thought of as what a family of four needs to earn to reach 100 percent or 150 percent of the federal poverty level. It is then adjusted for the geographic area's cost of living.

market capitalization   Market capitalization is a way of describ-ing the size of a company in terms that make it easy to compare two companies. The market capitalization is calculated by multiplying the number of outstanding shares of common stock by the current stock price. In other words, what would it take to buy the whole company.

microloan   This type loan is a very small loan granted to small busi-nesses for expansion or working capital. In the United States, these loans follow fairly traditional application procedures, but may have looser credit requirement. Overseas, microloans are often less than $100 and most often go to women so they can help feed their family through a business.

mid-cap stock   A mid-cap stock would have a market capitalization of $2–$9 billion dollars.

money manager   A money manager is a financial professional you turn your money over to along with the authority to invest it as they see fit. Money managers have discretionary authority over your money, meaning they can buy or sell when they feel the need to do so.

Money managers can also be stockbrokers, although they typically charge a percentage of assets under management as their fee.

mutual fund   A mutual fund is a pool of investors' money managed by professionals with stated investment goals and objectives. Investors leave the buying and selling decisions to professional managers. Investors own shares of the mutual fund and may cash them in at virtually anytime. The fund managers are responsible for making buy and sell decisions and sticking to the fund's strategy.

mutual fund families   Mutual fund families are groups of funds managed by one investment company. The funds are called a family because they share common management and investors can often move their money from one fund to another within the fund without penalty.

National Association of Securities Dealers   The National Association of Securities Dealers is a self-regulatory organization of securities dealers that licenses stockbrokers and others involved in the registered securities business. It administers tests that professional must past to be licensed and disciplines members for infractions of securities regulations. The Securities and Exchange Commission oversees its work.

outstanding shares   Outstanding shares of common stock refer to the shares owned by the public, including individuals, mutual funds, and institutional investors. A company may retain un-issued shares of its stock, but these are not considered outstanding.

portfolio creep   Portfolio creep is when a mutual fund manager begins investing outside the fund's objectives in order to boost performance. Typically, the stated fund strategy is out of favor or there is another sector or style that is currently hot in the stock market and the fund manager pulls in the hot stocks of the day to help him hit his performance marks.

prospectus   A prospectus is a legal document that must accompany any application or sales material for a mutual fund. It spells out the terms and conditions of the fund, the risks, the fees, and identifies the principal money managers.

sector   A sector of the economy is a grouping of businesses that have more in common than are different. Economic or industry sectors describe sections of our economy that function and are influenced by many of the same factors. Some examples of sectors include technology, retail, health care, or oil and gas. Stocks are also grouped into sectors.

separate account A separate account is a general term that refers to a high net worth individual or an institutional client. The financial professional manages the account much as a fund manager at a mutual fund works those assets. Typically, a money manager oversees the allocation and investment of assets. For large institutional accounts, this will involve a team of managers.

small cap stock A small cap stock has a market capitalization of $1 billion or less.

social justice Social justice is the concept that everyone in society deserves fair treatment. It goes beyond what the law prescribes and asks what is right and just. Different groups, however, may define "justice" differently.

stockbroker A stockbroker is licensed after passing a series of exams and works for a broker/dealer. Stockbrokers buy and sell registered securities such as stocks, bonds, and mutual funds. They are usually paid a commission—either a flat fee or a fee per share traded. Stockbrokers are the only financial professionals that can trade securities. Other financial professionals can also be stockbrokers and collect commissions and fees on the sale of securities.

stock option Stock options are contracts giving the holder the right, but not the obligation, to buy a certain number of shares of stock at a fixed price before the expiration date. Stock options are used as incentives to encourage directors and management to grow the company and raise the stock price. The option holders exercise their options, buy the shares at a lower price than the current market price, and then sell the shares for a profit if they wish.

sustainability Sustainability is the concept that companies respect the environment through all stages of product development, manufacturing, and disposal so future generations will have access to the resources they'll need. Many companies file sustainability reports detailing their efforts, such as controlling green house gases.

sweatshop Sweatshop is a derogatory term for a place where workers are treated badly and paid poorly.

value investor Value investing is a strategy that seeks stocks that the market has priced less than the companies' true value. The value investor counts on the market recognizing the company's true worth at some point and biding the stock's price up. Some of the most successful investors have been value investors.

Index

T